LANGUAGE FOR BEN

HUMAN HORIZONS SERIES

LANGUAGE FOR BEN
A Deaf Child's Right to Sign

LORRAINE FLETCHER

A CONDOR BOOK
SOUVENIR PRESS (E & A) LTD

For Judith
In memory of Mavis, her mother

ACKNOWLEDGEMENTS

Firstly and most gratefully I would like to thank my husband, Ray, and my children, Sarah and Ben, without whose co-operation and indulgence this book could not have been written.

Thanks also to Vivienne Cooper, June Fletcher, Kate Gilbert and Jane Weatherby for their helpful comments at various stages during the writing, to Sarah Clarke and Mary Whiting for their help with the typing, to Vivienne Cooper for checking the manuscript, to Jan C—— for her help during the final stages and to Tessa Harrow for her sensitive editing; also to Bob Duncan and Tyne-Tees Television for permission to use their transcripts. Grateful thanks are due to Barrie Clarke for help with the hardware and to Roger Fletcher for help with the software, without which this book would still be in twelve cardboard boxes on the workroom floor.

Finally, to Dick Gate, I would just like to say: 'I did get the b––––– thing written. Thanks for all the good advice.'

Lorraine Fletcher
February, 1987

CONTENTS

Acknowledgements 7
Introduction 11

PART ONE: The Story 13
1 Discovery and Diagnosis 15
2 The Support Team 26
3 Deafness: The Treatment 46
4 Looking for Signs: The Deaf Connection 64
5 Realising the Difference: The Nightmare 82
6 'Supermum': Commitments and a Cause 93
7 From Commitments to Priorities: Out of the Nightmare 118
8 'Formal' Education—The Right Place 134
9 Sydney Stone and the Beam of Light 153
10 The Right Person 171

PART TWO: The Diary 189
1 With Judith: The First Term 192
2 The Second Term 217
3 The Third Term 237

Conclusion 256
Postscript 258
Appendix 261
Recommended Reading 268

INTRODUCTION

Just seen the consultant and Ben is back, sleeping peacefully. During the operation they cleared some gluey stuff from his right ear and inserted a little tube, did an electrocochleograph (?) and got no significant response. Wait for proper results but definitely 'a very severe hearing loss'—will need a very powerful hearing aid as soon as possible. We have to see the consultant again before 11 tomorrow, and audiology to be referred to another hospital. Can achieve great results and have normal talking child GIVEN child's/ parents' intelligence, proper care and attention/education—but will take a lot of doing.

This is a verbatim diary extract. I wrote it, in the tiny space allocated to 8th December, 1981, in my five-year diary, minutes after my son's diagnosis. I was sitting at the foot of a large, white hospital cot in which my very small baby was recovering from an operation to drain fluid from his middle ear and to determine the extent of his deafness. This book charts his progress, and my own, over the four years which succeeded that diagnosis, and looks back over the year which preceded it.

By this I do not mean to infer that I have 'done it on my own'. This is patently not the case. Ben has a loving father, sister and grandparents, and the list of people who care for and about him grows ever longer, extending into the community and beyond. But I could not hope to tell their story with any degree of accuracy: I could not hope to represent events in exactly the way they felt or saw them. The only view I can present honestly here is my own. I did not have any great ambitions for this book when I began to write it, except that in writing it I would 'tell it like it is'. I have done just that, but it has meant that the story which emerged is mine as well as Ben's.

When the consultant spoke to me after Ben's diagnosis, he gave me a list of variables upon which Ben's likely progress would depend. It would depend on Ben's intelligence, but also it would depend on his parents' intelligence and proper care, attention and education—my part of the story.

Did I manage to give Ben proper care and attention? Have I ensured for him a proper education?

It depends, I think, on what you mean by 'proper'.

People's ideas about bringing up children and educating them differ widely: as soon as we decide to have children, we are faced with numerous choices. Shall we bring up our children alone or with a partner? Shall we have our children while we are young or shall we wait? Shall we choose a hospital birth or a home delivery? Shall we breast or bottle feed them? Shall we establish a strict routine in caring for them or shall we aim to be flexible?

In giving me his opinion, the consultant made an assumption about what I would want for Ben: he assumed that, as a hearing parent, I would want a talking child. Was he right?

I have tried not to speak for Ben in this book, only for myself. But in making decisions about what constitutes a 'proper' upbringing for him, I have had to put myself in his place, imagine how I would feel if I were him. If I were Ben, what would I want?

I have learned a lot about myself over the last few years. I have found that I am happiest when I am at peace with myself—when I like myself. I also know that the saddest times of my life have been those during which I have striven to be something I am not. Of these things I am sure—surer now than I ever have been. Consciously or unconsciously, I think I have based my choices for Ben on that knowledge—and before the knowledge, on a *feeling, which was just as sure.*

If Ben likes himself when he grows up, if he is happy, in the end, with the way he is, then I shall know that the choices I helped to make for him, when he was too little to decide for himself, were the right ones.

PART ONE

THE STORY

1 DISCOVERY AND DIAGNOSIS

It is perhaps thanks to the skill of the hospital staff in dealing so swiftly with what could have been a disaster that we do not worry after the birth. Ben is slow to regain a normal colour but apart from that seems fine. He has ten tiny fingers, ten tiny toes (the paediatrician counts them!), his limbs are strong, he has no blemishes, he looks around with interest when he is awake, and after a few hours he begins to feed well. His features are a bit squashed, but that simply makes him look oriental: he reminds Ray and me of a little Tibetan. Ray never mentions the shock and trauma he must have experienced being at the 'bottom end' during the birth; maybe he would rather forget. Perhaps it is true that fathers forget their fears just as mothers forget the pain of childbirth.

Once home, there is no time for either of us to think much at all. Sarah is not quite two and life is hectic, to say the least. When I brought the newborn Sarah home from hospital I would agonise over every breath, every little spot, the contents of each and every nappy; I almost lived inside this tiny being whose needs and whose actions were so new to me and so desperately important. I fit Ben in when I can and he rewards this more casual care with a placidness and a tranquillity I never thought possible in a child of mine. Yet he is not unresponsive, and at first we have no reason to suspect that he is any different from Sarah: he chortles when you tickle him, wriggles and kicks when you talk to him, appreciates having new and different things to look at, cries when he is hungry or upset, says 'A-goo!' to his grandfather, just as she did, and 'talks' to the toys hung over his cot.

As soon as Ben is past the newborn stage, we begin to establish a routine for caring for the two children. In the evenings, Ray and I bath them together, then Ray plays with Sarah in the bath while I get Ben ready for bed downstairs. Because I want to be sensitive to Sarah's feelings when both children are around, this time alone with Ben is precious. The kitchen is bright (we have decorated it in red and yellow) and warm; I put Ben down on his back on his changing mat on the table and I sing to him; I tell him all the things I've longed to tell him all day: how beautiful I think he is, how much I love him, what a wonderful baby he is . . . Sometimes I put the words to music and I sing them right into his eyes; he gazes at me the way only a new baby can, and he coos, and he gurgles back at me in the spaces between songs . . .

At the grandparents', he captivates everyone by his rapt attention to *their* attentions. He is so easily pleased . . . Yet there is something different about him.

My mother, who has 'feelings' about people, places, events, who knew I had given birth to Sarah before Ray rang to tell her, cannot look at Ben without a lump forming in her throat and tears springing to her eyes. Perhaps influenced by this, I resist impulses to call him an angel, fighting back images of its proper connotations. Maybe it is because he did almost die at birth . . . Maybe he has retained an 'other-worldliness'. We both feel that there is something not quite right, but the feeling is vague, unspecific, confirmed by nothing actually visible, though we watch him very closely.

Having had this nebulous sort of 'advance warning', then, we are not entirely surprised when certain aspects of Ben's motor development seem rather slow. Wary of comparing children, at first we give him a lot of leeway. But we have to recognise that Louise, my neighbour's daughter, born two weeks after Ben, is rapidly overtaking him at all the physical milestones, and that all the other babies whose mothers did the same National Childbirth Trust course as I did are equally 'forward', even though some of them are boys and hence—we have assumed—slower to develop.

7.4.81
NCT reunion. Noticed that Ben's the oldest and

biggest baby—but the floppiest. The others all seem to have much better control over their heads . . .

Later, I try not to worry when I discover from my diary that Sarah was beginning to crawl at an age when Ben still has difficulty holding up his head—but Ray and I now consciously, if unhurriedly, begin to 'work' on him. We begin purposely to put him into situations where he has to use those neck and back muscles; we play games which will strengthen them. Ben's favourite resting position is on his back on his changing mat; we encourage him to do sit-ups by holding onto our fingers and pulling himself up; we sit him in a baby chair rather than allowing him to recline in his bouncing cradle. (This is a good idea anyway because Sarah has discovered the thrill and excitement of using it as a kind of catapult when Ben is strapped into it, pulling it down at the back and allowing it to shoot forward—which sometimes makes Ben giggle but most often makes him cry.) Ben's legs are strong; he bounces happily and sturdily on anyone's knee, stands upright holding onto people's hands—but it is as if his head is attached by a loose spring; like Zebedee's, it wobbles constantly. Ray and I are confident that as Ben matures the problem will diminish: how can there be anything wrong with a child who appears so sturdy from the neck down? So we stay calm, but the grandparents are not so sure; they worry much more than we do, but quietly, so as not to upset us.

Unbeknown to them, though, and at the same time, another suspicion is forming in our minds. For a while now, I have known that, when I go in to vacuum Ben's room, he is unlikely to notice unless he can actually see me. Sitting on cushions in his room, feeding him, I have wondered idly why some people distract him when they come in and others don't: Ray can come and go unnoticed, but Ben always turns and looks when Sarah bounces in. One June morning—Ben is about seven months old—I am on my way next door to visit my neighbour. Ben is riding on my hip, wide awake and alert, when we meet Louise coming the other way, similarly perched on her father's hip, similarly alert.

'Hello, Louise!' I say, and she turns and looks at me, immediately, and smiles.

'Hello, Ben!' says Max, but Ben doesn't respond. He is looking at some washing, waving on the line in the wind. 'Ben!' Max calls, louder. Again no response. 'Look, Ben!' I say. 'Look, there's Max and Louise.' I turn him to face them and he smiles and bounces, thrilled to see them. Cogs spring into action in my mind and click away as, slowly, I piece these incidents together. He must be a little deaf. Maybe he's deaf in one ear, which would explain why he responds at some times and not at others . . .

Now, Ray and I subject this baby of ours to close scrutiny, aiming to make some sort of sense of his responses to sound. But his responses are very erratic; we look for a pattern but it is impossible to predict what he will respond to and where. His routine hearing test is due; we decide to wait for that and see what the health visitors say.

When they arrive to do the test, I do not mention my suspicions to them; I want to see if they notice any problem without influencing them by my own observations.

20.6.81
Ben's hearing card came. I'm becoming more worried that he might be deaf in his left ear—and I'm sure he won't respond to the tests.

24.6.81
Ben's hearing test. They couldn't get him to respond either, but said as he's still very young they'll try again in a few weeks. So no worry as yet—and after much persistence today I got him to turn to his left a couple of times in response to things.

14.7.81
I think that left ear DOES function OK. Perhaps it was just immaturity causing the problems with the test.

These little extracts from the five-year diary only hint at what is going on at this time. Even Sarah puts herself in 'testing' mode as the whole family sets about trying to ascertain whether Ben is deaf, and if so how deaf. We slam doors, we drop pans behind him, we call him, we squeak toys behind him, we rattle things, we bang lids together, we shout, we whistle, we whisper. Sometimes he turns, sometimes he doesn't. Just as I knew that I could vacuum his room without him realising, but didn't allow the implications of that knowledge to register in my mind, so now I close my mind to what might be.

* * *

There is lots to think about at the moment, lots going on. Ray starts a new job in September, up in the North. We are excited about moving 'back to our roots', for both of us were born there, closer to our parents, and into a part of the country whose hills and moorland we love. We are also in the process of selling our house—and it is not a straightforward matter: we live on a modern estate, there are dozens of houses exactly like ours and about one in ten of them is for sale. Worry thrives on spare time, and I have little of that: simply coping from one day to the next is a full-time job with a two-year-old and a baby to look after. If I worry at all, it is about whether we shall be able to sell our house in time for the family to be able to move when Ray starts his new job. I do feel a little uneasy from time to time about Ben's hearing problem, and we carry on spasmodic impromptu testing, and we watch Ben's reactions carefully; but thinking, actual hard cogitation, is rather a forgotten art: I just take each day as it comes and am thankful if by the end of it there are enough clean nappies for the morning, there are still two Weetabix in the packet and the pedal bin hasn't overflowed yet.

17.7.81
Ben's hearing test. They couldn't get him to respond again on the left side and are trying to get him referred to a hearing specialist before we leave. If he is deaf on that side he'll have to be fitted with a hearing aid or he won't learn to speak. We're still hopeful that as he becomes more alert he'll respond on that side, but meanwhile are doing a lot of face-to-face talking to him so that at least he SEES the sounds being

made—since his 'speech' at the moment has no consonants at all . . .

18.7.81
Noticed two BLUE spots wide apart on his upper gums—hope he's not going to have black teeth as well—he's such a beautiful baby now.

'. . . black teeth *as well* . . .' I may not consciously be thinking about it overmuch, but this little phrase, written quickly and without deliberation the day after the health visitors' comments about treatment, gives an indication of how my subconscious is working. By the deafness—or by having to wear a hearing aid?—my beautiful child would be scarred, spoiled, marked. Again, the defence system springs into action. We don't exactly deny the deafness—in fact in our day-to-day behaviour we are already accommodating it by dealing with Ben in a slightly different way, relying increasingly on visual rather than auditory stimuli, finding him new things to look at and touch, taking note of the kind of games he likes and repeating them—but we do postpone the deafness: having been told that Ben will need to see a specialist we reserve judgement till then. For now, we live for the moment, as usual.

*   *   *

In July 1981 we move house. Due to a hiccup at the buying end we expect to spend some time living with Ray's parents. Rather than waiting, we continue 'investigations' there, but without mentioning the deafness to the grandparents: we see no sense in upsetting them—for they will be upset, that is certain—until we ourselves are sure about it, until we have it confirmed.

6.8.81
Ben saw the doctor at Clinic. She's not sure about his ears, says they're a bit catarrhy, has given some Actifed syrup to clear it up, will do a hearing test with the health visitor in about a fortnight. She says that the hearing problem might simply be due to his always having blocked ears because of sniffles. Let's hope it is.

18.8.81

The health visitor and I checked Ben's hearing; she also tested the other aspects of his development—he's just a little slow with sitting, but hearing's the main problem. Saw the doctor straight away and she referred Ben to a specialist. They were both very nice. Parents all shocked but Mom F. had suspected it. Just have to find out now how much affected he is. Feel very tender towards him and trying very hard to help.

25.8.81

Ben's proper deafness tests—no conclusions drawn because of his inability to concentrate (to be expected in such extensive tests—rattling and banging all kinds of things behind him and at each side). So a different kind of test arranged Friday at children's hospital—hope it's not nasty for him.

28.8.81

It looks as if Ben may be totally deaf. Today's tests got no response—electrodes stuck to his ears and neck to monitor muscle reaction to really loud noises registered no response, and he didn't react to ANY of the things they sounded behind him, even a very loud drum. They said his reactions at home may be due to very good, quick eye perception and sensitivity to vibration, e.g. of floor if someone approached. Said to watch him and note down any instances of responses unaided by sight/vibration and today there have been none. Feel fiercely protective and very loving towards him, as does everyone we've told. More tests with big boss specialist 9th Sept.

9.9.81

Ben's appointment. Specialist thinks definitely some hearing loss; recommends op. to clear fluid (if any) which may be affecting his hearing, then electronic tests while he's still under anaesthetic.

The operation over, we have official confirmation that Ben is deaf. Sitting at the foot of his hospital cot, looking through its white bars at my sleeping baby, I think back. Could we have known before?

Incidents spring to mind, insignificant singly but when viewed together and in retrospect giving powerful indications that the differences we observed in Ben might have been attributable to a particular cause. There were the obvious ones, of course, the ones which originally gave rise to suspicions—but there were others, too. That wobbly head . . . Might that have been caused by a problem with balance rather than with muscle control? And Ben is by no means reliable now: all babies fall often when they are first learning to stand upright—but Ben's falls are spectacular, more like fainting than tumbling, with no intermediate stage. One second he's upright, holding onto a chair arm or other support, the next his head hits the floor. It's frightening, and at the moment we're grateful for Ray's parents' thick carpets and wooden floorboards. He obviously has very poor balance. Is this connected with deafness?

My mind wanders back to the very early days, days when we were still getting to know Ben, working out the best way to look after him, discovering differences and similarities between him and his sister . . . days before we even suspected that he might be deaf . . .

Travelling . . . On our way home, after Christmas. Ben is six weeks old. Having had a horrific outward journey with him, we've waited till bedtime for the return trip, so that both children can sleep. Sarah, in a safety harness between Ray and me, chatters away. I know that the noise and vibration of our ancient Volkswagen bus will soon send her to sleep, as it has done since she was a baby. We have found that the opposite is true for Ben: even the shortest of journeys has always seemed intolerable to him. On the way up North, in his carrycot in the rear of the van, on the floor, he fretted and cried for much of the trip. Because of fears for his safety, I was unwilling to pick him up and hold him, but eventually his cries became so piteous that I climbed over and cuddled him, sitting on a rear-facing seat in the back of the van. Even then he was not happy until he could see out of the window. I am resigned to doing the same on the return journey, but I intend to feed him, in the hope that he will settle down to sleep. As soon as we start to move, he cries; I feed him as planned. But, even though it is dark, he does not go to sleep. It is as if he is forcing himself to stay awake—behaviour quite common in his sister but unprecedented in this placid baby, who throughout his time with the grandparents has gained a reputation as the most contented child ever. He takes a little milk, breaks off, looks around, whimpers, starts again, obviously disturbed, resolutely refusing even to close his eyes. I talk to him reassuringly, try singing . . . nothing works. The journey seems never-ending. He falls asleep just as we arrive home, exhausted by his own crying. I take him up to his room; he wakes again as I turn on the light, but this time he is his 'normal' self, relaxed, calm as ever.

Another night, in his room . . . Ben, at three months old, tormented by wind—or whatever else it is that wakes babies up again soon after they have been put down for the night. In a similar situation, Sarah used to enjoy being rocked, in the dark, and sung to sleep. It appears that in this respect, too, Ben is different. I pick him up, check his nappy, which is still clean and dry, try feeding him—no, that's not the problem; I wrap him up in a soft, warm blanket, turn off the light, hold him upright against me in the rocking chair. He carries on fretting, wriggling about in my arms. Sarah used to do this for a couple of minutes, until I got into a proper rhythm and relaxed, so, undeterred, I rock, and I sing, one in time with the other, slowly, quietly. This is one of the pure joys of parenthood: the warm room, the smell of baby shampoo and the feel of that little downy head against my cheek, the prospect of cradling a sleeping baby in my arms while I rest myself, in the darkness, away from the bustle of life downstairs, in peace . . . But I can't relax, because Ben can't. The sweetest of singing and the most rhythmic of rocking have no effect.

Reluctantly, I get up, turn up the light a little and put Ben back in his cot, face down. He lifts up his head and cries. I try turning him onto his back; he catches sight of the row of toys strung across his cot and he is quiet. A dreamy expression replaces the look of anguish on his face and his eyes flicker backwards and forwards along the row, as if he is greeting each little creature in turn. I tiptoe out of the room; he does not notice me go. A little later, I creep in again. Ben is asleep.

That Christmas, the weather icy cold and with the prospect of a walk over the fields to an aunt's house. Impossible to use the pram—I'll just have to take Ben in the baby sling. I know that he doesn't like it, having made several attempts to carry him around the house in it, but I have promised this visit, and it will only mean ten minutes in the sling, so I decide to try again. I feed him so that he is full, peaceful and ready for sleep; I lie him down, change his nappy and dress him in warm clothes.

He looks around, calm, interested, accepts the baby sling. Ray helps me to strap it on; the grizzles of protest begin. I resolve to carry on: maybe brisk walking will pacify him as it used to pacify Sarah. I fasten my coat around the sling, tuck in the little head. Ben starts to cry. It is snowing. I tell this baby about it and everything else I can think of as I walk, fast and easily, down the road. The crying persists, getting louder all the time. It's pitiful. Two old ladies tut-tut in sympathy as they make their way slowly towards us up the hill.

'Poor little mite!' one comments as we pass. I feel so cruel and guilty I could weep, but I plod on, still talking, but to no avail. I begin to sweat, my heavy coat feels sticky, my chest wet against the little hot body.

'How true it is that kids differ,' I console myself, thinking of Sarah as a baby, riding untroubled in the sling, as much calmed by it as Ben is agitated. At my aunt's house I throw off the coat, struggle to release Ben quickly from his prison. I put him down on his back, on the floor, to extricate his legs. The crying subsides. Almost immediately he is quiet, sociable, content.

'That's better,' says my mother, also visiting. 'You just wanted to have a look round, didn't you?'

. . . And what of the cause? Maybe we could have been more aware even before Ben was born, more careful, perhaps? Yet, during this pregnancy, I was even more careful than during the last one: no alcohol, no drugs—not even an aspirin—and before even trying for Sarah I had an immune test for German measles . . . but, yes, I was ill. I struggle to remember. We had visitors. Their little girl went down with a tummy bug. After they left, suffering as I was from the kind of permanent nausea I took drugs to relieve whilst pregnant with Sarah, it was a while before I realised that I had caught the bug—but then it took hold; the vomiting became more frequent and was accompanied by debilitating stomach cramps. I was really ill for about a week, couldn't keep down any food, lost weight and, for a while, worried about losing the baby. I must have been about eight or nine weeks pregnant. Just when organs like the eyes and ears are starting to form—just when a virus like German measles is at its most dangerous.

And the birth. Should we have suspected then that something was wrong? Could we have known then? I was certainly well-prepared for the birth: my classes had familiarised me with every detail of what would happen to my body and how I should deal with each stage of the labour. I read every book I could find, and I had memories of Sarah's birth—hospital controlled and quite frightening for Ray and me—to help me through this one . . . but I resolutely avoided reading the sections on 'birth trauma' . . . I could anticipate my own body's suffering without fear, but I found the thought that my baby might suffer birth injuries too awful to contemplate. Like every mother, I was tormented from time to time by the thought that I might give birth to a handicapped child.

I remember a motorway journey when, pregnant with Sarah, I was sharing some of the fears I had then with Ray. His response came instantly, almost without thinking.

'Well,' he said, 'you know, even if it is . . . different in some way, it'll still be ours, and we'll still love it.' I remember that now, as, in the quiet of the children's hospital, I remember that other hospital where, just over a year ago, Ben was born, with the umbilical cord looped twice around his neck. He was a 'blue baby'; he needed oxygen before he would regain consciousness. Afterwards, he appeared to be fine . . . Too little oxygen at birth? Too much? Both can cause damage. Was it then that Ben became deaf?

Now, I tiptoe around Ben's cot and I conduct my own examination. Despite the insertion of the grommets, the operation has left no marks; there will be no scars. The operation has not changed Ben, and neither, I realise suddenly, has the diagnosis. 'It'll still be ours, and we'll still love it.' Ben is still the same child, the child that Ray and I brought into the world in shared labour and the child we love. Just as the blue marks I noticed on Ben's gums all those months ago have been replaced by healthy white teeth, so the idea of deafness I had at that time has been replaced by a healthier one. No longer is it something ugly, a scar, a blemish. Faced with it, here and now, I see it as it has always been for Ben: a fact of life, and as it has to be for us: a difference.

2 THE SUPPORT TEAM

The day after the operation Ray and I meet the consultant at the Department of Audiology. He repeats the diagnosis for Ray's benefit, arranges to see us again when the results of the electrocochleograph have been properly analysed, and hands us over to the audiologist.

The audiologist explains a little about the nature of Ben's deafness: it is a sensori-neural loss, which means that the problem is with the nerves, not with the mechanical structures of the ear. Although the consultant has cleared out some fluid from the middle ear cavity in Ben's right ear, that was not the cause of the hearing loss—but the grommet, the little plastic tube, will form a permanent airway through the eardrum, which will hopefully prevent the middle ear cavity from getting clogged up again, and this should help a little: if Ben has any hearing at all it will be far more effective if the middle ear is clear of fluid. She explains that Ben will be prescribed a hearing aid; she is aware that we shall shortly be moving house and she arranges for Ben's notes to be transferred so that the local hospital can prescribe one for him, or possibly two, depending upon the opinion of the consultant there. She recommends that we have earmould impressions taken right away and makes an appointment to have this done. We have no idea what an earmould is; she explains that it is the part of the hearing aid which sits in the ear, and tells us that the impressions are made by injecting a soft rubbery material into the ear and allowing it to harden. These impressions are then sent away and permanent, hard plastic moulds are made of exactly the same shape. Receivers are then embedded in the moulds so that the amplifier can be attached. I am nodding; I look across, so is Ray. Maybe he, like me, is feeling a bit saturated, and a bit taken aback by all this. We haven't thought of Ben's deafness as a medical problem, yet because of it he has been into hospital, had an operation, he has had a foreign body embedded surgically into his eardrum, and here we are, having a discussion with a woman in a white coat about equipment. It feels strange. After all, Ben is not ill . . . or is he? Is he? Is deafness an illness?

Perhaps sensing that we are not really listening any more, the audiologist gives us a telephone number so that we can call her if we need any more information. Then she asks us if we would like to meet the social worker; the consultant has arranged for him to be there in case we need him.

The social worker? Ray and I look at each other in amazement. Ben has a medical problem, and now, it seems, we have a social problem. I don't know whether to be amused . . . I am certainly confused. The social worker seems to be prepared for confusion—but not amusement. He is very quiet, very grave; he talks of grieving. But, for me at least, he is about six months too late. The closest I have come to grief was when the idea of deafness was still new to me, when I saw it as a scar on my beautiful baby, when I coped with it by forgetting about it, when I was desperate to know, but would not look beyond the knowing into the future. The social worker is treating us as if yesterday's diagnosis were a bolt from the blue—yet how can it be a bolt from the blue when it has been expected for so long? The extended period of testing gave us plenty of time to get used to the idea that Ben *might* be deaf—not that he *was* deaf, but that he might be. As our suspicion grew, gradually, so confirmation came, gradually, a little with each test. Far more traumatic than this diagnosis was the one we made ourselves as we sat in that soundproofed room with Ben when he was nine months old and watched, incredulous, as he played, oblivious to ear-splitting shrieks and bangs from the speakers behind him. If we were to experience any trauma, surely we would have been at our worst on that day, the day we realised just how deaf Ben was. Yet on that day we had to go home without even having the truth of what we had just seen officially confirmed: we were allowed, even encouraged, to go on hoping.

Even that seems light years ago now, as we sit with the social worker in his quiet little room and try to explain how we feel . . . how we knew about and accommodated Ben's deafness for months without really worrying about it, how we have come to regard it simply as a difference, not as a problem. Denial can be harmful, says the social worker gently; if we hold back our grief and try to control it we are likely to suffer more later—and I can see the sense in that. I will admit that my defence system slowed down recognition of Ben's deafness for a while, and that the day we realised how deaf Ben was our first—crazy—reaction was to buy him a musical radio—with moving pictures, admittedly— but, nevertheless, a musical box . . . but just now, I can't find anything to grieve over.

Yet the events of today *have* given rise to a new feeling, just there in the back of my mind. I struggle to dig it out, to categorise it. It's a familiar feeling: butterflies in the stomach, buzzing in the head . . . It is fear. Not fear of deafness—I'm sure we have got over that—but fear of the unknown. We have grasped that there is much we have to learn; we have been told that there is a lot of work to be done, but we don't even know what it is, let alone how to do it . . . Yes, there is something this social worker can do for us. We do need his help. He can help us to find out more. We have to discover what Ben's deafness will really mean, for him and for us as a family, and what we can do to help him.

Ray is on the same tack: he is asking, can the social worker recommend any books? The poor man is taken aback. Still worried about us, still not quite convinced by our calm reaction that we are not in a state of shock and distress, he advises us against reading too much at this stage. This response does worry us. Does he feel that we should be protected from further knowledge? Is life with Ben going to be as dreadful as that?

Eventually, worn down by our persistence, he recommends three things—a book, a correspondence course and a society: *Your Deaf Child's Speech and Language*,[1] the John

Tracy Correspondence Course,[2] and the National Deaf Children's Society.[3] This last he feels would be particularly helpful, and he lets us have a copy of their quarterly magazine, *Talk*.

Once home, we almost eat that magazine. By the evening we have read it from cover to cover and back again. This morning, we knew nothing about deafness except what we have observed in Ben. Now we are beginning to form a picture, a picture of the deaf child at school, the deaf child at home, the deaf child growing up—*the deaf child*. We are beginning to make generalisations and to draw conclusions about what we can expect for Ben and for ourselves in the years to come.

This morning we were an ordinary family. Now, we have a handicapped child who needs special equipment and special treatment. We have suddenly acquired a team of advisers to provide the equipment and to give us advice—to help us in the daunting task of bringing up this deaf child.

Ben is the same child as he was this morning—but how our picture of him has altered. He needs doctors, he needs technicians, he needs us to have a social worker. Now, the shock waves begin to register. To us, Ben was simply 'different'; we accepted that quite readily. But now we are finding out just what that difference will mean. To the support team, Ben is a patient, a client, a handicapped individual in need of technical aids. That picture of our son is new to us, and it is one which we are far less ready to accept. *Talk* is full of success stories, of people who have 'overcome their handicap'. But it has not until now occurred to us that Ben might not be successful! I look at him: happy, healthy, lively, cheeky . . . He is *not* handicapped. But all my experiences of today come together to tell me that he is. And I don't like it.

I am reminded of the way I felt towards the hospital staff when Sarah was born—how ambiguous my feelings were then. Sarah was *my* baby; my maternal instincts were functioning as they should; I had read all the books I could find; technically, I knew all about babies, but still, faced with this vulnerable little newborn, I needed the expertise of the hospital staff and I was grateful for their experience.

Despite the strength and intensity of my attachment to her, Sarah was partly 'their' child, partly their responsibility, until the time came for me to take her home. There was a lot I had to learn from them.

Ben is our second child, and we have brought him up so far with great faith in the relevance and appropriateness of our own experience in bringing up Sarah. We have found differences, but so far we have been able to accommodate them. Yet suddenly, there are things about Ben's care and upbringing that we do not know and for which bringing up a first child has been no preparation at all. Here is the situation I encountered when Sarah was born, but reversed, turned on its head. I had professional help immediately Sarah was born; I watched the professionals, and under their guidance I learned slowly how to handle my new baby, so that a few days later I felt confident enough to leave their protection and carry on on my own. With Ben, I started off confident about how to take care of him, and continued to be so; then, suddenly, this battery of professionals has arrived on the scene and, in a sense, my child, the child I know and love, has been taken away and a new one substituted, a child for whom my previous experience has little relevance.

This situation is intolerable to me. I want to regain the confidence I had in myself before today. I want to find out all that the professionals know and more, so that I am no longer in a state of ignorance about my own child's needs. I wish that I could go back in time, get some books, read up on deafness in the same way as I read up on pregnancy, on childbirth and children . . . but I can't. I've got to look after Ben, and I've got to find out how I should be looking after him, at one and the same time. That's where the fear comes from. I didn't choose this. I don't know anything about it. What if I can't handle it?

The afternoon is dark and wet on the day Ray's father runs Ben and me into town to have the impressions made for his earmoulds. I squeeze out of the back seat of the car with Ben under my arm, Ray's father takes the baby buggy out of the boot; I strap Ben in, he waves bye-bye to Grandad and we run, Christmas lights reflecting on the wet, black pavements, across the road to the hearing aid shop. I've passed the shop several times with Ray since we suspected Ben's deafness, and looked curiously at the window displays: huge cutaway diagrams of the ear showing all its workings; photographs of suave, smiling people wearing invisible hearing aids ('Fits INSIDE the ear'); models of the latest designs . . . What will Ben's hearing aid be like, I wonder. I force my unwilling brain to think about it—Ben in a hearing aid . . .

I wheel Ben into the shop, slightly nervous, wondering how he will react to the experience. The technician is a middle-aged, greying man, confident, kind. He asks me to take Ben out of the buggy and sit him on my knee while he has a quick look at his ears. Ben co-operates happily, accustomed by now to having his ears looked at. The technician disappears into the back room to prepare his materials and I try hard to calm my rapidly escalating state of nerves. Then he returns, holding an enormous syringe, and I cannot suppress a shudder of shock and fear. I have been told that the process is painless; the audiologist has explained it and the technician does so again before and as he works. Ben is not frightened; I know that my own fear is irrational, but I can't control it. I watch, forcing myself to breathe, as the warm compound is piped into Ben's ear—but it goes in easily, like jam into a doughnut, really, and with as little fuss. Ben sits perfectly still throughout, then I, too, am able to relax at last, relieved at his calm. The technician seems pleased with the impressions, and says that we should receive the earmoulds within a couple of weeks.

Outside the shop I hug Ben furiously. Then I wheel him down the road, into the nearest department store, and I buy him a snowsuit. He doesn't need a snowsuit—but I feel a great urge to compensate him. For what he has just undergone? For what he will have to undergo? I can't say, but I do know that the purchase of the snowsuit is the direct consequence of the visit to the hearing aid shop.

Ray and I have often laughed when other people's children have talked of being given sweets 'because I was so good at the dentist's'. Now, I am starting to understand. As a child, I had to go into hospital for minor operations, and my parents would bring me a present every time they came to visit. The presents certainly cheered me up—but, looking back, I can see that they also served a purpose for my parents: bringing me presents was a way for them to show their love at a time when I might be doubting it. It made *them* feel better, too . . .

We have an hour before the shops close. Maybe I can find the book which the social worker recommended. Ben and I tour the bookshops. In every one, I have to ask. Not only is this book not on display, but there is not a single other book on deafness, either in stock or on the shelves. We get up to the university bookshop just before closing time, and our persistence, at last, is rewarded by the purchase of one slim volume, called *Learning to Hear*.[4]

Now, this idea is completely new to me. We were told that Ben's deafness was permanent. I know that some physical handicaps can be alleviated by various kinds of training and therapy, but it has never occurred to me that deafness might be curable in this way, and certainly none of the professionals we have spoken to has mentioned the possibility of Ben actually *learning* to hear. But wait a minute . . . I struggle to remember the consultant's exact words. Something about having a normal speaking child if the parents are intelligent—well, yes, we are, and if the child is intelligent—well, Ben seems so . . . but he was talking about learning to speak, not learning to hear . . . but of course, the two must be connected . . . My mind can hardly keep pace with its own deliberations and I can't wait for the chance to read.

The chance comes sooner than I expected. Ben falls asleep on the bus home and I am able to skim through the book. In that short time I discover two new concepts: *auditory training* and *residual hearing*. I learn that total deafness is extremely rare, and that most deaf children have something called residual hearing, which can be trained, sort of coached and coaxed, so that the child is able to make full use of it in appreciating sound. Fitting of hearing aids is of course vitally important, since these amplify the sounds so that a greater proportion of them can be perceived by the child. But with auditory training, the number of sounds perceived can be significantly increased as the child 'learns to listen', and the earlier the training starts the greater the chances of success. Deaf children in ordinary schools, deaf children with normal speech . . . all this accomplished by training, sometimes simply by mothers speaking into their children's ears. Success has been achieved by born deaf children, by severely deaf children— what did the consultant say? 'A very severe hearing loss.' All this sounds very positive, very hopeful . . .

My mind is buzzing away, desperate to make a start. Ben wakes up as we get off the bus. I do not strap him into his buggy. I put the shopping bag in the buggy, push it with one hand and carry Ben in the other arm, talking into his ear, all the way home.

Once home, I am anxious to show Ray what I have learned so that he can do it, too, but, despite my enthusiasm, Ben will not co-operate. Back on familiar territory, he would far rather chase the dog, or tease us by attempting to eat from its bowl or by approaching the fireplace—both of which little acts he knows will bring instant reactions— either a waggled finger if he catches our eye or a mad dash to move him or the object of his attentions. Unperturbed, though, I tell Ray about what I have read.

'Talk to him all the time?' he asks. He knows of my theory about the 'running commentary' approach with children: I feel that, if a child is talked to all the time, the sound of the parent's voice will become like a radio or a TV always on in the background—will, in effect, become background noise. I think that exposure to such 'noise' impedes children's concentration and will make them poor listeners when the time comes actually to get and remember specific information from what they hear. Meaningful conversation, fine, but talk for talk's sake I think can do more harm than good with little children: it can become like nagging, habitually ignored. It seems strange to Ray that I should actually want to subject Ben to a barrage of sound when I have purposely avoided it with Sarah. He does have a point.

Once Ben is in bed, Sarah watching TV with Grandad, Ray marking books at the kitchen table, I look carefully through *Learning to Hear* again and try to relate the information contained in it to our own situation. It becomes clear that the crucial factor, the major resource in the education and training of young deaf children, is the time and patience of their mothers. Not technical aids, not schools, not the support services. Their mothers.

The significance of this suddenly hits me, like a blow between the shoulder blades. At the moment I have not a great deal of confidence in myself as a mother. Apart from the blow to my self-assurance caused by the realisation that I need professional help in bringing up Ben, I am finding life in general much more difficult now that he is no longer an immobile baby. Just living with my two youngsters is proving to be a greater challenge, both physical and mental, than I ever thought possible. An only child myself, life at home as I remember it was quiet, trouble-free. I find the conflicts that arise now that both children are mobile almost intolerable. Not used to so-called 'sibling rivalry'— except in books—I waver between guilt and panic whenever there are disputes. When Sarah provokes or attacks Ben my first response is always to be angry at her, but then my anger is quick to turn in on myself: I brought her up, I must have done something wrong; it must be my fault she's so aggressive; I can't be handling her properly. Ben is still at an age when caretaking is ongoing: he has to have his nappy changed, he has to be fed, he has to have attention when he cries, he has to be protected from danger, watched constantly unless he is asleep. Sarah must feel neglected a lot of the time: her frequent 'accidents' (puddles every-where), attacks on her grandmother, acts of physical damage—crayoning on things, even at one stage tearing two pairs of net curtains at my mother's home—must indicate a high degree of anxiety or unhappiness . . . how am I going to give Ben all the extra time and training this book says I must give him when his physical care takes up so much time and Sarah needs me so much? When shall I find time to acquire the expertise I am determined to gain for myself regarding Ben's upbringing?

Ray is still marking furiously; since he started his new job he has brought work home most nights; he has also increased the amount of time he spends running: a swift few miles in the open air before the evening meal gives him breathing-space between the teenagers he teaches at school and the babies he lives with at home. Sometimes, I count myself as one of those babies: my behaviour towards the children these days is often anything but 'adult'; I lose my temper with them, vent my anger in words and then, as often as not, sulk, just like a four-year-old, locked in my own little cage of frustration, quietly tormenting myself. It is Ray who brings me out of these moods, makes me laugh, cheers me up . . . but he has a lot on his mind just now. He is at a stressful time in his career, having just taken over as head of department in a large school. How much support will he be able to give me? How much time will he have for Ben? This is a time of life when husbands have every right to expect support from their wives—yet I feel more in need of support than able to give it.

We have lived with Ray's parents for five months now. Watching Sarah, cuddled up in an armchair with her grandfather, I think about how much I have come to take his help for granted, and Ray's mother's: someone to babysit, someone to take one child shopping while I give some time to the other, someone to do all the cleaning and most of the cooking . . . How did I manage before we came? And how shall I manage once we move? Just learning to run a household again seems a daunting task in itself. Coping with the children on my own, and training Ben, and educating myself . . . it all seems too difficult to contemplate.

'Let's go out,' I say, when Ray finally closes the last book. As usual, he talks me round. We're about to move into our dream home, he reminds me. It's in the hills, right on the edge of the country, below a meadow, surrounded by trees. It took us a long time to find it and we've waited for it for five months. Soon it will be ours. It's a big house, it will be perfect for the children, lots of room to play; they can each have a room of their own; I can take them for walks in the fields. We were always busy in our old home, but we managed. Think about that. Think how pleasant it is to move into a new home, finding new little places to put things—it'll be like playing house. And Ray will be much closer to his workplace, so he will have more time, and the first few months in a new job are always the hardest . . .

So we start dreaming, about what it will be like to live in our new house, and I forget my worries. One thing at a time. Let's get the move over with first. Let's settle the children into their new home first. Let's settle down ourselves. There's no hurry. Everything's going to be all right.

Then the date arrives to meet the consultant again to discuss the results of the hospital tests. Thanks to the break, and the book, and the audiologist, and *Talk*, and the social worker, we are now better informed and better able to understand what he tells us. He says that the results have confirmed his original impression: Ben has a hearing loss of 100 decibels or more. I think back to the book. I remember reading of 20 dB losses, 70, maybe 90 . . . but over 100?

'Will he be able to hear anything, then?' I ask. The consultant explains that 100 dB is about the volume of a heavy lorry at close quarters. He tells us that Ben's hearing can be boosted with hearing aids, 'but don't let anyone tell you that the kind of aid will make much difference, because, quite honestly, it won't.' He is reluctant to appear too pessimistic; he explains that fluctuations in the results of these tests can sometimes occur . . . If Ben was in a bad mood when he 'went under', the result might be worse than if he went to sleep peacefully . . . I think back. Ben was in a horrible mood. He wanted a breast-feed and he couldn't have one because of the anaesthetic . . . he was really miserable by the time he finally fell asleep.

Ray and I are confused. We expected concrete information from this meeting, a kind of confirmation. But we are still left with uncertainty. Will Ben hear or won't he? Is his loss over 100dB or under? What will he get through his aids? I actually ask this last question. Again, the reluctance. 'He might get a sort of low rumble.' He might. We ask a few more questions. The answers are equally vague. Precise information is obviously hard to come by. It is not that this man is being deliberately awkward; he does not appear to resent the questions, and it is not that he is in a hurry; he seems to have plenty of time for us; his face is open and his eyes are immensely kind. Is he unable to say—or unwilling? I am reminded of the health visitors who examined Ben before we moved up here. If they suspected deafness, they didn't say so outright; it was 'immaturity', maybe. Even when they decided to refer Ben to a hearing specialist it was 'just in case'. Here, after each test, even the one which convinced Ray and me that Ben was completely deaf, no firm opinions were expressed; we were always simply referred 'for more tests'. At each stage, every possibility of error was checked and double-checked, almost as if they were waiting to be proved wrong. Or maybe they were all waiting for the specialist's opinion. Yet here is the specialist and he isn't giving any firm opinions either.

I am sure that all these people mean well; in our contact with them we have always been treated with genuine kindness and concern. Everyone has been so very nice to us, almost as if . . . Yes. I recognise that kind of concern. From books, from films, from my own experience and that of my mother I recognise it. The evasive answers, the quiet voices, the sad yet resigned faces, the understanding smiles. That's sympathy. That's the kind of sympathy you extend to someone bereaved. As if Ben were dying. Dying, not deaf. We have been protected throughout, in much the same way as people are protected from knowledge of impending death, as if knowledge of what was suspected would be too hard for us to bear.

As we leave the consultant's office for this final time, I feel somehow let down. We thought that we were going to find out how deaf Ben was. We thought that after this visit we would have more idea about how his deafness would affect him. Yet we are no nearer the truth than before. We must 'wait and see' yet again. We must see how he responds to his hearing aid, then we might have a clearer picture.

So what have we gained from all these visits and from all these meetings with professionals? Ben has gained a grommet in his right ear, a prescription for a hearing aid, a

set of earmould impressions and record cards in several
different departments. Ray and I have gained a lot of
sympathy, a smattering of information, and a totally new
image of our child. We are the parents of a handicapped
individual. With the arrival of the support team I have been
forced to acknowledge that fact, forced to see Ben's
deafness not as a difference easily accommodated in the
day-to-day running of things, but as an illness, a disability,
a *handicap*, which I shall have to struggle to help him to
overcome. Part of me feels determined to carry it through;
the other part still feels unequal to the task, ill-prepared,
not ready.

I let the defence system take over once more. I focus my
attention on the new house, on the pleasure of moving in,
watching the children delight in the space, the views (the
viaduct, the village, the countryside) . . . and then I
concentrate on preparations for Christmas. The children
seem to be getting on better; Sarah is pleased with her new
bedroom 'of my very own', and Ben loves the low windows;
the sills are at just the right height for him to pull himself
up on and he spends a lot of time standing watching the
world go by: trains passing at eye level over the viaduct and
big red buses on the road below. We go for walks in the
snow, Ben in a pack on Ray's back, Sarah falling gleefully
into snowdrifts three feet deep. We feel healthy, free,
happy. This is the sort of life Ray and I mapped out for
ourselves when first we decided to stay together and have a
family. It has taken us ten years to get here, but it was
worth the wait. Now, we have no desire to move on or to
move up; we have all we need here, and more. People who
don't know me say hello to me in the street. There are no
curtains yet on the big bay window overlooking the village;
at Christmas time, our own little tree sparkling in the
corner, we can see everyone else's; coloured lights in the
darkness. We are part of all that; we belong. I feel a great
sense of peace and stability. I feel as if I have come home.

We meet our neighbours, including 'the other Fletchers',
a family along the lane with so many coincidental resem-
blances to our own that they feel special from the start.
Now, there are two Sarah Fletchers—our own and their

baby. And two Mr R. Fletchers—Ray and Roger. And elder children with birthdays one day apart . . . and the first people we get close to in our new home . . . and a dilemma.

At their house, our first 'official' visit. We are all there. Both families, their children and ours, grown-ups with sherry, children with Lego. Ben is cruising round the furniture. Annette is talking to him. He is not responding. I watch. Really, I should tell her. But what if she's embarrassed? What if there's one of those nasty awkward silences where nobody knows what to say? Out of all the activity in the room, all I am aware of now is this little child, playing, oblivious to anyone's attempts to get his attention. It must be obvious that there's something not quite right with him. I force myself to speak.

'If you notice anything strange about Ben, there's nothing wrong with him, it's just that he's deaf.'

Nothing wrong, just deaf. Denial or acceptance? Does his deafness really matter? There is a whole new community here which is going to know us, not as we were, but as we are, a family consisting of four people, one of whom is deaf. No change, for these people. Not the shock of our friends down South or the pain of our parents on realising that our baby was deaf—but the understanding that this new family has a deaf baby. A subtle difference, but important. Another chapter in our lives: Ben, our deaf child. And a new environment in which to begin it: this northern village, our new home.

'I hadn't noticed anything strange about him,' Annette is saying. 'He just seems like an ordinary, normal little boy.'

I smile at her, relieved. The telling wasn't so hard.

Just after the Christmas holidays, we are surprised to receive a telephone call from the social worker we saw after Ben's diagnosis. We are technically off his patch now, he says, but he only lives just up the road. Would we like him to call and see us one evening? Maybe, now that we've had a little time to think about things, we would like the opportunity to have a chat? He would like to help us in any way he can.

The post-diagnosis meeting seems a long way behind us now; we have indeed had time to reflect and, although the

idea of having a visit from a social worker still seems
strange to us, and although we have mixed feelings about
what the various professionals have to offer, it would be
nice to talk to someone. We are very touched that this man
has not forgotten us and that he is prepared to give up his
own time to come and see us 'out of hours'. So I ask him to
come and we arrange a time.

He duly arrives, early one evening; we sit around the fire
and talk. Ben's earmoulds have also arrived; tiny, in
smooth, hard, transparent plastic, two little glinting
jewels, they sit above us on the mantelpiece, while the
children play between us on the hearthrug, unusually
demanding little attention, Ben occasionally crawling off to
kneel at the window and watch the traffic gliding by in the
orange light of the road below. The conversation starts off
general: how have we settled in? What are the neighbours
like. . . ? But very soon it focusses on Ben: how are we
coping? Have we had any contact from the social services?
Or the education service? No, as yet, no contact. As well as
talking to us, the social worker talks to Ben and Sarah. He
has plenty of time for both children, but when he talks to
Ben I'm sure there is a special intensity, a sort of
determination to notice and be noticed. Any overture from
Ben is remarked upon and replied to, almost made a game
of. Asking how we are managing to communicate with
Ben, the social worker mentions this himself; he tells us
how important it is for Ben to learn to look and pay
attention to people's faces. We may have been encouraging
this ourselves quite naturally, he says, but it is as well to get
into the habit of responding in an interesting way, of
holding and making the most of Ben's attention whenever
possible.

He gestures towards the earmoulds: have we tried Ben
with them yet? It hasn't occurred to us that we could; we
saw them as an attachment for the hearing aid we haven't
yet received, and anyway we have no idea how to put them
in. He suggests that we try. Young children, he says, often
show a resistance at first to wearing earmoulds, but the
younger Ben is when we first try them, the more likely it is
that he will accept them without a fuss. He demonstrates,

and it quickly becomes apparent that we haven't caught Ben quite early enough. He accepts the first quite placidly and we are able to note—and applaud—the man's technique, but the second is refused and is swiftly rejoined by the first, which Ben is able to wiggle out of his ear with one twist of a chubby little finger. It is with some trepidation that we replace them on the mantelpiece: what if Ben won't wear them? The social worker's response is good-natured; it is comforting to talk to someone who has known lots of children like Ben. It is useful to observe and to copy his tactics in encouraging Ben to communicate.

But it is not until the last few minutes of his visit that the most significant aspect of it—for us—emerges. By now the children are beginning to make it obvious that they are ready for bed, and the social worker is sensitive enough to take this as his cue to leave. But just as he does, he reaches down into his briefcase and hands us two books—almost as an afterthought. One, he says, is by the president of Gallaudet, the college for the deaf in America, and is about the use of sign language in educating the deaf in a college setting, *How a Special College Serves Deaf People*.[5] The other is a newly-published manual about deafness, written by two British experts from Manchester University, *The Hearing Impaired Child and the Family*.[6] Very cautiously, with a studied air of non-committal, he explains to us that there are two bodies of opinion regarding the use of sign language with deaf children. Some authorities reject it altogether—in fact, he says, if we had still been in his authority, the need to conform to educational practice there would have prevented him from even referring to it in his dealings with us as parents of a newly-diagnosed deaf child. He hopes that the two books, together, will give us a fairly balanced picture.

Sign language! My mind immediately flashes back to our post-diagnosis meeting with the consultant, to the scrappy bit of paper we took with us with all our questions written down on it. Hadn't Ray written, 'Should we learn sign language?' What happened to that question? Did we ever ask it? Why haven't we thought of it since? It seems such an obvious—the obvious—response to an absence of hearing. If you can't go in via the ears, use the eyes instead.

I can't wait to get the children to bed so that I can read the pamphlet. In fact, I'm in bed myself before I get the chance to have a look at it, but once I start reading I can't put it down. It reveals how deaf students at Gallaudet are not disadvantaged by their deafness because all the teaching there is done in sign language. This little book does not seek to advise or instruct; simply, it offers a glimpse of very real possibilities: here is a language that any deaf child can learn, no matter how deaf and no matter what his potential for speech—those two variables which have so far eluded us in our attempts at foreseeing Ben's future. Sign language can open up to *any* deaf child, as it has to these students in America, education at the highest levels. It all seems so logical, so fair. Reading the *Learning to Hear* book, after the first, short-lived flush of enthusiasm, I felt weary, anxious, under pressure, and I was unwilling to respond. But this little pamphlet brings with it relief, confidence, a sense of pleasurable anticipation, even excitement! Sleep is a long time coming as I plan a future for Ben. He will be able to learn sign language! If he learns sign language he will no longer be disadvantaged. I can't wait to get started. I feel happy, full of energy. This is what I should have read the day after Ben's diagnosis. This is what I should have read the moment I suspected that Ben was deaf. How different, how much simpler my feelings about him would have been if I had. These people at Gallaudet are not handicapped—far from it. Ben can be like them.

Next day, as soon as I can snatch a moment between chores and the demands of my own children, I take a look at *The Hearing Impaired Child and the Family*. The cover bears an engaging photograph of a small boy, complete with hearing aids. It looks as if he is on a see-saw in a swing park. He is a beautiful child: chubby, healthy, rosy-cheeked. My eyes flick from the face to the hearing aids; back to the face, then to the hearing aids again. I recognise in myself a deep feeling of pity, of sadness. This is what Ben will look like. And other people will look at him, and do what I have just done, and feel as I did . . .

The book is sensitively written; obviously the authors

have had a lot of experience both of deaf children and of their parents—and their attitude to deafness is the one I have come to expect of professionals working in the field: deafness is a severe disability. Contrast with the Gallaudet pamphlet could not be more marked. There was optimism, here is sympathy. There the handicap could be ignored, here it can be worked at. In many cases it can be largely overcome—they do not use the word 'cured', but it springs to my mind—by the use of hearing aids (technology is the answer) and hard work. This is a larger and more up-to-date volume, but the message it gives is the same as *Learning to Hear*. There is much information about types and causes of deafness, the internal workings of the ear, surgical procedures, hearing aids, test equipment, the science of audiology, auditory training and testing . . . the information is detailed and involved; it takes days to wade through it, but I do so, conscientiously. I notice that in this manual deaf children are never referred to as deaf. Hearing impaired—the authors' term—seems to fit in with their view: the 'impaired' part of the phrase jumps out at me from the page wherever it is used. The term 'hearing impaired' carries with it the constant reminder of a fault, something wrong, broken. I don't like to think of Ben that way. But the manual is certainly comprehensive—everything you need to know about your hearing impaired child. Or is there? I flick through its many pages again, then the index, searching for something. These people are experts. What do they think about sign language? What is their advice to parents about that?

I cannot find any advice. I cannot even find a reference. For the two very experienced authors of this family guide to deafness, sign language is not worth a mention. I seek out *Learning to Hear* (which has conveniently lost itself under a pile of other books so I don't have to think about it), and I look through that. I find a brief reference to sign language in the introduction: 'There was a controversy between the advocates of sign language and finger spelling (the manual method) and the advocates of lip-reading (the oral method). Lip reading was the orthodox method in this country although signs were also used to a varying extent,

sometimes officially and deliberately, sometimes unof-
ficially.'[7] Then nothing. Controversy, says Learning to Hear,
two bodies of opinion, says the social worker . . . quite
obviously there is some nervousness about sign language
in official circles, at least in this country, some reluctance
even to mention it, let alone to make use of it. The seeds of
doubt are sown. As I read the Gallaudet pamphlet in bed
that night the proverbial light-bulb appeared over my head
and flashed into life. Now, I can almost feel its light fading
because of the implications of what I have just read. The
idea is still there, but I can't ignore the warnings: implicit
in the fact that these respected educators of the deaf
choose not to include it in a manual for parents; implied by
a local authority which advises its social worker not to
mention sign language to new parents. Signing seems such
a logical solution, such an easy way out of communication
difficulties. But people don't appear to be taking it. Why?

Indecision, with me, quickly translates itself into inaction.
I'm no longer certain about sign language, I am as yet
unable to face up to the rigorous training routines
advocated by these other books . . . so I do nothing.

It is, after all, very easy to do nothing at this time. I'm
very busy with the new house and much preoccupied with
settling a very nervous Sarah into nursery school. I don't
feel any great sense of urgency. Ben, at fourteen months, is
a delightful baby. The problems we are aware of are few:
we have to head him off physically if he is approaching
danger because it's impossible to call him; if he cries we
have to find some kind of visible distraction (flashing the
light on and off works); he wakes frequently in the night.
But none of these problems is serious. Once we have
eliminated obvious dangers around the house—as you
would for any baby—so that it is safe for Ben to crawl
about in, we find him by far the easier and the less
demanding of the two children. Sarah's needs at this time
are many and varied, but difficult to ascertain, and when
one is satisfied, another immediately arises to take its place.
Ben is oblivious to adult conversation, whereas for Sarah it
seems to trigger off an urgent need to exercise every
muscle in her body—especially her vocal cords—in the

closest possible vicinity to the people who are talking. Ben eats anything that's put in front of him; Sarah changes her mind four times between planning a meal and serving it, and then rarely eats it, demanding biscuits half an hour later. A quick breast-feed sends Ben into deep and peaceful slumber; Sarah needs songs, stories, more songs, more stories, cuddles, drinks, the light on, the light off, Mummy to do it, Daddy to do it, the curtains drawn, the curtains open . . . just coping with Sarah is a job in itself. We do elaborate our home-made gesture system a little for Ben, and we continue to use the social worker's communication techniques and those we have evolved ourselves, but this seems to be enough for him. Basically, we treat him as an ordinary child, pleased that this is still possible. 'An ordinary, normal little boy', Annette said. Yes, he can be that, to them, and to us also. He is deaf, but he has a right to be ordinary and normal, too. We should not let concern about his deafness deprive him of that right. He is happy; we are happy with him. We see no need, and have no great inclination, to make changes. We don't want to change Ben. We like him as he is.

Notes

1 COURTMAN-DAVIES, M. *Your Deaf Child's Speech and Language*, London: Bodley Head.

2 The John Tracy Clinic, 206 West Adam Boulevard, Los Angeles, California 90007, USA.

3 The National Deaf Children's Society, 45 Hereford Road, London W2 5AH.

4 WHETNALL, E., and FRY, D.B. (ed. R. Niven). *Learning to Hear*, London: Heinemann (1970).

5 MERRILL, E.G., Jr. *How a Special College Serves Deaf People*, Carlisle: British Deaf Association Publications.

6 NOLAN, M., and TUCKER, I.G. *The Hearing Impaired Child and the Family*, London: Souvenir Press (1981).

7 WHETNALL and FRY *op. cit.*, Chapter 1, p. 1.

3 DEAFNESS: THE TREATMENT

Ben is sixteen months old. We feel as if we have lived in the village all our lives. Sarah has settled reasonably well into nursery school, and now I am able to spend some time with Ben, giving him the sort of attention which Sarah so loved at this age, the kind which it is easy to give to a first child, but which is so difficult to find time for with a second if the first is still at home.

Just as when he was a baby I used to look forward to those after-bath sessions when we were alone, and even enjoyed early-hours feeds for the same reasons, I love our afternoons. But we do have one problem.

Ben has hearing aids now, two little grey pocket ones which fit neatly into his dungarees . . . but they spend most of their time on top of the fridge. Sometimes I manage to get them into position when Ben is asleep, but if awake he sees them as pull-apart toys rather than equipment to help him to hear. There is no way he will actually leave the earmoulds in place and the aids in his pockets.

My feelings about the aids are ambiguous. Ben is a beautiful baby. Hearing aids are ugly things: what mother could honestly say she felt happy about seeing her child festooned in this way with electronic equipment, other than in a situation where it was necessary to save or preserve its life? Ben in pocket aids, wires sprouting out of his ears, makes me think of a baby in an incubator, tubes protruding from every orifice, and provokes in me the same kind of reaction: immense sadness and sympathy, an urge to see the child out of there, well and healthy, in its mother's arms. So, yes, I try the aids every so often, but half-heartedly, struggling all the while with that part of me which cannot bear . . . to interfere with him in such a way.

On walks, Ray and I have carried the aids with us,

waiting for Ben to fall asleep; we have fixed them in place and inserted the earmoulds, and we have had to witness an immediate change in the reaction of passers-by. Everyone looks at a baby, especially one as pretty as Ben. Sarah bouncing alongside is the picture of health, all red cheeks and curls . . . People smile as they pass us, they talk to Sarah, they beam at Ben, who beams back. But once Ben is wearing his aids, it is as if people dare not look—or they look quickly, avert their eyes and walk on. If anyone talks to us it is to offer pity. It is as if all the health, all the vitality, all the attractiveness of this little family is eclipsed by the fact that the baby has wires coming out of its ears. Of course, I understand how they feel completely because my instinctive reaction is the same. But, unlike them, I can't ignore the aids. I have to handle them daily, test them, keep the earmoulds clean, check the wires for fraying, find ways of fitting them to Ben's clothes, and, worst of all, I have to attempt to get Ben to wear the damned things against his will. Yes, I understand their reaction: it's the same as mine, but I have to suppress mine; I am supposed to see these things not as the cause of a problem but as a solution to one; I am supposed to be grateful for them.

So at home I allow myself time to get used to the things. I don't force them on Ben and I don't force them on myself either. I use opportunities as they arise and the rest of the time I forget about them, in much the same way as I have allowed myself to forget about *Learning to Hear*. I was not ready three months ago and I am still not ready. The urge to help Ben is still there, of course it is, but I feel I am helping him now, in my own way, by playing the games he likes and by following his lead, just as I did with Sarah.

One afternoon, having delivered Sarah to nursery school, I arrive home to find a little note on the doormat:

> Sorry I missed you.
> Will be in touch.
> Jan C——
> Teacher of the Deaf

Teacher of the Deaf. The title is vaguely familiar. As I play around with the thoughts it provokes I recall the social worker's question, and passages from the Manchester book . . . I remember that there are special teachers for the deaf . . . and Ben is to have one—now! I look at my baby, asleep in his buggy, mouth open, snoring gently, then I look again at the note. Do we need help teaching him? The idea of teaching this sixteen-month-old still seems, somehow, inappropriate. In fact, it is exactly what I have been avoiding.

I think of Sarah at sixteen months. Her environment itself seemed to result in her learning things, and the motivation came from within her: her own curiosity and determination to widen her experience of the world and increase her effect on it resulted in her learning, quite naturally and without pressure, all that she needed to know. At Ben's age she had no teacher . . . but she did have adults, she had parents and friends. What was our rôle in her natural learning process at that time? How did we help her? We provided a stimulating environment, we provided new play ideas or repeated old ones, as she liked. But did we teach her? Actually setting out to teach Sarah anything usually met with resistance. Whereas for us to follow her inclinations seemed to be great fun for her, the reverse situation soon became boring; her busy little mind was already somewhere else. She learned at her own pace—but it was fast . . . I remember that at Ben's age she understood practically everything we said to her . . .

And here, unavoidably, the difference is clarified. Possibly the most important aspect of our rôle in helping Sarah to learn surfaces: communication. We talk to her. We don't teach her, but we tell her about things and we answer her questions. And at an age when Sarah was starting to talk, Ben understands only a few gestures. As far as is possible with a second child, we have provided Ben with the same environment for learning as his sister had, but he gets no commentary about what he does and he has only the rudiments of language with which to manipulate his environment. We talk to him, but he doesn't hear us, and not even the most stimulating of environments can result in much learning if communication is limited.

Teacher of the Deaf. My idea of her rôle takes shape. If

we need help with anything, we and Ben, it is with language. Some kind of language. Thinking about it, language is the one area in which we must be failing him. In struggling to decide what to do, I have ignored this fact for long enough. Really, something has to be done.

Ben wakes up, wet through. Changing his nappy these days is not a simple operation. Once free of nappy Ben crawls away at top speed; catching him and getting him to keep still for the clean one is not easy. I keep a stock of little-used toys in the hope that examining one of these will keep his attention for long enough. I think of Baby Sarah along the lane, younger than Ben but at the same stage, kept riveted by her mother's constant patter, gazing up into Annette's face, babbling, hardly noticing the nappy change in her fascination with the latest silly rhyme or nursery song, infinitely distractable by voice and tone of voice alone. Not so Ben: if he is looking at something other than my face there is no contact at all; when I do get his attention I can't hold it for long; he would rather crawl off and find something to do than watch my lips move . . . I crawl after him and carry him, struggling and protesting, back to the mat, hand him another toy from a rapidly diminishing pile. If my time and patience were infinite, I could manage without being physical like this, but Ben is only one out of a family of four. With the exception of weekday afternoons, this particular couple of hours in the day, there are always other demands on my time. It would help if I could temper my actions with words, as I do with Sarah. It would help if I could explain. Yes, the sooner we meet this teacher of the deaf and get some sort of communication established, the better.

When she arrives, I like her at once. She is the sort of person I would have chosen as a friend. She has a bouncy manner, a friendly smile and a reassuring way of talking. She gets down on the floor with Ben and me and she plays with him. He likes her. When she isn't talking to Ben she is asking me questions. Does he have a hearing aid? How is he responding to sound? Do his earmoulds fit OK? I show her the pocket aids, embarrassed that they are on top of the fridge rather than attached to Ben, and I explain that he won't wear them. 'Well, they're not very good,' she says, 'I'll try to get him a Phonic Ear—but we might as well start by trying to get him used to these ones.' Energy and enthusiasm just shine out of her as she fits all the component bits together, hooks the aids onto Ben's dungarees and deftly slips in an earmould, talking cheerfully all the time. I watch, incredulous. So far, with us, Ben has only tolerated the earmoulds whilst asleep. Ray and I are so clumsy and nervous, so anxious not to hurt him, so very tentative in our attempts to fit the earmoulds into those tiny ears, that Ben reacts at once: the whole apparatus is wrenched off and discarded in one easy movement. It's like a game with us. We approach with the aids. Ben prepares himself. We give him something to hold or to eat; in the momentary distraction we make our move; Ben parries; the moment is lost. It soon transpires that, despite her expertise, Jan's only real advantage is surprise; as soon as Ben realises that this new person plays the same game, the earmould flies out as swiftly as it went in. Jan laughs. 'You'll have to be firm,' she says. 'It'll take a while but he'll get used to it.' She gently but firmly repeats the operation several times, matter-of-factly, showing no reaction, until Ben begins to show distress rather than annoyance.

'OK,' she says, 'we'll stop there. But you must keep trying so we can start training his hearing.'

Ray is home when we have our first training session. Jan does indeed want to help us in our efforts to get through to Ben, and we are both relieved when she says that the best way to do it is through play. She demonstrates. With Ben in his high chair, the tray empty in front of him, she sits opposite him, her face level with his, and produces a toy from behind her back. Ben's eyes follow the toy, a brightly coloured ball, as she raises it to her face, careful not to obscure her mouth.

'It's a ball, Ben,' she says. Suddenly she throws it up, catches it, brings it close again.

'Here's the ball, look!' Ben is watching all the time. She puts the ball behind her back. Ben knows it's there; he is waiting for it to come back out. He's enjoying this game.

'Where's the ball?' Jan asks, and, to us, 'Make sure he

watches your face. Whenever he looks, say something.' Ben is craning his neck to see behind her, where the ball is. She moves so that her face is within his field of vision.

'Where's the ball, Ben? Do you want the ball?' Ben's gaze has shifted again, from her face, past it. He wants to see the ball. It doesn't emerge. He looks at Jan's face again.

'Do you want the ball?' Ben makes a sound. Jan's face lights up. 'YES!!! Good boy!' The ball appears, as if by magic. Ben holds out his arms but the ball stays where it is, next to Jan's face.

'Here's the ball, look. Here it is. Do you want the ball?' Ben is holding out his arms even further, straining over the empty tray towards the ball, looking alternately at it and at Jan's face. Whenever he looks at her, Jan asks if he wants the ball. At last, he vocalises. She beams at him.

'Oh, I see, you want the ball!' At last, she gives it to him. He holds it for a few moments, then looks at her. He wants to continue the game.

'Give me the ball, then,' she says, and starts again. No opportunity is missed. Eye contact must result in communication. If he looks, talk. This is the social worker's advice extended into a teaching session.

'OK? Now you try,' says Jan. I take the ball. No problem, we've played similar games before, except that now I capitalise on the eye contact. Ben holds out his hands for the ball, I hold it by my face while I ask if he wants it, then I pass it to him.

'Hold on a minute,' says Jan. 'He didn't ask for it.'

'Yes he did,' I reply, 'he held his hands out.'

'Yes, but he didn't ask. You must wait till he vocalises, then give it to him, or he won't learn to talk. If you want him to talk, you'll have to get him used to the idea that talking gets results where not talking doesn't.' I try again. Ben shows in his whole demeanour that he wants the ball; his body speaks volumes but his lips make not a sound. I can't resist such an obvious demand. I give him the ball.

'Oh, you're going to have problems, you are,' says Jan. I explain that it feels cruel and unnatural to me, to hold something back that Ben so obviously wants.

'I do know how you feel,' says Jan, 'but if you want him to

learn to use his voice you're going to have to be firm. You'll get used to it and so will he. He's a bright kid. It won't take him long to make the connection between using his voice and getting what he wants. Watch.' She demonstrates again. This time it takes longer. Ben is very nearly at distress point, but then he makes a sound and is rewarded by a beaming smile and the coveted ball. 'You can do the same with his food,' says Jan. 'Have you got a drink for him?' I fetch his beaker, am about to put it down on his tray.

'Wait a minute,' says Jan. 'Don't waste your opportunities! Ask if he wants a drink.' I learn quickly. Beaker at my cheek, I ask Ben if he wants it.

'Do you want this?' I ask sweetly. 'Do you want a drink?' I am determined to wait this time. Ben reaches out. I hold the beaker near my face. 'Is it the drink you want, Ben?' His chin begins to quiver. He stretches towards me, arms out. I feel very anxious, torn between wanting to follow this teacher's instructions and not wanting to make my baby cry. I repeat the words, but without conviction. He is obviously baffled and upset, and I can't stand it. He whimpers. I'm so relieved I pass him the drink straight away. I know that the sound he made was the usual preliminary to a fully-fledged howl, but maybe it will pass as a vocalisation. It does. If Jan knows she's not telling.

'Well done!' she says. 'But you forgot to tell him what it was before you gave it to him.'

She tells us about the importance of being firm, of being in control of the situation and consistent in our responses: ignore any non-verbal requests or demands; respond only to vocalisation.

A persistent little voice inside my head is fighting to be heard. 'If this is deaf education,' it is saying, 'it could use a few changes . . .' But respect for Jan's professional status and obvious experience keeps blocking it out. We want to help Ben. She is showing us how it can be done. How can I tell her that her way is wrong when I have no experience of it?

When she has left both Ray and I are quiet. I have avoided this way of helping Ben for months; I could have followed the instructions on auditory training in *Learning to Hear*, but I haven't. And now I know why. It hasn't just been laziness or an unwillingness to face up to things. What Jan has just demonstrated is simply not our way of doing things. As well as trying to cultivate a relaxed attitude to parenting, help the children towards self-discipline rather than overtly disciplining them, we have our own ideas about teaching and learning. We have both trained as teachers, and together we have read and discussed theories about how children learn. The ones which most appeal to us are those which have as their basis a firm respect for the rights of children as originators and decision-makers in their own learning, where the teacher's rôle is seen as facilitating, not forcing, learning experiences. You can teach all you like, say those educators we have come to respect, but children will learn only what they want to learn, when they want to learn it. Effective learning is child-initiated. Our own experience so far with Sarah, and with the children in our classes, gives ample support to this view, and over the years it has become our own. It fits in with us as people, with our way of thinking and with the way we would like to relate to children, both our own and other people's. What we are being asked to do now, with Ben, though not exactly contradicting this view, sits awkwardly alongside it, and we are both uneasy.

Ray has very little time for a method of teaching which pins children down and delivers formal training. He has a superb relationship with Ben: when Ray is around Ben has little time for anyone else; they kiss and cuddle a lot, Ray holds him close, carries him about, shows him things, talks to him. They have special games which are theirs alone; they rough and tumble; they make each other laugh. Ray values their relationship as it is; he is reluctant to change the way he operates just for the sake of extracting a few sounds from Ben. Ray's view of language is much wider. Anyone can see that he is communicating with his son, that they both derive a lot of pleasure from exchanges which do not require either of them to speak or to hear. They are attached to each other by an invisible cord; they are on the same wavelength. Ray refuses to jeopardise this by making demands on Ben which he feels are inappropriate, unfair and educationally ineffective.

I start with the same set of ideals but my judgement is blurred: in this kind of situation the anxious schoolgirl aspect of my personality comes to the fore: this person in authority, this teacher, is asking me to perform and I have to do well. When I gave in to Ben she noticed, she commented, and I felt that I had failed. I could ignore advice from books, but I can't ignore advice from a teacher. Even when my instincts are urging me to rebel, the voice of years of conditioning says that I must not, that teacher knows best and I must live up to her expectations of me.

Fear for Ben's future also leads me to conform. All my experience so far has been with hearing children; maybe deaf children do need handling differently; maybe I can't safely trust my own judgement—or Ray's—on this. I cannot risk my child's future; I must do my best for him, and Jan seems very sure of her methods. I don't have the confidence to defend my instinctive preferences against her professional advice, so I decide to play it her way and see what happens. Ray and I agree to differ.

From that first visit onwards, life is very different, for us and for Ben. Ray does agree that the hearing aid is a priority, so we embark upon an ongoing battle getting Ben to wear it. We try it whenever he falls asleep, whenever he is in his high chair, whenever he is sitting still and concentrating on a play activity. We seem to be constantly interfering with him, deliberately disrupting his old routines in order to establish this new one. But Jan offers us encouragement, assuring us that it is in Ben's best interests to wear the aid now, when he is small, to gain the best possible advantage from it. Thanks to her, Ben is able to borrow a Phonic Ear, a radio aid, with very high-powered amplification and excellent sound reproduction. I make up a harness for it so that it is impossible for Ben to dismantle or remove the aid once it is strapped to his chest. Eventually he accepts that it is put on every morning and kept on until bedtime. The aid becomes a part of his clothing: nappy, vest, jumper, dungarees, hearing aid. The earmoulds are more of a problem, though: they cannot be strapped on or glued in and Ben hates them. They dangle from their leads, swinging to and fro as he crawls about, being crushed underknee (not underfoot—Ben still isn't walking) and finding their way into obscure corners of the house and garden, acquiring unhygienic amounts of dirt in the process.

In our battle to 'persuade' Ben to tolerate the earmoulds, gradually we begin to tolerate in ourselves behaviour which a year or even six months ago we would have found totally unacceptable and abhorrent.

Ben and I are both still very attached to his bedtime breast-feed. It is communication without words; it is my way of letting Ben know that I love him and that I like to be close to him, that I'm his mother and that I'll take care of him, and it's his way of telling me that he needs me. In a busy and noisy household, it is one of the few chances we get to be quiet and alone. That changes.

Beside us on the cushion is the hearing aid. As soon as Ben begins to fall asleep I insert an earmould. The theory is that, once the earmould is in place, one must make sure that the child has something to listen to or for. So as soon as it is in position I begin to sing Ben lullabies, loudly, through the radio transmitter worn at my neck. What used to be a natural and peaceful event assumes the characteristics of science fiction, both of us cluttered up with gadgetry, clanking clumsily against each other like a pair of robots, every so often the roar of the lullabies interrupted by the high-pitched squeal of acoustic feedback as the earmould works loose. For weeks, Ben jerks wide awake as he feels the earmould against his ear, and he resists. Stoically, patiently, I feed him half asleep again and I repeat my attempt, sometimes three or four times, struggling with my own feelings of revulsion as well as with Ben's resistance. The bedtime feed becomes lengthy and tedious, all pleasure gone—but Ben does, eventually, accept the earmoulds and the first stage of the battle is won.

In the day, I persist in what is called 'conditioning', but really it is bribery and blackmail. If Ben accepts the earmoulds, he can have a biscuit, or a Smartie, or a drink. No earmoulds equals no attention. Earmoulds equals undivided attention, plus rewards, for as long as he keeps them in. The day is punctuated by the squeal of feedback as, for tens of dozens of times, Ben pulls out the moulds and the process is begun again. Three or four months of this and there is no more resistance from Ben; the battle is over. For me, too, in a sense, the battle is over. The fact that Ben is now able to accept the aid as a part of his clothing seems to help me to accept it in that way also. It is a nuisance at nappy change and mealtimes, when it has to be removed for its own protection, and the attention it needs during the day is time-consuming, but it is no longer repulsive. It might be a scar, but it's an old one now, and I'm used to it.

During and beyond the hearing aid battle, however, we have the training sessions for speech. We want desperately to establish some kind of formal language, so I attempt the sort of training which Jan demonstrated at least twice a day, and Jan does a session each time she comes. Ben is strapped into his high chair; playthings are lined up on the table and used to try and elicit speech. Once the hearing aid is established, sound-making toys are added; we operate them close to the radio transmitter and look for a response, beating drums, rattling shakers, squeaking rubber animals. I take my job seriously despite the lack of reaction in Ben and despite lack of support from Ray. I know that Ben is very deaf and that it will be a long process. I persevere, and Jan keeps me going. She sees responses where I do not; she delights in reactions which I would have dismissed as coincidental; she convinces me that we really are getting somewhere. We continue these sessions in a formal, planned way, and in our everyday interaction I try to insist on vocalisation whenever Ben makes a request. Of course, this makes every interaction between us much more lengthy than it would otherwise be. Conscious of Sarah's feelings, I try to include her in the process as much as possible, but it happens so frequently that she soon loses interest; sometimes, she hovers in the background waiting for her turn; sometimes she demands my attention constantly until she gets it, for herself, not as part of Ben's game.

The speech and auditory training sessions, the hearing

aid battle and the daily 'workload' with Ben take up a lot of my time and energy physically, but the mental strain involved is by far the most draining aspect: all the time, there is conflict with my own feelings about how a baby should be treated; surely this amount of pressure must be damaging, especially when it was imposed suddenly and is in such contrast to the way I dealt with Ben before the onset of training. Surely he must feel hurt and rejected when his obvious but non-vocal demands are ignored, or when I refuse to play with him because his earmoulds are not in place, or when the precious bedtime breast-feed becomes a battle of wills . . . Ray agrees; he can see my relationship with Ben becoming distorted by the demands I am making of him, and I feel very much alone in what I am attempting to do. Ray feels no need to please teacher—he never sees her. He just carries on doing things in the way he feels is right. Feelings of resentment arise between us, ill-founded, perhaps, in that theoretically I have the power to change things, but very real nevertheless. I persist in the training, but all the while I long for the kind of easy relationship I can see blossoming between Ray and Ben, jealous of the fact that he can still enjoy what I have had to give up, and angry that by taking this 'natural' stance he is avoiding so much of the 'real' work and the unpleasantness, forgetting that I, too, avoided it for as long as I possibly could.

Ray is highly sceptical when I try to report progress in 'my' work with Ben; I am increasingly defensive and discussions rapidly become heated and hurtful. There are too many conflicts, on too many levels, and eventually we just stop talking about it. In general, Ray and I talk less and less. My job with Ben is the dominant thought in my mind, almost an obsession. I never ease off; I have to do the job well, I have to succeed. Whatever else I appear to be doing, the pressure is still there in my mind, predominating, taking over. Ben is the motivating force in my life and time for Ray becomes harder and harder to find. But I do need his support; I lean on him constantly, giving less and less in return. We used to be so close; now, it is as if we are losing touch, being pulled apart by our feelings rather than drawn together. We are very polite to each other on the surface, but the underlying tension is severe.

Then there is Sarah. Her little figure, hovering in the background waiting for my attention, or her little voice, repeating over and over again what she wants until at last I take notice . . . Only just three herself, in the course of a year Sarah has had to cope with a catalogue of disruption: the birth of a new baby, selling our house, the five months with Ray's parents, discovering that Ben was deaf, moving up North, starting nursery school . . . She needs my time, too, desperately, yet the demands on it, instead of diminishing as Ben grows older, increase with each new task I take on in his education. Every extra minute given to Ben is a minute lost to Sarah. No sooner has she got over the invasion of her world by this new little person than the attention given to him by everyone around her is redoubled because he is deaf.

People are not as considerate of her feelings as they were when he was a new baby, either. At least when he was born she got presents, too, and people made a point of asking about her first. Now, it seems that everyone's first question is about Ben. 'How's Ben getting on . . .? What's happening about Ben . . .? Is he wearing his hearing aid yet? Is his teacher coming today? When's his next hospital visit? Is he starting to talk yet?' We make visits, or people come to see us; usually, it's something to do with Ben, and the conversation reflects this, even when people are tactful. Play sessions with Ben are a priority; play sessions with Sarah are fitted in around them. Each of Ben's demands is an opportunity to 'work on' him; Sarah's are all too often met with delaying tactics: 'Just a minute, Sarah . . . Can you just wait till I've . . .?' The ease of communication there is between us works against Sarah at these times: because it is easy to ask her to wait, she is often kept waiting. Despite resolutions to the contrary, she is given second place far more often than I would have wished. I am hypersensitive about this, doubly aware of the injustice, the imbalance, in my treatment of my two children. Always a difficult area for me, it is ten times worse now because of the added pressure. I watch Sarah anxiously, full of guilt, waiting for her to crack; the thought that she might suffer preys on my mind and fights with my determination to do my best for Ben. I am constantly weighing up, which one first, what for whom, and when. My conscience pricks me remorselessly, about all my family. I cannot relax, I cannot ease off.

For the first time in my life, I have to evolve a priority system for people. There is no other way I can cope.

Undoubtedly, Ben comes first in this order of priorities, with Sarah a close second. Ray follows, a very poor last. Jan sees improvements, though, and that keeps me going. I am one of her 'best mums', I attempt to follow her instructions, and the slower Ben's progress, the more determined I am to work harder. It can be done, Jan says it can. She encourages me to persevere; she knows that I rely on her for support and she gives it. Though she never promises that Ben will talk, she gives me every encouragement to hope that he will.

But life feels strange, strained. The deafness itself we can cope with. But, just as contact with the medical team forced on us a view of deafness which was alien to us—deafness as an illness—so now the approach we are being encouraged to use to alleviate the deafness feels alien to us; it does not fit in naturally with the way we like to do things. It is not a relaxed approach; it is not easy going; it demands responses which do not come easily to us and an attitude to discipline which neither of us possesses. Attempting to pursue such an approach provokes a degree of conflict, both within myself and with Ray, with which I feel ill-equipped to cope, yet fear for Ben's future, combined with an enormous sense of responsibility, makes it impossible for me to abandon it. I feel trapped, uncertain, unhappy, and powerless to make changes. In six months, we have become a family under stress. Another social worker has been and gone, having uttered the following words of wisdom and comfort:

1 Watch your marriage—it's likely to break up.
2 Get Ben potty trained as soon as possible, then send him as a boarder to a school for the deaf.

3   Don't worry about him—he's only deaf, after all.

How are we supposed to react? We're new to this
professional intrusion by outsiders into our family life. A
year ago we were an ordinary family. Suspicion was
growing in our minds that Ben might be deaf, but we could
cope with that; life was hectic but enjoyable, we had our
move to the hills to look forward to. Now, we have a
handicapped child, one whose beautiful features are
constantly cluttered up with an enormous hearing aid, and
about whose education and handling we cannot agree
among ourselves, let alone with the professionals employed
to advise us. One says, 'He's deaf—so what?', one advocates
education at home, the other recommends a residential
school and predicts the break-up of the home anyway . . .
Ben endures a battery of tests and hospitalisation so that
the medics can obtain better results—to which no one pays
much attention and from which no one is prepared to draw
any definite conclusions . . . One says the type of hearing
aid doesn't matter, another says the one prescribed is no
good . . . One even recommends that we shout all the time.
I wonder if he has ever noticed his expression when he
shouts. Is Ben to think we are always angry with him? One
body of opinion thinks we should be talking, the other
suggests that we should sign. My conscience tells me that I
should be doing more for everyone; my tired body tells me
that I can't. There has to be an easier way. We can't go on
like this.

As the pressure intensifies, the idea of using sign
language seems more and more attractive. It does not
surprise me that Jan does not mention the possibility: like
most of the professionals we have consulted so far she
appears to have complete faith in the effectiveness of the
methods she uses. This of course adds weight to my
suspicion that sign language must be somehow inappropriate—or even harmful—and best avoided.

But it becomes more and more obvious that the natural
gestures we are using are effective in getting over the very
basic messages essential to everyday functioning in a way
that talking is not. It is, quite simply, far easier to gesture

once than to repeat an oral message five or six times, especially when both children are involved and it is necessary to get through quickly for the sake of peace.

Ben points a lot, and so do we; just by pointing we are able to exchange quite complex information, particularly when the pointing is combined with an appropriate facial expression. Ben seems instinctively to understand and to react to expressions: by watching our faces he can tell if something is likely to hurt him, or if we find something amusing, or if we are not amused and are likely to disapprove. He 'reads' anger, of course, and affection. It seems silly not to build on this mutual understanding and consciously develop these skills. Since we are all actually using home-made gestures and are comfortable with them, it would seem sensible to use 'proper' signs rather than to continue to invent our own as the need arises. Life would surely be far easier for Ben if he could tell us things in an unambiguous way, rather than in the hit-and-miss manner in which he operates at the moment. If we are frustrated at the amount of time and effort it takes us to get an oral message across, how must he feel, this child who has no oral language at all?

As I watch Ben struggle, as I watch Ray enjoying a pleasant, easy, uncomplicated relationship with his son while I wear myself out trying to make him speak, I feel that something has to be done, that we must at least consider the possibility of using sign language.

At last, I find the courage to broach the subject with Jan, confidently expecting to be advised against it. After all, if she agreed with it, she would have suggested it, wouldn't she?

In view of what I have learned so far about other professionals, and surmised about Jan's attitude, her response is completely unexpected. She reveals that she can sign. Not very well, she says, she's been on a couple of courses and sometimes works with further education students who sign. But yes, she will sign with Ben, if we are sure that that's what we want. I am completely taken aback and, now that she has agreed so easily, full of 'buts'. I want to know why the books don't mention sign language, why the professionals are so cagey, why, if Jan knew about signing, she hasn't mentioned it to us before. What's the catch?

Jan qualifies her agreement. She will sign, she says, and she will teach us what she knows, but we must all be sure always to try voice first, and sign only if Ben doesn't understand, because *too much signing will make him lazy and prevent him from learning to speak.*

At last, I understand. Here, in plain terms, is the root of the professionals' objection to sign language. Signing is obviously the easier option for a deaf child (this, after all, is why we are considering using it), and the professionals believe that giving a deaf child a choice of means of communication early on will obviate (in the child's mind at least) the necessity of vocalising. In other words, using sign, offering an easier option, might destroy a child's motivation to learn to speak. All is now clear. For a hierarchy of professionals dedicated to the training of hearing and the production of speech in children who are not naturally inclined that way, sign language constitutes a threat, a serious barrier to the success of their methods. Their approach relies on fostering in a child a determination —a desperation—to learn to speak. As Jan had said, 'If you want him to speak you'll have to get him used to the idea that talking gets results where not talking doesn't.' Add sign and you take away the intensity of that motivation, thus making the professionals' job that much harder. Hence their resistance. So now we know.

Jan advises me to think very carefully before making a decision, and when Ray comes home we talk about it. It is now obvious even to me that Ben's oral progress is going to be painfully slow anyway, and the 'talk if you want something' approach is causing all of us considerable distress. The pressures imposed by adhering to it have taken their toll on family life and on the relationship between Ray and me. Now, the prospect of a way out seems attractive to both of us. The situations where we really need to get through to Ben are multiplying as he grows in mobility and in maturity. An approach which consciously includes some signing and which is endorsed—

however cautiously—by Ben's teacher, will allow me to
relax a little. It is, after all, what I instinctively wanted to do
when the idea first occurred to me, and Ray was thinking
about it as early as the post-diagnosis meeting. Apart from
being 'the easy option' for a deaf child, it could also be the
easy option for that child's parents. We now know why
there is resistance to the use of sign language, but for us,
now that the mystery has been removed, the benefits of
using it far outweigh the disadvantages. At last, we are
sure that our grasp of the basic facts is adequate enough for
us to make up our own minds.

I am rather nervous about the possibility that by using
sign we might ruin Ben's chances of talking but, all things
considered, I would rather take that chance than continue
the way I am doing, trying to walk a tightrope between
Jan's approval and Ray's disapproval, and pushing aside my
own ideas about child care and education in pursuing
methods which are so far removed from those I would
freely choose.

The 'easy option' is far more suited to our personalities
and to our way of life. We need to relax; we need to agree,
both with our instincts and with each other. We choose to
sign.

Jan is very supportive. Once assured that we have made
our decision in full knowledge of all the pros and cons, she
starts to use signs with Ben and to teach them to me. But
she has never done this before; no other parents have ever
requested this provision and she has not been trained in it.

We are all aware, also, that the overwhelming majority
of schools for the deaf are 'oral', which generally means,
Ray and I discover, that signing is not used at all with very
young children and is avoided as far as possible with older
children also, at least within the four walls of the school.
Some schools have a policy of trying oral methods first and
using sign later, usually reaching a decision for each child
individually at about age seven, so that the teachers have
the opportunity to ascertain whether the profoundly deaf
children (who are universally slow to start to speak) can
achieve success under an oral regime first. If Ben were to
attend such a school, the fact that we have signed with him
might be seen as counterproductive, in that it would
undermine the school's attempts to foster oral communication.

Slowly, the implications of such an approach sink in . . .
such a system would mean that, no matter how poor a
child's performance orally, he or she would not be allowed
access to sign language until the age of seven, if at all, so
that a child who was slow to talk would have little or no
language for seven years of its life.

One of the 'ground rules', the fundamental principles,
behind my postgraduate training in nursery education,
leaps into my mind and refuses to go away. The preschool
years! The precious, highly significant, highly productive
preschool years! What is going to happen to them under
such a system? What a shocking, what a criminal waste of

time those years will have been for a child who has to wait until the age of seven before being judged unable to benefit from an oral education! Seven whole years without communication. What a dreadful prospect!

I am still shouldering the burden of the possibility of Ben's motivation to speak being dulled by our use of sign—but now my overriding concern is that, for Ben, those years should not be wasted. I find the possibility of a child being without any effective means of communication during the first seven years of its life unthinkable. I simply cannot believe that trained teachers, responsible for the education of young children, could advocate a policy whose effect, as I see it, would be irrevocably to damage their ability to learn and to develop normally.

Whatever the theory behind it, whatever the arguments for such a plan, I cannot accept it for Ben. Whether or not the schools for the deaf will approve, Ben will sign. Whether or not it affects his speech, Ben will sign. Already many situations are becoming difficult because of lack of communication. The prospect of coping for five or six more years at this level is intolerable, out of the question. Ben is very deaf. Whatever happens, it will take him a long time to learn to speak. He needs an interim solution, and so do we, and we need it quickly. We have to sign; we have no choice. Not to sign would be to deprive Ben of the possibility of normal development, to waste the enormous potential for learning offered by the preschool years.

The immense significance of the decision to be made dawns at last. We are talking about more than a means of communication, about more than an easy way out for parents weary of trying to pursue an oral régime from a 'progressive' educational background. What is at stake is quality of life—Ben's life.

I feel intensely emotional, angry, terribly sad. Sad for all those children in schools for the deaf, whiling away their first years at school waiting for a decision to be made. Sad for their parents, condemned to years of hit-or-miss exchanges in place of conversation, all for the sake of possible attainment of a goal which can in no way be guaranteed.

And what of the feelings of those unfortunate children who reach the magical age of seven and are then judged to have failed? How must their parents feel then? I do not want to be put in that position, and I don't want it for Ben.

Ray is relieved. It must have seemed a long wait, for him, for my ideals finally to regain a proper place in my attitude to Ben's education. But at last, faced with the prospect of wasting Ben's precious childhood in an attempt to conform, my emotions—always my biggest motivator—take over and give me the push I need, and I leave Jan in no doubt about my determination.

She teaches us all she can. For part of each of her sessions now she works with Ben; when he tires she works with me, painstakingly going through lists of signs, which I learn parrot-fashion. I teach them to Sarah, when she is interested, and to Ray when he comes home. We all use the ones we know with Ben, as best we can.

But we need more concentrated help. Despite her lack of experience, Jan is trying her utmost to cater for our needs as we see them, and she, too, is aware that we need more help with signing than she can offer. Constantly on the lookout for a solution, she discovers that the school for the deaf in a neighbouring town does, in fact, have a small group of older signing children, and that the teacher of that group is running a small signing class for their parents and interested professionals. She visits the school and obtains permission for Ray and me to join the class.

We are all highly excited about this; my heart races as we follow Jan's little yellow Renault through the city traffic to get there—and I don't think it's because of the speed with which Jan negotiates traffic islands . . . At last, I feel that we are *doing* something, actively building on our determination to make progress, actually doing something we believe in. The class is to be held at the deaf club and this is exciting, too, another 'first' for us. What will it be like? Shall we manage to communicate with the deaf people there?

In fact, we do not meet any deaf people; the room has been booked on a night when the deaf club is not officially open, so the only people about are the hearing people who are there for the class. When we arrive it is already in progress: a teacher is going through a reading book with her group arranged in a circle around her, and the students are signing each word of the text as they read it, very competently, it seems to me. Another teacher is waiting for us.

Elspeth, our 'personal tutor', like Jan herself, and indeed like the teacher of the main group, has an air of warmth and cheerfulness, a ready smile, an eagerness to help which we find immediately reassuring. Jan stays with us ('I don't want to get left behind'), and we talk about what we want to learn and why we want to learn it, cautiously at first. But our confidence increases as it becomes clear that Elspeth not only understands our way of thinking, but actually approves of it! Eventually she laughs, and gives us a lovely example both of her signing ability and of the extent of her knowledge and experience:

'What you need is TOADAL CARMUNICATION!!!' she cries, the exaggerated American accent accompanied by flamboyant signs quite unlike the prim and compact little efforts to which Jan and I have been restricting ourselves: a huge circle is drawn in the air, both hands working symmetrically, parting at the north pole of the circle and meeting again at the south, then index finger and thumb of each hand form mirrored 'C's, which see-saw alternately through the air in large arcs, forwards and backwards in front of the body, narrowly missing each other as they pass, almost, but not quite interlinking. The image is a powerful one, the term new to us, but it encompasses everything that we are trying to do. The teacher explains: speech, amplification, drawing pictures, signing, mime, acting, pointing, showing, gesturing . . . we should feel free to use any or all combinations, whichever seems appropriate at the time. She shows none of Jan's hesitation over signing: she does not discriminate. Use it all, she says, and we feel she means it. Her attitude gives us a whole new confidence. It is obvious from what she says that she, at least, is convinced that we are doing the right thing.

She asks us what signs we are most in need of, and teaches us the ones for a whole battery of everyday things: activities, clothes, toys. Time flies by; only when she asks us to bring a list of useful phrases for next week do we realise that it is time to finish. I have noticed out of the corner of my eye that the main group has been signing whole sentences, with an ease and a fluency which amazed me. I'm in such a hurry to be like them, to be competent rather than a stumbling beginner.

At home, Ray and I practise the signs we have been taught, and are soon word-perfect and ready for more. Learning the signs is so easy for us that we soon progress into the advanced group, but now that we are more practised ourselves this group no longer appears quite so fluent. The work is a little more demanding, but still well within our capabilities, and we repeat the sessions at home between classes to keep ourselves up to standard.

The feeling of working together towards a common goal is very precious to us after those months of underlying disagreement, and the trips to town, with my mother babysitting, give us the chance to talk and consolidate our views, something which has been sadly lacking in our lives recently but which is vital to any partnership. There is lots to talk about that is pleasant: we know that at the signing class we are regarded as rather special parents: despite the fact that the class has been set up to help the parents of children in the 'Total Communication' class at school, we are the only parents to attend; the teachers see in us the sort of attitude which they had hoped to encounter in the parents of children they teach, and they respect us for it; this in turn gives us confidence and increases our enthusiasm and determination to learn, knowing that any progress we make will result in progress for Ben. Most evenings find us sitting by the fire, 'testing' each other on vocabulary; we often find it difficult to get to sleep at night because we are signing in our heads. It's a good feeling: communal, joyous effort.

But the town is a long way from our home. My mother (grandparents are the only people I feel I can ask to babysit) has to travel twenty-five miles to reach us, then we have another twenty-five to reach the deaf club. Maintaining this commitment weekly is quite difficult. Jan, ever watchful, is aware of this, and one day she bounces in with good news: she has managed to organise a class, she says. A few teachers are interested, and some parents of older children, so the adviser for special education has arranged for an experienced social worker with the deaf to put on a course at the Teachers' Centre. Jan can hardly contain her excitement: it is tacitly understood by both of us that this arrangement must imply a certain degree of agreement within the Authority with parents learning to sign. I'm sure that, like us, Jan has felt rather isolated and unsure of herself about using signs; we know that there has been a general feeling of concern from above and elsewhere in the support team, from the medics in particular. So setting up the course shows real progress, and for us it is yet another indication of Jan's genuine willingness to give us the kind of help we feel we need. How different this feeling is from our first reaction to Jan, my desperate attempts to conform to her way of doing things, the arguments between Ray and me about techniques – here, we are all in it together. Facing Jan across the hall at signing class, Ray by my side, I see the three of us as a team, working together for Ben's good, and I am happy.

Ray and I never miss a session. The way this tutor works is to hand out typewritten lists of words and then go through them giving signs for them, her students copying. There is a new list every week, two or three pages of vocabulary; what we have done already is revised at the start of each session. At home, after the class, we teach the signs to my mother, we give each other fingerspelling tests, and we generally revise the vocabulary. We are all very proud of our progress.

But before long, the realisation dawns that our acquisition of signs is the easiest part of a process which is going to involve much more than rote learning by adults. The idea of learning to sign is, of course, that Ben should learn. For Ben to learn signs he has to see them in use, and just as hearing children pick up their first words by hearing them used in context over and over again, so Ben has to see signs used in context, not once, but regularly. Frequently. Just as hearing children say 'daddy' only after hearing the same person referred to by this name over a period of months and realising for themselves the meaning of the word, so very young deaf children will not pick up the sign for 'daddy' until they have seen that sign used often enough in a meaningful context to result in understanding. Copying a sign does not necessarily mean understanding it; only when a child uses a sign spontaneously, in the right context, can you be sure he or she knows it. It's no good pointing to daddy, making the sign and hoping that if and when the child copies it the sign has been learned.

This realisation takes me by surprise. I expected oral progress to be slow, but I did not anticipate such a long time-delay between us using signs and Ben producing them himself. Even though I studied languages at college, even though I faithfully recorded Sarah's every utterance when she first began to talk, and observed that there was a delay of weeks and sometimes of months between her understanding a word and her actually using that word herself, it takes me a long time to come to terms with the fact that Ben's acquisition of signs might follow a similar pattern.

Besides the inevitable delay, I realise that there are also other factors which might be impeding Ben's progress in learning to sign.

The first is one which I had no difficulty in recognising as far as spoken language was concerned, but which is just as relevant for signing. Because she can hear, Sarah is surrounded by language; all of it is in some degree accessible to her. She might not understand everything that is said, but she can at least begin to process it; bits of it will make sense and she can use those bits to help her to understand the bits which don't. Ben's experience is very different. 'Seeable' language for him is on the lips (imagine watching, without sound, a foreign language speaker on TV and trying to distinguish words and phrases, let alone understand them), or single signs, whose context does not always make the meaning obvious.

Ray and I use the signs we know, but although they are impressive as a vocabulary list, they are in reality not a great many compared to the range of possibilities we have in spoken English.

When I try to use a lot of signs when I am talking my

speech becomes hesitant and stumbling; I feel awkward and selfconscious. So I tend to stick to using one or two at a time. But this is what I was taught always to avoid when talking to children: in order to learn, they need proper sentences. You say even to a baby, 'Come on then, let's put your shoes on'; you don't say, 'Come. Shoes'. The limitations of my signing mean that Ben is simply getting clues from my signs, not language.

Embarrassment at my own incompetence makes me reluctant to sign in public: when pushing Ben through the village in his buggy I find myself looking around to make sure no one is watching before I make my attempts at communication, even though I know that my embarrassment is causing me to sign far less often than I should.

Ray's approach, thank goodness, is different. Even before we knew any signs his communication with Ben was something of a phenomenon. Now, rather than adding signs from a vocabulary list to his spoken English, Ray seems naturally able to incorporate them into his unspoken communication—though equally naturally unable to speak and sign at the same time. If Ray is signing, he is signing. If he is talking, he is talking. There is no in-between. Try as he might, he cannot combine the two. At signing class, this puts him at something of a disadvantage sometimes, but with Ben it is very effective: Ray is still able to make full use of the facial expressions which Ben understands so well—so that, if at first he does not understand the sign, he does have a clue as to the general meaning. I am so involved in the mental juggling that is needed in trying to combine signs with speech, I find the process so uncomfortable and awkward, that whatever I am trying to express, my face as often as not registers confusion. However, I am reluctant to abandon spoken English as Ray has done; I am glad that his communication with Ben is naturally becoming more complex, and I can see that Ben is learning from their 'conversations', but I agree with Jan that Ben needs to get used to watching lips and listening for sounds, so I see myself as the English part of the partnership, and I plod on, trying not to be selfconscious, sure that practice will eventually make the process easier.

We sign during the formal training sessions; when not working together (one signing, one holding toys), both Jan and I become adept at holding things while we sign— between our knees, under our arms, under our chins . . . We also learn to manufacture situations where we can use certain signs, because in everyday life, the inevitable time lag of a mainly visual means of communication presents some practical problems: Ben loves birds, for example, but how often does a bird stay in one place for long enough to be pointed out and signed? And of course, any of this can only be done once you have Ben's attention; if he is not looking, there can be no communication. Birds seem amazingly well camouflaged when I try to show them to Ben, and it is a long time before it occurs to me that the reason I have noticed them in the first place is because they were singing! We try pictures, and photographs, but, like any baby, Ben is far more interested in real things, and above all he is interested in *action!* It is with great joy that I discover a realistic-looking rubber seagull in a local toyshop: with a little practice it can be made to fly through the air. Ben likes it, never tires of seeing it perform its aerobatics (with a little help from its friends) during training sessions, and in the end our persistence is rewarded. At nineteen months, Ben signs 'bird' spontaneously—his second 'naming' sign, after 'dog'.

Although getting the signs over to him is very slow, signing requires nothing of Ben that he is not able to do, and from Ray and me it requires no compromise in our philosophy of life or of education. Despite our different techniques, we both feel that we are on sure ground, that we are doing the right thing. Learning to sign, and signing with Ben, is something we can undertake as partners, encouraging each other, helping each other along and, in doing so, sure that we are helping Ben. We are prepared to work very hard, together.

But courses over, signs learned, I seem to have reached a plateau. I cannot seem to make any progress in my use of signs as I speak; in a sentence, only one or two signs are added. Ben's attention span is short, and I count myself lucky if he watches me for long enough to take in any more than one sign at a time. I feel very frustrated; I know lots of signs and I endeavour to use them, but talking to Ben I am thwarted either by the limitations of my vocabulary or by Ben's unwillingness to watch. Yet he watches Ray, as he has always watched him. . . .

Elspeth contacts us at about this time and tells us about a new course in sign language starting at the deaf club. It is being organised by the senior social worker there, and differs from the school-run course in that it is to be run in conjunction with the deaf club and will have deaf tutors. We are keen to go; it will be good to try out our skills on real-live grown-up deaf people; with them there will not be the problem of attention span I encounter daily with Ben; I should find it easier to get through to people who will actually look at me.

The first few classes are run by the social worker himself. From a deaf family, he is an expert interpreter. He does not do much vocabulary work, but concentrates on sign language in a wider sense. He begins with a set of objects on a table, for example, and he asks individual students, in a kind of signing very closely resembling mime, to fetch one of the items at a time.

Later, deaf tutors, working closely with the social worker, give us vocabulary sessions. We are surprised to encounter differences between the signs we have learned and the ones these deaf people use for the same words; we have heard that there are regional differences, but I had not expected there to be so many differences, or that the differences would be so great as to render the signs we knew unrecognisable. It is interesting to note that, when we give our version, the deaf tutors can often tell us in which part of the country that particular version originated: there are 'Oldham signs', 'Preston signs', 'London signs', just as for hearing people there are recognisable accents. The differences don't seem to bother or to confuse our tutors: one laughs them off and, with a shrug, signs: 'Same, different, same, different.' He is very flexible about the whole process: if you can convey a meaning, it doesn't matter how you do it. This flexibility, I soon learn, is possibly the most essential requirement of a hearing

person who is learning sign language from deaf people—
and I soon find out that it is a quality in which I am sadly
lacking.

At one memorable session each hearing student is paired
off with a deaf tutor, given a newspaper cutting and asked
to 'read' it so that the deaf person can understand what it is
about. My partner is a man a little older than me. As he
introduces himself he uses his voice on its own. I can't
understand what he says. So he tries again, but signs as
well. I still can't follow; I don't know whether to look at his
hands or his face. Starting to panic, I can feel my face
reddening and I can actually hear my own pulse. The man
smiles patiently and repeats what he has just said. This
does not help at all; it only increases my feeling of panic
because I still don't understand. I try concentrating on the
voice alone; when that fails, on the signs, still to no avail,
until I realise, as he slows down, that some of it was
fingerspelling and I haven't even noticed. He repeats his
message again, even more slowly. I home in on the
fingerspelling and I find out his name; I spell mine out to
him. By this time I am ready to go home. But I still have the
newspaper cutting to translate! I scan it. Oh no! It's about
the Beatles. This man is deaf. Will he know about the
Beatles? Will he even know what pop music is? Here I am,
trying to communicate with someone whose experience of
life is completely different from mine . . . how can I find out
what is common ground? I have words in my head;
vocabulary lists flash through my mind . . . but they don't
even include the sign for 'song'. Fingerspelling again, I ask
the man if he knows the Beatles. He nods and smiles. Does
he know they wrote songs? I ask lots of questions; there is
much nodding and smiling, and I discover another response,
which is neither yes nor no, neither a nod nor a shake of the
head, accompanied by a disarming smile and an expression
of utter incomprehension. This deaf man does not understand me. I have acquitted myself very well at two signing
courses, learned my signs to the letter, yet this deaf man
has difficulty understanding what I am saying to him.
Whose fault is this? Is it his—or is it mine? I begin to
suspect that he has been instructed to be deliberately

awkward—and immediately I regret the suspicion. I recognise the nod/shake of the head, the bewildered/ encouraging smile, in my own response, and I am not trying to be awkward, I am simply doing my best to avoid embarrassment . . . just as he is with me. Time up, I retreat thankfully, and jabber away to Ray in a language I can be sure of.

I have been knocked off balance, absolutely baffled. On the way home I think about it. I can't relate my success at signing class to my failure in communicating with this deaf man. To make matters worse, Ray has not experienced much difficulty; he felt that he got through to and understood his partner fairly well. 'Why didn't you mime?' He asks. I am not a little piqued that I, a linguist, have found the experience more difficult than Ray, a mathematician with, supposedly, relatively poor linguistic skills. My confidence dwindles, so that apprehension rather than excitement heralds our next visit to the club.

Communicating with deaf people 'in the flesh' is not easy. Every deaf person is different, with a different way of communicating. Quality of speech varies enormously, and there is little opportunity to get used to one voice or another. Signs and the way people use them vary, too; sometimes it seems that we are dealing with straight translations of English words, but sometimes the order and the delivery are so much at odds with English that the signing is almost impossible to follow. This is sign *language*, as the deaf use it, and the more we see of it, the more certain we are that it varies as much as English, if not more, in dialect and in complexity of usage.

In each 'chat' session, I find that there is a choice to be made. I can either nod and smile and shake my head and learn virtually nothing, or I can admit that I don't understand, and face a lengthy exchange of very simplified information that eventually results in mutual understand-ing—and actually teaches me something in the process. Here again, Ray is more successful than I am; we find that we have different preferences in these sessions: he finds that the less a deaf person uses his or her voice the better able he is to 'clue in' and understand, and the more comfortable he is, whereas I rely on voice if at all possible, and find it enormously taxing to 'read back' sign alone.

The deaf people's tolerance and patience with both of us is infinite. I feel inadequate for much of the time, but not because of any lack of consideration on their part. The fact that we have a young deaf son seems to give them an added determination to help us, and the fact that they appreciate, and approve of, our efforts on Ben's behalf, gives us a tremendous feeling of worth, even when we are struggling to understand or to make ourselves understood. It is hard not to try, when they so much want us to succeed.

Elspeth is in the habit of meeting one of the deaf tutors in the pub after the signing class, and one evening they invite us to join them. Ken is the mainstay of the team of deaf tutors; Elspeth has known him for a while, and Ray and I sit and marvel at the extent of the conversation they are able to engage in, seemingly without effort and with little misunderstanding. We do a lot of nodding and smiling at first, terrified when both heads turn towards us and we realise that they are waiting for a comment or a reply; but slowly, gradually, as the weeks go by and the visit to the pub becomes a regular sequel to the classes, we do find that we can reply, and can participate, if only in a limited way at first. Ken seems to be able to modify his language for us, naturally adjusting to our different needs. He slows down his rate of delivery considerably and fingerspells if we are completely lost, more and more slowly until we understand, and with marvellous patience. Slowly but surely we learn, the visits to the pub becoming more useful and more significant to us eventually than the classes themselves. Just as it is easiest to learn a foreign language in the country where that language is spoken, so signing with Ken helps us to *use* our sign language. What started off as a vocabulary list is gradually transforming itself into a language: certain whole phrases and expressions come more and more easily, and I really begin to feel the benefit at home with Ben, not only because my signing has improved but also because my attitude has improved alongside it.

Now that I am accustomed to signing with Ken in the

pub, I feel much less inhibited about signing with Ben in public. People regularly stop what they are doing and stare at us in the pub, but it is simply because they are fascinated by Ken's silent conversation. We feel quite flattered to be included in the overall scene, and very privileged because we are starting to understand a language which these people can only observe. And I am starting to feel a similar sense of pride when I sign to Ben.

But language is not all we are learning from our contact with Ken.

Ken has no hearing and hence (he would say) no speech. He is, in fact, an example of what we and the professionals have been trying to avoid for Ben. The audiologist has fitted hearing aids, the teacher of the deaf has concentrated on speech and auditory training, specifically to prevent Ben, if at all possible, from growing into adulthood without intelligible speech, a social outcast with a severe disablement . . .

Yet here we are, at the pub, in a social situation with Ken which he has completely under control, and in which he feels at ease. This is not the deaf club, this is an ordinary public house, yet Ken is able to order a round of drinks and pay for it, at the end of the evening he will catch his bus home, cook himself some supper in his own flat, and next day he will go to work and earn his living. He can be independent; he is self-reliant. His lack of speech does not prevent him from leading a life which is normal in every other respect. Realising this gives Ray and me a lot of comfort. As we get to know Ken better, and as our communication becomes easier, I can ask him all the questions I long to be able to ask Ben: the inevitable 'What's it like to be deaf?' (Answer: 'What's it like to be hearing?'), and, more specifically, 'How do you feel about being deaf?' I don't understand the sign he uses in reply to this, but the fingerspelled phrase he offers to explain matches the facial expression and body movements exactly: 'Not bothered.' I persist, wanting more, feeling that there should be more. Surely he can't shrug off his handicap in this way? What about music? What about not being able to understand the television? How does he use his time? He tells us that he reads a lot; information which he might get from TV he gets from newspapers instead, and as for music; Ken was born deaf. How can you miss what you've never known?

Through Ken, we are gaining insights into deafness which all our reading has not even touched upon. These insights, gained over a period of several months, exert a subtle and gradual influence on our attitude to Ben and to ourselves as a family. We begin to recognise that there is a very important distinction to be made between those born deaf and those who have lost their hearing later in life: from the professionals we have picked up on the idea that deafened people have a distinct advantage in that they are more likely to have and to retain a knowledge of English and the sounds of speech. Talking to Ken it becomes apparent that the born deaf, too, have an advantage. They lack hearing, but they have never actually *lost* it. Never having heard, they have no loss to grieve over. Like Ben, Ken has always been deaf: he grew from babyhood as a deaf person and he has organised his life around that. He tells us how lucky he feels he is in having had deaf parents: for him, deafness has always been normal.

This is another idea which is new to us . . . Or is it? Isn't this how we felt about Ben before the professionals in their various guises convinced us that his deafness would mean that he could never be normal? And Ken considers himself lucky to have had deaf parents . . . ? Of course! The penny drops. Apart from feeling 'normal', he has also grown up with a language! From babyhood his parents were able to communicate properly with him. Not for them this struggle over methodology and then the task of learning to sign—they just signed between each other and with him because that was the natural thing to do. He has been able to eavesdrop on their conversations and learn from them, just as a hearing child does in a hearing family. An all-deaf household is not the severely disadvantaged family unit it would at first appear; just the opposite, it is the ideal place for a deaf child to grow up. Our reaction against the professionals and the kind of assistance they offered arose because we wanted a kind of normality for Ben; not the kind which could only be achieved by 'curing' his deafness, but one which accommodated it. Deaf children of deaf parents have as their birthright this normality. For them, deafness is just a way of life.

As if to add weight to this very different picture we are beginning to gain of deaf people in general, and our son in particular, a new manual 'for those who care about deaf children' is published. Written by three Canadian authors, one of whom is the deaf father of a deaf child, it is called *Can't Your Child Hear?*,[1] and it offers support, in terms of statistical proof, for the information and ideas we are getting through conversation. From this book, for the first time, we discover facts, about deafness itself and about deaf people, their prospects and achievements in terms of speech and in terms of general education and patterns of social development, which no professional from the many employed to advise and inform us, has seen fit to pass on to us. This book pulls no punches. It is aimed at parents, yet it does not seek to 'soften the blow'; the information contained within it is precise, black and white. Not blurred by the sentimental concern for feelings which we have found in other books, it takes parents' reactions into account and talks about them frankly.

We read that deaf children of deaf parents have a significant advantage, and not only in terms of early language acquisition; that 85 to 95 per cent of deaf adults marry other deaf people; that auditory and speech training has not been shown to be very successful with children who have a severe hearing loss, *and* that signing has not been shown to prevent the development or use of speech. This last item we find immensely reassuring—but at the same time puzzling. If recent research proves that signing does not impede speech, why is there still so much unwillingness to use it? Surely professionals involved with the deaf should make it their business to keep up to date with research? Properly used by professionals, this book could bring tremendous reassurance to parents struggling to decide what is best for their children. Yet we heard about the book from *Talk*, not from a teacher or a social worker or a doctor. Jan is the most helpful and dedicated of teachers, yet we recommended the book to her, not she to us.

In the book, a quoted story tells of how a deaf boy with little or no communication with his parents, '. . . who had helped his father round up sheep and put them on a train to be slaughtered . . . believed that when he was placed on a train with a group of other children, he was going to be killed himself. He said that the sight of his mother on the platform, and some of the children in the train crying, as well as his father looking very upset, convinced him that this must be so.'[2]

We feel for the child, and for the parents who were powerless to explain to the boy what was really happening; this story and others strengthen our determination to work at our communication with Ben.

We read of other parents' anger at those friends and relatives who will keep ringing up with news of 'cures' rather than allowing them to come to terms with their children's deafness; we see our own worries and difficulties repeated many times in other people's experience. Reading this book is like talking to other parents, parents who have been through it all themselves, know how we feel, *and* know all the relevant facts. Rather than worrying us, the factual information, like our conversations with Ken, is immensely reassuring. It reinforces our belief that signing is right, and it makes us realise that by signing we could be saving both ourselves and Ben a lot of disappointment and distress. We can be sure that Ben will learn to sign. By not putting all our eggs in the basket of speech, we will never face that agonising situation encountered by some parents, who have persisted with oral-only methods until their children were in their teens, hoping and still hoping for the progress they have been told is sure to come 'later', only to discover, too late, that the goal, 'good speech', for their child anyway, was unrealistic and will never be reached, and that they have wasted their time—and the best part of their children's youth—in aiming for it.

We were looking for signs, and we have found them, but, much more importantly, we have found deaf people themselves, those people for whom deafness is not a disaster because they have developed a language which allows them to develop normally. We can't magically transform ourselves into deaf people, Ray and I, but we can aim to show the same acceptance of Ben's deafness as deaf parents would, and, from our contact with people like Ken, we shall hopefully be able to stay in touch with the way deaf people see themselves, and deal with Ben accordingly.

Notes

1   FREEMAN, R.D., CARBIN, C.F., and BOESE, R.J. *Can't Your Child Hear?*, London: Croom Helm.
2   DALE, D. *Language Development in Deaf and Partially Hearing Children*, Illinois: Charles C. Thomas (1974), p. 100. Quoted in Freeman, Carbin and Boese, *op. cit.*

5 REALISING THE DIFFERENCE: THE NIGHTMARE

Our philosophy, our ideals decided upon, we feel easier. But that does not mean that life is easy. We have managed to arrive at a mutually acceptable view of Ben and his needs. But Ben is only one person, and we are a family of four.

The birth of a child is not the first chapter in the book of any family. Before any baby is born, the family into which it will arrive has built up its own pattern of life; each member of the family has needs and wishes and good points and bad points and strengths and weaknesses that have to be accommodated by the other members of that family. And no family is perfect. There are always stresses in a marriage: as soon as one individual decides to live with another a subtle process of adaptation is begun, of 'giving and taking'; unwritten rules are established as each partner learns to accommodate the needs and wishes of the other, and the process is not over in six months; it lasts as long as the partnership. When children arrive the process becomes even more complicated: each child is another individual with specific needs, which can never be predicted and may turn out to be entirely opposite to what its parents expected . . . but these, too, have to be accommodated: more adapting, more 'give and take'. Ben was not born into an ideal family. It was all very well for us to decide that, for us, deafness would be normal. But we are, after all, a hearing family, and prepared as we are to adapt—for Ben's sake and our own—change is always hard. Our goal is to become as much like deaf parents as possible in our attitude towards and our handling of our son—but, as always, the reality is very different from the ideal. We are not deaf; we have not been able to develop a natural system of communication with him from birth as deaf parents do; we are all learning to sign at the same time.

At a time when communication between parents and their children is usually well under way, our communication with our son is only just beginning. At a time when a hearing toddler would be learning from the constant chatter of an elder brother or sister, Ben is cut off from Sarah because she can hear and he can't. His situation at present is not ideal by any means, and neither, it must be admitted, is ours. Penelope Leach, that sensitive writer about babyhood and motherhood, discussing the physical and emotional demands made on new parents, describes how they 'must struggle straight from giving birth to caring for the baby'[1] . . . and we feel much the same way. Much as we feel our responsibility towards Ben, and determined as we are to accommodate the difference we have discovered between him and ourselves, we did not have a lot of time to prepare properly for it: valuable months were wasted between our first suspicion of his deafness and our decision to sign with him; the oral training is slower still to yield results, even though it was begun much earlier. And Ben is no longer a baby, as easy to care for as any other. Of our two children, now he is becoming the demanding toddler, without language and with the extra and unfamiliar needs imposed by the physical requirements of a deaf child with hearing aid and grommet. His need for communication is fast outstripping our ability to satisfy it. Our situation is far from normal.

Summer comes; Ben is twenty months old. Thanks to the generosity of friends, we prepare for a long holiday: a trip down to the South Coast, first to visit friends in Kent, then across to Somerset. The journey down is planned to the last detail: a stop overnight in the Midlands; 'lucky bags' for both the children with little, individually wrapped presents to keep them amused along the way. Sarah's safety harness is fitted on the back seat of the van now; facing her is Ben's baby seat so that they can see each other; I plan to sit with them in the back and talk to Ben; we will travel during the day so that he is not worried by the dark.

The journey is like a bad dream. Bored after an hour or so, Ben starts to experiment with his harness; within minutes he has learned to unclip it and is out of his seat.

The motorway is busy; the thought of a baby crawling about unrestrained in a moving vehicle worries me. I replace Ben in his seat dozens of times; he thinks it's a game and gets out again. Sarah stays in her straps; she understands the danger; she joins me in frowning at Ben and repeating the 'DANGEROUS' sign. But he does not know what this means; he refuses to take us seriously; eventually I hold him in his seat, close the catch on the harness and hold it in place, while he screams and tries to bite the restraining hand. Through London, I point out the sights to Sarah with one hand and hold Ben's harness with the other. He refuses to be distracted; his 'lucky bag' was emptied long ago . . . Eventually he sleeps. 'Will you read to me *now*?' asks Sarah.

In Kent, we camp on the sunny and secluded back lawn of our friends' country cottage; we take all our meals outside with them, collecting, cooking and eating together the produce of an enormous and well-tended fruit and vegetable plot. We go down to the harbour every day and find a bit of sandy beach where Sarah can build sandcastles. Good food, good company, idyllic surroundings. A restful family holiday.

But Ben, at the precarious and highly unpredictable learning-to-walk stage, has to be watched constantly. The garden has steps to fall down, a greenhouse to crash into, poisonous plants to eat . . . The house has crockery at a reachable height, an accessible pantry full of goodies . . . and a dog. Ben crawls around after the dog, an enormous—and placid, thank goodness—English Setter; he pulls and twists all the animal's extremities to such an extent that at times I wish the dog would bite him. He terrorises the cat, when he can find it (when Kitty sees him coming she runs and hides); he gets into all kinds of mischief. Our friend Jenny's look of disapproval is famous—and effective on children from one to fifty-one—but it doesn't work on Ben, who blithely moves from one location to another, leaving havoc in his wake.

On the beach, I seem to be continuously plugging up and unplugging his ears, removing then replacing the hearing aid, removing sand from earmoulds and microphones. I am tired all the time; when the movement of the sea lulls Ben to sleep, I sleep, too, thankful that the others will play with Sarah: I just don't have the energy. Somehow, Ray finds time to run; Barrie runs, too; together they navigate the clifftop paths and inland tracks; they return refreshed, cheerful, happy. Running is Ray's pleasure: healthy, harmless enjoyment. To me, it is his means of escape from a stressful situation, a means of escape which I do not have but want desperately.

In Somerset, after another horrific journey across country, we spend a week with more old friends. A pleasant daily routine is established: in the morning we prepare an evening meal and pack a picnic while their children amuse our children. Then we take off in the van and spend the day at the coast, stopping for a drink at the pub on the way home and returning to eat at about nine.

This routine suits everyone, until the end of the day, when Ben, who is ready to sleep at about eight and hates the journeys home at dusk, makes it clear that he is not happy. Strapped unwillingly into his baby seat, desperate to be held and comforted, wanting his bedtime breast-feed, he screams all the way home. I spend those journeys kneeling in front of his seat, holding him or stroking his head, wiping the tears from his face—and sometimes mine—while the other children sing travelling songs and their mother wrings her hands at our distress and her powerlessness to help. I won't take him out of his seat; he is only just learning that he must stay in his straps; to give in would only confuse him and make other journeys even more difficult. The situation seems surreal, nightmare-like, and the thoughts going through my mind at this time verge on the murderous. I am in a trap; there are lots of people here; eight of us, all with different needs. I can't expect two whole families to rearrange their timetable for Ben's sake, neither do I want to opt out: I could stay in with Ben and save us all this misery—but I came here for a holiday; I want to be with our friends; I want to see different places and do different things. I grit my teeth and wait: for home, for night-time, for the blessed relief of mealtime, Ben in bed at last, another day over. And when

Ray runs I hate it. As he goes upstairs to change into his shorts I look down and see that my knuckles are white from clenching my fists. I want to hit out—at him.

*   *   *

As term begins again, Jan reminds us that we have the right to claim Attendance Allowance for Ben. Guidelines from the National Deaf Children's Society advise that before filling in the form parents should spend a little time trying to ascertain in what ways their child needs special attention. So I begin to write things down. It is only then that I realise to what degree Ben is different; how much adapting we have had to do and how much there is still to be done.

Emotionally, I am on a knife edge when I compose my letter to the Attendance Allowance Board, and I am in no doubt about our right to claim that money. I want some independence; I want to have lessons and pass my driving test; I want to be able to afford holidays which don't entail miles of driving; above all, I want paying for the job I am doing because I am beginning to realise just how difficult it can be.

Slowly the letter takes shape. Bits of it make me cry. The word 'handicap' springs to mind frequently as I write. A few months ago I rejected the word, and the idea. Now, after our so-called 'summer break', I feel that the whole family is handicapped by Ben's deafness. I need support. I want compensation.

The finished letter is seven pages long. It gives detailed information about Ben, our life with him, the changes we have undergone and the strain we are under.

The doctor from the DHSS who comes to examine Ben after the Attendance Allowance Board has received and processed the form and the letter, does what many doctors have done before: he claps his hands behind Ben's back. I think of the detail in my letter and I have to suppress a smile. Which will carry more weight? My seven pages or the crude evidence obtained in a matter of minutes by this doctor? He asks us a few questions: does Ben need help going up and downstairs? Does he need attention in the night (has he read the letter?) . . .

I feel extremely miserable after the doctor has left. Demonstrating the extent of Ben's dependence on us as parents has caused all kinds of conflicts within me: parents like to show off their children's achievements; I remember how proud I was of Sarah when, at her development check-ups, she performed all that was expected of her and more—and how annoyed I was if ever she refused to co-operate, because her ability or lack of it reflected on my success and competence as a mother. Here, for this doctor, I was being asked to display incompetence, to show what Ben could not do rather than what he could do, and it hurt. I am finding some aspects of life with him terribly difficult; I have gone into great detail about them in a letter; I did not expect to have to provide living proof of my inability to cope with my child while a doctor looked on and took notes.

A few weeks later we hear that Ben has been awarded the full allowance. Later still we receive the allowance book: 'Dis. Person Mr. B.J. Fletcher'. I look at it in distaste. 'Dis-?' Diseased? Displaced? What negative words the 'Dis-' words are. It is a while before I conclude that it stands for disabled. But he won't be, not if I can help it. All the determination of that decision returns. The extra money helps; it is a relief not to have to keep an eagle eye on the bank balance, not to have to contemplate going out to work. Now, I can concentrate on the work I do at home, and now I tackle it with a vengeance.

Obviously, it would be to everyone's advantage if Ben's social behaviour could be improved; Sarah in particular would benefit—so Ben and I join the local Mother and Toddler group. This is a big step, for Ben and for me, because I am painfully shy in large group situations, and gave up on Toddler group with Sarah in our former home town because I found the experience too stressful. Making conversation took enormous effort; I was ill at ease with social chit-chat and would spend the whole session looking into my coffee cup and hoping that I would not have to talk to anyone.

I expect to feel even worse now; it will be impossible for

me to merge into the background because Ben is so obviously an unusual child . . . The Phonic Ear is going to draw attention to us; I am going to have to make conversation, to think of something neutral to say . . . And when we arrive at this toddler group, people do notice us; they do start talking to me—but that hearing aid whose presence I so resented becomes a talking-point. Rather than making the situation more difficult for me, it makes it easier. Children stare at it, but this prompts their mothers to ask about it, to ask about Ben, to talk to me. Straight away, I am accepted into the group. As time goes on I become aware of little friendship groups, cliques, I suppose, groups which in the past I would have found immensely threatening because of their exclusivity. But now I am never excluded, and it is because of Ben, because he is deaf. I would never have guessed that joining a social group could be made easier for me because of Ben's deafness, but it is: I feel welcome and secure. Being Ben's mum somehow protects me from the sort of pressure I have found so uncomfortable in the past; no one is going to reject me; they feel for me in the job I'm doing. Ben, deaf, brings me closer to these other women than Ben, hearing, could ever have done.

As Ben gets used to the group, anyway, my own social problems fade into insignificance beside his. One of the functions of a toddler group is to get little children used to playing together, and Ben is bad at that. He is not the only two-year-old to take toys from immobile babies, hoist innocent (but smaller) fellow-toddlers off tricycles and onto the floor, paint his chair rather than the paper in front of him, eat the playdough and throw the sand—but he is the only one who can't be deflected from his mischief by a well-aimed yell or a well-timed (verbal) distraction. Other mothers drink their coffee in peace and leave most of the child-care to the supervisors; my coffee goes cold as I chase after Ben, rescuing one innocent victim after another and cleaning up after countless little acts of vandalism. It is like the tussles of home but with ten times the responsibility: at least Sarah is bigger than Ben and can fend for herself and, if I choose, I can ignore their battles; but here I feel I have to intervene: people are inclined to make allowances for Ben and blame their own children even if Ben is at fault; I have to discourage this and be scrupulously fair myself, even though it is much easier to distract a child who can talk, and much easier to explain rules to a hearing child.

Convinced that, with Ben anyway, prevention is better than cure, I watch him like a hawk, ready to haul him out *before* he breaks up the jigsaw, knocks down the tower, scribbles on someone else's paper. For a lot of the time I play with him rather than risk him sabotaging another child's game, for proper social contact is a mystery to him: he doesn't hear other mothers—or other children, for that matter—repeating the universal rules of sharing and turn-taking and respecting of property; the only guidance he gets is from a mother who keeps physically removing him from what he wants to do, or showing by her face that what he is doing is unpopular, or telling him in the few signs she knows he understands now, 'Stop', or 'Wait', or 'NO!!!' which must be thoroughly frustrating for him. I am heartily glad when other children, not as tolerant of this little deaf boy as their mothers are, retaliate or make it clear to him themselves when Ben's behaviour is not acceptable. I feel that this is the best way for him to learn, and I have to explain this to many mothers who can't bear the sight of their own children pushing away a little boy in a hearing aid . . .

The toddler sessions are particularly exhausting, both mentally and physically, but the everyday routine in general is increasingly difficult. Even the walk home from nursery becomes problematic: as Ben gets steadier on his feet he rejects the buggy and insists on walking; at first I try reins, since much of our journey is along busy roads, but Ben either pulls like a badly-trained dog on a lead or hangs from the reins, inert, and it is impossible to walk. Trying to keep hold of the buggy, and Sarah's hand, and Ben's reins, and walk in a straight line on a busy pavement, is virtually impossible, especially when I need both hands to communicate with Ben. Trying to replace Ben in his buggy when he has decided to walk is like trying to squash a plank into a shopping trolley . . . So I abandon the reins and try to train both children to walk alongside the buggy, holding a handle each as I push it along. Sarah conforms, eventually, but Ben without reins is a monkey out of its cage. And he is thorough. He has to try the doors of every parked car, climb on each wall, run up and down each path, climb up and down each set of steps. He shows a blissful disregard for traffic, and because I think that it is vitally important to distinguish dangerous occupations from just plain annoying ones, I concentrate my efforts at discipline on keeping Ben away from the road. So on the journeys home I fluctuate between panic and boredom, as Ben fluctuates between the road and people's paths. Sometimes Sarah joins in with Ben, but she is tired after nursery; mostly she waits, with me, while he conducts his little diversions. Eventually, most nights, one of us loses patience; Sarah begins to walk off on her own, or I decide to be firm, grit my teeth and strap the plank remorselessly back into the shopping trolley, tickling it to achieve the necessary bend, and being rewarded with screams.

Occasionally our slow trips home coincide with Ray's return from school; once, my heartfelt 'Beam me up, Scottie!' was actually answered in the form of a big blue Volkswagen van pulling up behind us—but usually I arrive home absolutely shattered, as often as not with a ringing headache, feeling more inclined to go to bed than to cook a dinner. The children are at their worst then, too; both are hungry and tired; hanging around the kitchen in the hope of getting a bit of attention, they get under my feet, slowing down the cooking, far more inclined to fight than to play. I wish Ray were around at these times, but he is usually working late or doing 'a swift five miles before tea'.

At teatime, in the kitchen, furious with Ray for not being there, furious with the kids for being unable to be together for five minutes without fighting, hot, tired, hungry, I feel as if I am going mad. I take out my anger on the kitchen, slamming doors, banging pans onto the stove, dragging ingredients out of cupboards and cursing when more fall out with them. Other mothers would prepare the meal during the day, I tell myself. Other mothers sit their families down every day at five-thirty on the dot to meat and three veg. Other mothers are better organised than me. And other fathers don't mess things up by coming home at a different time every day and expecting to run before tea . . .

And I am so *tired* by evening; the day draws to a close so slowly . . . I feed Ben to sleep; the episode with the hearing aid was the prelude to a period of very difficult bedtimes, when Ben neither wants to give up his breast-feed, nor go to sleep with it, so it takes him ages to settle, sometimes hours at a time. I scour the baby books and other people's experience for a solution: 'Leave him to cry,' most people say—but Ben doesn't just cry. Even with the light on he screams; he rattles his cot ferociously and soon learns that he can climb out of it; he arrives downstairs scarlet in the face and with his eyes half-closed and puffy from yelling. We try visiting him every few minutes to reassure him that we are still there: each visit distresses him more when we leave. Eventually I give up looking for a way out; I take a book in with me and use the time when Ben is going to sleep to read, toddler at the breast in one arm, book in the other. When Ben is finally so fast asleep that he no longer wakes up as soon as I move, I lay him down in his cot, turn down the light and go downstairs.

Maybe I can carry on reading once Ray and I have tidied and washed up . . . maybe there will be something we can watch on TV . . . These days, it is as if we would rather not spend time talking to each other about what's been going on in the day. Each of us knows that this seemingly innocent and universal habit of parents everywhere is risky for us at the moment: all too often the most harmless of discussions ends in an argument. The friction which erupted at the end of the holiday is still there, bubbling just under the surface, ready to flare up at the slightest provocation. And the resentment is no longer just one way. We both feel it; each of us believes that, at the moment, life is very tough and the other is not being very helpful. There is little understanding between us, little tolerance, little patience. Each of us feels neglected, unloved. Time and time again, after each bitter little dispute, we try to rationalise things, to tell ourselves that it is because life is so full that we feel this way, that life with two young children is a challenge for most couples, that Ben's special needs make it even more of a challenge, that we should work with each other, not against each other, because now is the time that we most need each other's support. Loving feelings resurface, only to be replaced within hours by another bout of resentment, another crisis of responsibility, another row over who should do what, and when, and why.

Some people can ignore unhappiness and carry on regardless. Ray can emerge from the most heated dispute between us and still have fun with the kids. I can't. If I am unhappy the unhappiness pervades my entire life. Depression saps my energy, decimates my conversation, sabotages the well-being of all of us. Deep and bitter feelings of dissatisfaction build up inside me; anger surfaces at the slightest provocation, and not only in words. For the first time ever I hit Sarah; during one particularly vicious argument I even hit out at Ray, and there are times when the anger inside me, at myself, reaches such a pitch that I feel ready to tear apart my own head or to beat it against a wall. Ray and I both feel tired, constantly, but he continues to run, which infuriates me. We argue frequently. Our relationship has never been under such strain. For the first time, in the middle of another sleepless night, in the heat of another bitter row, the word 'divorce' is mentioned, and we fall asleep, back to back, not touching, unable even to cry.

Note
1   LEACH, P. *Babyhood*, Harmondsworth: Penguin Books (1974), Ch. 1.

Some parents of newly-diagnosed deaf children embark upon a countrywide—sometimes worldwide—search for the best of everything: the best clinic, the best audiologist, the best audiogram, the best earmoulds, the best school for the deaf, in their desperation to help. Some scour the literature and travel the world looking for cures. We have not done this. We accept that Ben will always be deaf; we are not interested in cures. As for technology, we feel that Ben has the best of hearing aids, and we are grateful that our own Area Health Authority has prescribed it: he now has a Phonic Ear on the NHS.

So we do not feel the need to search, for cures or for new technology. But in our own way, we have embarked upon a search—a search within ourselves for resources with which to combat a problem which we are only just beginning to accept that we have. Ben does need a lot of help, that is obvious now, if he is not to suffer because of his deafness. He was already seventeen months old when we began to sign with him. He has a lot of catching up to do, and it seems that we are the ones who must help him to do that. His progress is slow; lack of communication with our two-year-old is making life very difficult for all of us. We have to do more; we have to do all we possibly can to combat the problem . . . Then our lives will be easier.

At Jan's suggestion, I send for the John Tracy Correspondence Course, for deaf babies and their families, which our first social worker suggested all that time ago. Free to all parents of preschool deaf children, it presents a programme designed to stimulate language development, and it is personally supervised by individual tutors, who study the questionnaires filled in by parents at the end of each section, writing back with comments, advice and encouragement. It sounds perfect, except that for us its range is limited, for by language the Tracy course means spoken English—but the producers of the course seem so confident of the success of their methods, the literature is so sympathetically written, the writer seems so well to understand the feelings of parents and to take them into account, that I decide to follow the course anyway and integrate it with our signing. It will mean extra input; it must help Ben.

Preparation of teaching materials for the course is very time-consuming; it is well worth the effort when whatever has been prepared captures Ben's imagination, but often he is not remotely interested, and when I have spent an hour making sorting boxes and cutting out pictures for them it is hard to sit back and relax when Ben would rather look out of the window than at paper cars or planes or boats, and my task-sheet instructs me blithely simply to go on to the next activity. Sometimes it seems that the benefits to Ben in terms of enjoyment and stimulation are minimal compared to the effort I have to put in to keep up the momentum— but at least I feel that I am *doing* something. I inform my tutor that we are using a Total Communication approach; she does not discourage it, but she does not encourage it either; when I submit my reports she is unfailingly encouraging about Ben's oral progress whilst at the same time seeming not to have read my comments on his progress in sign! I am reminded of the techniques I was taught at college to cope with 'deviant' behaviour in the classroom: ignore the bad behaviour and heap praise on the good—works every time!—and I am furious that this technique is being used with me, that Ben's signing skills are being ignored when we have worked, and are working, so hard to achieve them. Every time I send in a report I hope that it might result in recognition for signing, an ac-knowledgement that it seems to be helping rather than hindering Ben's oral progress: the more we sign with Ben, the more fluent we all become, the more he uses his voice. I feel that I have to 'spread the word', somehow believing that my experience with one child will alter views they have formed over years of working with others. Total

Communication is becoming a sort of cause rather than a method or a philosophy.

At the same time, the debate which began all those months ago when Jan first started work with Ben is always in my mind. What do I really want from education? Do I really want to sit Ben down at a table several times a day and put pressure on him to use his voice and to listen to mine, or do I want his education to be natural, ongoing, an integral part of his everyday life, the inevitable result of him doing what he wants to do, i.e. playing freely? Do I really want to begin the same battle to persuade Ben to use an auditory trainer, a powerful amplifier with headphones, capable of giving out sound at 135 decibels—about the volume of a jet engine at close quarters (latest in the arsenal of equipment recommended by the John Tracy Clinic), as I did to persuade him to use his hearing aid? His own attitude to auditory training is very clear: the moment he sees me approaching with the little carrying case that holds the amplifier and headphones he decides he has urgent business in another room. Once I have persuaded him to sit still and try it his reaction is the same as it used to be with the earmoulds: I fix the headphones in position, he takes them off, this sequence repeated until we are both rigid with tension. He agrees to talk into the microphone—but only if I wear the headphones. The routine is not pleasant for either of us, yet, time after time, it is the speech work—noise making and noise perceiving—which gets the comments and the praise from my tutor.

At about this time, Jan leaves to take up a promotion in a different Authority. I miss her badly; she gave me a lot of encouragement and she really was interested in Ben's signing. Ben's new teacher is fresh from the Manchester training course, and she does not sign—in fact we feel quite fortunate when we discover that she actually knows what Total Communication is, for the Manchester course still feigns to ignore the existence of anything but oral methods in educating the deaf—but we are thankful for her open-mindedness; she really does mean well, and whilst teaching Ben orally she does make an attempt to learn to sign. But she has no confidence; in supporting a family using Total

Communication, she is being asked to provide a service for which she has not been trained. Our still clumsy attempts at signing seem highly proficient to her, and she feels inhibited by what she sees as our expertise. As teachers ourselves we both vividly remember the demands made upon us by our first year's teaching; we feel for her in this new post; she has never taught a two-year-old before and she is finding her feet. Her situation is difficult enough; we do not want to put her under any more pressure, so we are placed in the incongruous position of feeling we have to support her and boost her confidence, when really the situation should be reversed . . . And she is worried. Relying almost entirely on the aural/oral approach, she is very concerned about Ben's lack of interest in sound. She tries vainly to establish the basic premise of auditory training work: with practice, even a profoundly deaf child will eventually respond to his name. But Ben does not respond, despite all our efforts.

'Ben! . . . Ben! . . . BEN!!!' the teacher calls, her voice verging on the hysterical, every time she comes. I hate these sessions, and the emotions they arouse in me. I feel embarrassed for the teacher, annoyed with Ben for not responding, and guilty in myself for not having managed even this small achievement in my months of trying. I feel angry, and when the teacher has gone and Ben wants attention I have to struggle with a little gremlin inside me.

'That child doesn't deserve attention,' it is hissing. 'He's messed you both about for the whole of the session; he hasn't made the slightest effort to co-operate; he's screwed up the teacher's nice picture cards, he's rolled about under the table and refused to come out, he's thrown the headphones onto the floor . . . and now he wants to play. Don't play with him. He wants a drink? Don't give it to him. Tell him he's a naughty boy. Turn your back on him. Refuse to look at him—he's just spent a whole hour refusing to look at you. Let him know he's done wrong. Horrible child.'

And when Ray comes home there's pressure. The teacher has a theory that it's because our voices are so light that Ben won't listen to us. Would Ray do some of the auditory work? Ray tries, and at first Ben co-operates. It seems that he does hear something—but whatever it is it is not interesting enough to make him want to prolong the exercise, and Ray is unwilling to coerce . . . The amplifier of the auditory trainer is on maximum. Every time Ben pulls off the headphones there is an ear-splitting shriek as the loop of auditory feedback comes into play; at the same time as frantically adjusting knobs and levers to stop the terrible noise, Ray has to attempt to keep Ben entertained enough to want to try again. This is not the sort of activity that I would want to come home to after a day's teaching and, if I am honest, one of the reasons I am happy to pass over the responsibility for it to Ray is that I find it so difficult myself.

The situation would be very different if Ben were interested, but he is plainly not interested, quite the reverse. It is hard to find anything of value in the auditory training aspect of work with Ben and much that is harmful: it is a cause of tension between Ray and me and engenders within me feelings about my child which are positively damaging. After each failed session it feels as if Ben has done something badly wrong, yet, on examination, really the misdemeanour he is guilty of is out of his control: he has not behaved badly, he has simply failed to hear. To be annoyed with him for failing to respond in the proper way to an auditory stimulus is to be annoyed with him for being deaf. How must he feel? Does he actually know what is expected of him when we ask him to listen? How perplexed he must be at the despair, the anxiety, the disapproval which he must read on my face during those sessions, and how hurt he must feel when I am angry with him afterwards, when I then ignore his efforts to communicate and his need for reassurance because I have been so embarrassed by his behaviour.

But putting my views to a Manchester-trained teacher is another matter altogether. So, for a while, I say nothing. I grit my teeth as I watch her and Ben struggle, I try not to get too involved, I try not to let my emotions show and I try to remain patient with Ben both while she is there and after she has left. And I become more and more anxious. Ben is failing. At every session he is failing. Whilst in our normal day-to-day communication now he babbles away as he signs, he is obstinately quiet during the oral sessions. The more the teacher tries to get him to voice sounds, the quieter he becomes. And yet I cannot bring myself to point this out or to complain. The teacher is inexperienced; Ben is still very young; I am reluctant to challenge authority in any form. But the child is suffering. He is learning little or nothing at these sessions and he is beginning to show a stubborn resistance to teaching which bodes ill for his future education. I can see him 'turning off'; he either looks away altogether or he develops a glazed expression which suggests that he is in a world of his own, thinking thoughts entirely unconnected with what this teacher is trying to teach. I would expect this—and have seen it—from bored teenagers in a classroom, but I would not expect it from a two-year-old in his own home. Children love to learn. It is their very existence; they learn more in the preschool years than at any other period in their lives. To see Ben, who is normally curious, interested in everything, active and bright, to see him switch himself off in this way is heartbreaking.

At a loss how to cope with this, Ray and I decide to visit Jan, and tell her in confidence about our worries—about our concern that, although this teacher is making such a valiant effort, she appears to be getting nowhere with Ben's speech. We ask her if there is anything else we could be doing to help Ben, maybe a different method. Jan, I think, still sees us as incurable softies in our approach to Ben. She asks how we are getting on with the 'talk if you want it' approach, and I have to admit that this is an aspect of training that I have allowed to slide, for practical reasons: when you're in a hurry, it is easier to sign. Her solution will be hard for us, then, she says, but we might like to have another go. We should renew our efforts to encourage speech, but not formally, as training. We should aim to make it part of Ben's everyday life. If Ben wants something, we should again insist on vocalisation. This would not be the same as when he was a baby—now, we can use our improved communication to help to 'soften the blow' for him; it's not as if we would be withholding things without an explanation—and at other times we would be signing, so we would not be depriving Ben of communication altogether, just teaching him another skill.

Put this way, it does not seem such a cruel proposition, so we try it, and for a while, it seems to be working. Ben gets accustomed to the routine of asking for things using his voice. He points or signs, we smile encouragingly and sign, 'Wait! Can you say ————?' and, as in the early days, we bring the object up to our faces so that he can match it with the lip pattern—and now, Ben makes an attempt at the word. Once he is used to the routine, it is not particularly time-consuming. He never does it spontaneously, though. We always have to remind him to use his voice, and we always have to give him an example to copy. In other words, he is starting to mimic on demand, but his spontaneous spoken vocabulary is still limited to a few words. Whether this prompted copying can be called learning is questionable; Ray and I are aware of this, but it does not seem to bother Ben or annoy and frustrate him in the way that auditory training does, so we persevere, knowing that this is one of the stages that has to be gone through when a deaf child learns to talk.

Some time passes before we get any indication of how Ben really feels about this new routine, but, eventually, he lets us know. One evening, Ray and I are clearing up in the dining-room after tea. There is a bowl of tangerines up on the bureau out of Ben's reach. He toddles in and points. He loves oranges.

'Do you want an orange?' Ray signs, bringing one up close to his face. 'OK, then. Say "orange". Orange, look. Do you want an orange? Say "orange"!' We know that he can; he has said it before. But this time, Ben does not say 'orange'. His face expressionless, he turns away and walks out. I follow him with the orange. He doesn't want it; he won't even look at it, even though I offer it unconditionally on the palm of my hand, at his level, not mine. Close to tears, I take it back into the dining-room and replace it in the bowl.

What are we doing to this child? Would we treat Sarah in this way? Would we treat any fellow human-being like this? Ray is thinking exactly the same thing, has thought it for a long time, became unhappy about it long before I did. Perhaps we have read too much into this little incident; maybe Ben's reaction simply meant that he had changed his mind ... but his behaviour provokes in both of us immediate acknowledgement that treatment which we felt inappropriate and unfair before we could sign is equally inappropriate now. Communication is more important to us than mimicry; an easy relationship with our child is more important to us than pursuit of speech. We reached this decision long ago, when Ben was too young to tell us how he felt. His behaviour now confirms it. He refuses to talk for his teacher; he refuses to comply when we coerce. The only time he can be relied upon to use his voice is when he is in a natural, relaxed situation where communication is happening—genuinely—for a purpose and not as part of a lesson. 'Bye-bye' comes naturally to him, 'hot', 'warm', 'aaah' when he is cuddling. He signs and says 'car' spontaneously, and 'cat', but although we have been working on 'food' words for weeks as part of this new regime, he does not spontaneously use a single one of them. The oral approach just does not seem to be working, with Ben. Yet, all around us, now, everyone seems to be advocating it, pushing us to continue.

At National Deaf Children's Society meetings, the other parents are, without exception, pro-oralism, anti-signing. We joined the Society shortly after Jan started to work with Ben; though neither of us are natural 'joiners' we felt we needed contact with other parents and that Ben would benefit from contact with other deaf children. At first, it was vastly comforting to share our hopes and fears with people who had been through the same problems themselves. But as our views about Ben's deafness and his education developed, it became increasingly difficult to find any common ground. The more we talk, now, the more differences we discover between our approach and theirs, between Ben and their children. Although all are finding life with their deaf children more or less of a challenge, although all admit to problems of communication at various levels, none has reached the same sort of conclusions as we have. All are still following an oral approach. Our insistence on *Total* Communication, the use of signing in addition to oral work, marks us out as exceptional parents, and Ben as an exceptional child—and I don't mean in the complimentary sense. The other parents feel that their children—regardless of degree of hearing loss—have a good chance of succeeding orally and that signing is not appropriate for them. All are relying on speech and lipreading, in some cases even without recourse to gesture. For these parents, speech is of paramount importance. They want acceptance of their children by a society which is predominantly hearing; in their opinion the only way to achieve this is by teaching their children to talk, and they believe what they have been told by their professional advisers: that the quickest way to get deaf children to talk is to avoid signing with them.

It gets harder to sit through meetings and hold conversations when our views are so different; we needed a support group; what we actually have now is a social situation which is full of tension, for all involved, as we skirt around topics which are important to all of us but about which we know we shall disagree.

I have kept in touch with the Society for Ben's sake; we have been going to parties and attending socials so that he can become aware that there are other children like him, so that he can begin to make friends with other children who are deaf. But to me, in the heightened emotional state in which I find myself for much of the time these days, these socials, too, are fraught with tension, and intensely depressing. Nowhere is the plight of these deaf children more painfully evident to me than when they are together. Hearing aids at optimum volume, acoustic feedback emanating from many as the children get excited and dislodge their earmoulds, the children mouth at each other, calling in voices that cannot be understood to friends who can't hear if their backs are turned. Each child frequently turns to a known adult for interpretations or explanations, each adult performs his or her own version of oral gymnastics in response; the air is full of the debris of failed communication, and Ben thrashes about unheeding with the rest of them, together, but apart. How very sad it is to see eight-year-olds relying on physical horseplay to establish relationships, when Sarah, at half that age, is able to hold proper conversations, to share experiences and make observations with the help of language, to introduce herself to other people by name and make friends with them—and how infuriating to have to stand there and accept it.

Watching these children, I feel that they are truly handicapped, through no fault of their own but because of the narrow-mindedness, the blind faith in oralism, of the people employed to advise their parents. Surely all children have a right to be able to communicate easily with others? It seems to me that these children's rights are being deliberately ignored for the sake of a goal which may never be reached. It seems criminal. Yet, just as I am convinced that their parents have been misinformed, deluded, so those same parents are certain in their own minds that I am the deluded one, that what they are doing is right, that by insisting on speech now they are laying the groundwork vital for success in the future, that if they can only put up with the frustrations and difficulties of an oral approach for a few years, they and their children will reap the benefit of it in years to come.

If there were not so much at stake, I would admire their patience. As it is, I cannot understand how they can bear to wait that long. I am concerned that Ben's early childhood should be as free as possible, as soon as possible, from the terrible frustrations caused by lack of communication—I want to avoid them for myself, as well as for him. Our children's early childhood is providing us with enough of a challenge as it is, without deliberately obstructing everyone's progress by following the snail's route to communication and insisting that a child who cannot hear should speak . . . I want Ben to do more than mimic at five years old; I want him to be able to converse freely; I want him to be able to use language with ease, independently. And for him to do that, it is even more obvious at times like this, the language he does that with just has to be sign language.

There is a choice to be made, here. Although throughout my life I have learned that the easy way through is to conform, to adopt the majority view, I cannot do that now. Perhaps I should sit back and let them get on with it. But that, too, seems impossible. It hurts to disagree, when other people's opinions have always meant so much to me, but I have never been so convinced that my path is the right one, never before felt secure enough in any conviction to be able to follow it through in the face of disapproval from the majority, never been prepared completely to swim against the current in my pursuit of what I feel is right. But now I begin to do just that. The idea that an enormous tragedy is under way in the field of deaf education eclipses the difficulties that beset my personal life; what began as a search for a way to make life easier for us and for Ben becomes in a sense a crusade: I want easier communication for *all* deaf children and better information for *all* their parents, not just for us and Ben.

The only proper explanation for these parents' wholesale acceptance of what seems to me a totally inappropriate and needlessly narrow system of education for their children, is that they have been misinformed. This is not their fault and, in some cases, not even the fault of their advisers. They are at the receiving end of a long chain of misinformation, which must have begun—and must still begin—at the teacher training establishments. Ben's new teacher came out of Manchester not only unable to sign, but with no knowledge whatsoever of research and developments in Total Communication, despite its rapid progress in America, despite the fact that in Sweden deaf children have a legal right to be taught—and to be taught in—Swedish Sign Language. Schools in the United Kingdom are now adapting, slowly, to accommodate signing . . . and yet a highly respected university department, one which should be at the forefront of developments in the education of the deaf, is still turning out teacher after teacher with no expertise whatsoever in the area of manual communication. And the other professionals in deaf education, the heads of schools, the heads of service, the teachers in charge of units . . . They must be aware that a change is under way . . . Why are they not informing parents?

I conclude—fairly quickly—that it must be the work.

Admitting the relevance and usefulness of signing, admitting that in fact it does not impede the acquisition of speech, would involve those professionals who do not sign in an enormous amount of retraining, firstly, in bringing up to date their knowledge, secondly, in learning how to sign, thirdly, in learning how to make use of their new knowledge in teaching. There must be teachers at all levels who are very comfortable as they are, happy to teach what they always have in the way that they have always taught it . . . And the Catch 22 is that as long as they continue to provide such a narrow education for deaf children, as long as the only successful deaf are the ones who have been able to benefit from an oral education, there will never be enough non-oral deaf with the academic credibility necessary to challenge these teachers, to insist that a proper education is provided for those many deaf children who cannot survive in an oral setting, who need sign in order to learn. The old order seems set to continue undisturbed . . . unless parents intervene. Not individually, but as a body . . . an action group, such as we would have an ideal basis for with NDCS . . . if there were more parents who thought as we do. It all boils down to information. They have been misinformed, as we were in the beginning. All they need is access to information, and they will change their minds.

So we start up a library of information for NDCS. This means extra work, of course, but it gives a new purpose—and new hope—to meetings, and I tell myself that running the library, apart from keeping us all in touch with the latest literature about deafness, gives me much-needed intellectual exercise: collecting information, filing it, ordering, reading and reviewing books, is useful recreation for my academic brain, a change from the everyday routine—training, perhaps, for a future job. The Supermum I want to be needs outside interests, and she must think of her career.

Our first acquisitions for the library are two more copies of *Can't Your Child Hear?* Surely this book will influence at least the parents of severely and profoundly deaf children to think again about their children's needs? As the months go by and the library grows, we give this book pride of place in the collection and we keep our fingers crossed, whilst dutifully continuing to stock the literature recommended by the professionals as well, so that we cannot ourselves be accused of the bias we complain of in their provision of information. Now, parents have access to a complete picture of the possibilities and the prospects for their children . . . but each time *Can't Your Child Hear?* goes home in someone's bag I feel we have made progress. In my mind, it is progress for Ben, too. I want there to be other children with whom he can sign.

The country as a whole is making progress at this time. Slowly, articles on Total Communication are creeping even into *Talk*, whose oralist bias has been depressingly consistent up to now. New recruits to NDCS, those with younger children, are showing an interest in learning to sign; some actually request Total Communication for their children. Another course is set up at the Teachers' Centre as the peripatetic teachers rise to the demand; slowly, even some of the stalwarts amongst the parents begin to enrol. The tide seems to be turning, gradually; I no longer feel that I am swimming against it; I no longer feel so alone; things are definitely changing, and as more parents of younger children start to sign I can allow myself to look forward to the prospect of there being a group of children with whom Ben will be able to sign. His horizons, like Sarah's, will be able to widen to include his peer group. For the younger children, there is a great deal of hope.

But what of the older deaf children? How are they reacting to their parents' efforts to learn to sign? How do they feel about the breakthrough, the changes in attitude that are developing? Conversations during coffee break at the classes, and, inevitably, at NDCS meetings, reveal that some of the children's reactions are not at all what I would have expected. I thought that they would welcome the relaxation, enjoy the prospect of having a break from the strain of lipreading, be pleased at their parents' efforts to make communication easier . . . But in some cases, particularly with older children, this is not what happens.

'D—— doesn't want me to sign,' says one mother. 'He

says signing's only for deaf people and he won't sign to me.'
One boy refuses to help his mother to learn 'because
signing's stupid'. I am amazed. Where can these attitudes
be coming from? All these children sign at school, in the
playground if not in the classroom, and some are actually in
Total Communication classes at school . . .

I search about for reasons for such reactions as these,
and I come up with a theory. The Total Communication
classes at schools for the deaf were set up originally to
accommodate a few 'oral failures', the real no-hopers who
failed repeatedly to get anywhere in their oral classes until,
at age seven, they were removed from those classes and
transferred to Total Communication groups. For the
children still in the oral classes, who have watched this
process, signing could quite easily have become synonymous
with 'stupid'. Just as in an ordinary school which practises
streaming the kids in the bottom set are looked down upon
by their brighter peers, so the oral kids in a school for the
deaf could easily feel superior to the ones who 'have to
sign'. Needing to sign in the classroom might well have
marked out that group of children not only as different, but
as academically inferior. So, although signing at home
would make life easier for them, some children are
resisting it because they have worked out for themselves
that clever kids don't need to sign with hearing people, and
also that talking deaf kids are better deaf kids. And who
could blame those children if they have reached such
conclusions? They will simply have absorbed criteria for
self-worth that have been laid down for them throughout
their school—and home—life, through hours, and days,
and months, and years, of auditory training, of articulation
work, of lipreading practice, of talking, talking, talking, and
being talked, talked, talked at. Their parents bring home
from meetings a magazine that is actually called *Talk*, full of
articles about people who have 'overcome their deafness',
who have learned to function as hearing people with
hearing people by learning to talk. ORAL success. No
wonder these children have speech as their only criterion
for success. No wonder they are so reluctant to give up the
'oral' habit which they and their parents have worked long

and hard to establish in the home. To relinquish that would be to lose the 'oral' status that goes with it.

It is a real shock to me to discover that resistance to signing is not just endemic to the teaching profession and to parents. Ray and I learn just how deep that resistance runs when with deaf children ourselves. In our contact with them, we make it very clear that, for us, signing is an effective and acceptable means of communication. Their responses vary. Often they appear to understand, but they will not sign in reply; they speak to us, hands almost obstinately still, and if we do not understand they will bring in Mum as an intermediary. Some even write in the air or on the backs of their hands rather than sign back, so important is it to them to be seen to be using English. One tells us in no uncertain terms that it is bad for Ben for us to sign with him, that he has to learn to talk because that will be better for him. We resist; we tell them clearly that we want to sign, that signing is wonderful, that we and Ben like signing. They remain unconvinced.

All of these children are deaf, some profoundly so, some have speech so indistinct as to be unrecognisable as speech, but they are still trying to resemble hearing people, so convinced are they that speech is the key to success, that signing is second-best. Ray and I are stunned by responses such as these. It seems to us that these children have come to deny something which is as much a part of them as their right- or left-handedness. They are deaf; they will always be deaf, but they are determined not to appear so.

The ideal is, surely, a way of educating children which seeks out their good points and builds on them, which encourages children to discover their own talents and make the most of them. But for these children, it seems that only one talent is acceptable or desirable: the ability to speak. It seems so wrong to us, so unfair, so damaging . . . What psychological problems will ensue if these very children discover, in the end, that they are still not acceptable to hearing society, that the speech which they have worked so hard to acquire is so poor that it alienates them from the very people they have struggled so hard to emulate . . . what then? How will they see themselves then? Will they then be forced to admit that they are deaf? And how will they feel then about being deaf? Sorry, surely, and miserable, and powerless, and infinitely, unarguably, inferior . . .

We can aim to avoid this, for Ben. It was thoughts like these which pushed us into making the decision to sign with him. For the younger children, there is the prospect of change. But for the older children, the choices have already been made. For them, all we can do is to hope that they make it, that they succeed, their way, and that, if they don't, they and their parents will find the inner strength necessary to cope with what they will see as their failure. For they are loved, these children. All are cared for by parents who are trying their utmost to do what they think is best. We fear for the children—but we also fear for the parents who, having loved, having tried their best, will blame themselves if things go wrong, will think that they didn't love enough, that they didn't try hard enough. And we can hear, in advance, the excuses of those teachers who will encourage them in this belief, who will not, in the end, have to take the blame for the children's failure. For we know that, having pushed the parents down the wrong path, they will blame the parents for the impasse to which that path has led, will refuse to acknowledge that they themselves didn't really know the way—or that the map they were using was out of date. These teachers will blame the parents' laziness—these parents who have worked so hard—for their children's failure, not their own incompetence.

We have to accept that there is not a lot more that we can do. We have provided information; now we have to sit back. Very conscious of the delicate state of parents' emotions, including our own, reluctant to subject them or ourselves to any more pressure, we join them in seeking other ways to help.

One of the parents has heard that they are doing wonderful things with computers at schools for the deaf; NDCS invites a teacher to give a talk. She fires us all with enthusiasm: whatever our views on communication, no

one can deny the effectiveness of the computer in teaching
the deaf; here, whatever his or her oral proficiency, the
deaf child can achieve a productive dialogue with the
machine, can really explore its possibilities on a one-to-one
basis, without teacher interference, thus giving the child a
rare opportunity to be independent, to initiate and to
control learning experiences, to find out for him/her-
self.

At the next meeting we discuss the possibility of fund-
raising for computers; support is unanimous. Ray teaches
maths and computing; he is duly elected to supervise
the project; within a month we have our first BBC
microcomputer in use in someone's home. Before long we
have four micros; Ray is in charge of hardware, software
and basic training, and the children are thrilled. 'Hands on'
experience is available to all who request it, including the
youngest children. Just by tinkering about with the
keyboard, Ben learns to recognise the alphabet. The
computers are a great success; we hope that by providing
this service we shall be helping some of the older deaf
children towards a marketable skill which does not depend
on the ability to speak. But now there is much more work
for us. The library has expanded to include toys; this
involves liaising with the peripatetic service and the Toy
Libraries Association (now Play Matters)[1] to choose suitable
ones, ordering, labelling, cataloguing . . . I have also
inherited the masses of informative leaflets and booklets
which the Society has accumulated over the years. Enjoying
the challenge, and always on the lookout for useful, maybe
persuasive, information, I sort through them, setting up an
alphabetical file and index, clearing out the attic to provide
proper storage . . . My tired evenings come alive as I hare
up into the attic once Ben is asleep, to file or look up
information, to back a few books, to order some toys, to
write another begging letter for funds.

Doing more seems to make me feel better, seems to help
me to forget the things that are bothering me. Running
through my head is the old advice: 'If you want something
doing, ask a busy man'—or woman, as the case may be. The
energy generated by this new activity, the feeling that I am

responding well to a new challenge, seems to result in more energy. Maybe I need to take on more—different things, to broaden my interests. I look at Ray; the more he runs, the more he wants to run, and the fitter he becomes. Maybe I could find something else to do—something outside the family, perhaps—a proper outside interest, one that has nothing to do with deafness . . . Some of my friends have joined a women's discussion group in the village; several times I have been asked to meetings and I have made excuses . . . but now I feel able to take on something new . . .

It is not so much the discussion that impresses me, at the first meeting, but the women. Here are Supermums galore, their active brains and busy bodies proving that there is more to life than family commitments, that it is possible to be a good wife and a devoted mother without stagnating, that it is possible—and desirable—to develop a wider view of life. A lot of these women are involved in other groups; they are political, knowledgeable, articulate in a way that I have never been. I want to be like them; I want to be less insular, more aware . . . I have always had gut feelings rather than reasons for my politics; within weeks I have determined to convert these gut feelings into action; I have joined two political groups; I am now a *very busy woman*. The spare time that depression thrives on no longer exists; I have filled it up. Every minute of my day, I have something to do. I have developed a new purpose, a new briskness. The woman I see when I look in the mirror—when I have time—is as close to Supermum now as she possibly could be.

But still, Ben is on my mind. We are working hard with him, but we seem to be working blind. We have no way of knowing how he is getting on or what we should be aiming for next. His new teacher is able to comment on his acquisition of speech—if her experience is limited she has certainly read all the appropriate literature—but she has no experience of children learning to sign, so she cannot comment on this. There is not even another child with whom we can compare him; the chldren who are signing now are just beginners. Could we be doing more? How does Ben's linguistic progress match up to that of other children of his age who are signing? How is he progressing in general terms?

It is perfectly obvious that the bulk of his language is manual, and that if we as a family were limited to spoken communication we should be lost indeed—but the lack of support and the lack of direction really begins to upset us. We keep looking for advice and encouragement about signing, professional and from other parents; locally, we find none.

It takes a television programme to cover the distance it is necessary to cover to find parents who have more experience of Total Communication than we have. One Sunday, on *See Hear*, BBC Television's magazine programme for the deaf and hard of hearing, we watch a film of a family whose philosophy seems to match ours exactly. We watch as a London couple, Riki and Clive Kittel, tell their story. When their son, Piers, was born profoundly deaf they decided immediately that they should learn to sign, and they quickly found out that the best way to do that was with and through the deaf community; once involved with the deaf community they realised that there was a great need for proper employment for deaf people; this resulted in the setting up of a printing co-operative with a deaf workforce. This had two very beneficial side-effects for the family: it provided the Kittels with signing practice (the language used within the factory was BSL[2])—and Piers with lots of new deaf 'aunts and uncles'. The results are plain to see: Riki and Clive are actually able to 'sign for themselves'— there is no interpreter on screen with them—and when the cameras follow the family at Piers' bedtime, Clive and Riki can tell him a story together in sign, the little boy participating actively, obviously following the story and understanding it—and he is starting to talk! How limited our own communication seems compared to this. Yet Ben and Piers are about the same age, diagnosed about the same time. We were looking for comparisons; we are shocked at what we find. So this is what can be done. What a lot we still have to do! But I am encouraged; the process which led to the decision to sign, and the process of learning to sign, has been terribly slow in our case compared to theirs, but this little boy is living proof that the way we have chosen can have spectacular results.

Immediately after the programme I rush upstairs and write to Riki and Clive, telling them how inspiring we found watching them, writing a little about Ben, and tentatively suggesting we make contact. In March, Riki calls to see us on her way from London to Carlisle on a business trip.

Over supper, we exchange experiences, stages in our lives with our deaf children, ideas about how they should be educated, complaints about the system. The similarities in our ideas and our ideals are remarkable, and it is wonderful to be able to talk frankly with another parent without there being disagreements. We talk until the early hours, and the next day, as she leaves, I ask her whether she has any advice for us, whether there is anything we should be doing that we are not.

'Yes,' she says. 'Signing.'

I can't think of anything to reply. Perhaps I did not expect such a frank response; certainly the truth of what she said hit home with deadly accuracy, but it hurts to acknowledge it. We are signing, as well as we can, but, yes, we are only signing with Ben. Between ourselves and with Sarah we don't sign, we just speak. This is one significant difference between Piers' home life and Ben's, and between Ben's home life and that of a deaf child with deaf parents. Riki and Clive, as they did on TV, attempt to sign whenever they speak, when Piers is around. So he has access to their conversation in exactly the same way as hearing children have access to their parents'. As well as with him, they are using a language Piers can see between themselves as well. As far as possible, Piers' home life is like Ken's was as a child. When talking to him, we appreciated the value of that situation, but we have never considered trying to establish it in our home. Now, we talk over the question a little: our circumstances are very different from Riki and Clive's; apart from the obvious advantage they have of working with deaf people, Piers is an only child. We have Sarah to consider, and we feel that her life has already been vastly disrupted by our preoccupation with Ben and his needs; to attempt to use another language, purely for Ben, would be unfair on her. If we were fluent in Signed English we could use it as we spoke; there would be no problem, but Ray is incapable of signing and speaking simultaneously and when I try to do it for any length of time my spoken English deteriorates beyond belief: it changes in pace, I stammer and hesitate, I simplify my language to fit in with the signs I know. Surely this would not be fair on Sarah, whose own use of language is still developing, and surely our communication in a wider sense (which needs all the help it can get at the moment) would suffer?

Sensitive to our feelings, maybe sorry she was so abrupt, Riki does not pursue the matter. We exchange warm goodbyes and promise to keep in touch.

When she has left, Ray and I debate the question over and over again. Each of us sees the immense benefit to Ben of a signing environment, and every so often we attempt it, but practicalities defeat us. We find it impossible to use a language constantly in which no one in the household is anything like fluent. We just cannot do it, and the fact that we are not doing something which could help Ben so much weighs heavily on my mind. Up to now I have followed every single avenue suggested to me to help Ben to develop language, even those which have been terribly difficult for me; now, in this, I am failing him. The guilt that this realisation engenders is overpowering; it is obvious that if we want Ben to make progress with his signing we have got to make more effort ourselves. I go to the Teachers' Centre for the repeat of the signing course, hoping that I might learn something new—but it is a vain hope. Learning signs parrot-fashion is no substitute for sign language tuition from deaf people, and nothing like as effective as conversation with deaf people; this, we realise is the ideal; this is what we need, but it just does not seem to be available locally. We have no contact with our neighbouring town now; the signing classes are over and Elspeth has begun a university course which takes up most of her weekends; we don't see Ken and we have no excuse now to go to the deaf club . . .

I begin to write letters to 'helping' organisations, not now to raise funds but to try to gain for ourselves some contact with the 'deaf world' that we have discovered we need so much in trying to help Ben. Replies to these only confirm what we already know, that locally there are not many deaf people. There is no deaf club nearby; the few deaf people living in the area tend to use clubs further afield; our social worker is on indefinite sick leave so cannot help us.

But my mother is learning to sign; we hear through her that her local deaf club is planning a weekly play session, on a Saturday afternoon, for local deaf children and the hearing children of deaf club members. There will be deaf adult helpers and it will be a good social occasion when parents can meet and chat while their children play. It sounds ideal; we often visit our parents anyway; we could combine shopping in the city with sessions at the deaf club. Then Ben would be able to mix with other deaf children in an environment where signing was the norm, and we would be able to improve our signing by chatting with the deaf people there.

But the reality is very different from the dream. The deaf adults in charge are very friendly and helpful and welcome us warmly—but they all speak! Sometimes we see an elderly couple in a corner signing together, and there are two club officials who sign, but they are there to conduct deaf club business; we can hardly interrupt either couple and insist they include us! The deaf parents bring along their children—but the children can all hear, they all speak and their parents speak to them. The only deaf child present apart from Ben is a little girl of about nine, and she, too, is 'oral'. As in our early contact with NDCS, Ben is a curiosity and the fact that we sign with him is a cause for concern. Sarah enjoys the playgroup, the children have fun playing with some lovely new toys provided by local charities, and we attend regularly for a few weeks, hoping each week that someone will sign to us, or that another—signing—deaf child might turn up, but gradually numbers decline and when one Saturday we are the only customers we decide, reluctantly, that we have maintained this commitment long enough—and another door closes, for us and for Ben.

But in May of 1983 our 'unofficial' social worker, who, bless him, is still 'looking out' for us in his own time, lets us know about a workshop on Total Communication which is planned for one Saturday at the school for the deaf in a town some miles away. There will be some sign tuition and the opportunity to meet other interested parents, also some talks by professionals: 'Total Communication in Home and School'. At last, some help, some appropriate help!

On the day, we listen—and watch—as Peter Llewellyn-Jones and Susanne Turfus from the British Deaf Association[3] put their views. They give us background information, then they put over the reasons for the development of Total Communication—absolutely brilliantly. Ray and I listen fascinated as the argument emerges—flawless, ultimately convincing. As Peter Llewellyn-Jones talks, Ray scribbles furiously on bits of scrap paper. He rarely takes notes, but all this is worth recording. It is as if this man is talking to us personally, talking for Ben and for the thousands of other badly educated and shamefully mistreated deaf people, children and adults, whose rights are ignored and whose language is ridiculed by the people employed to help them. The man is a brilliant speaker—but in addition to speaking he is able to sign, fluently, gracefully. I watch him as one watches a religious leader, intently, determined to take in each word, each gesture, and to remember it all. Tears are close to the surface for much of the time, the tears that come when you talk to someone who understands completely at a time when you most need to be understood. The experience is uplifting, a turning point. We reached our decision painfully; through months of observing and arguing and agonising we have arrived at a philosophy to adhere to in educating Ben. These people, representing the adult deaf community, have thought of everything we have thought of and more; they are telling us that it is right.

We travel home on a high; we have been inspired. Here is the support we needed! I grab hold of Ben when we get home and I hug him. You're going to be all right, kid, I tell him in my mind. There are other people who have tried what we're trying and it works. We've got the backing of clever people; we're not on our own.

But Monday comes; Ben's teacher arrives; out come the auditory trainer and the speech cards . . . I tell her about the weekend; she listens, then forgets . . . Nothing has changed, really, for Ben . . . and we are still alone. Riki has gone back to London; Peter and Susanne have gone back to Carlisle . . . all we have brought back from the weekend is the address of an action group in case we want to know how *not* to persuade an LEA to accept Total Communication, and a determination to sign more . . . which is nothing new.

And then I am called upon by the LEA to give a talk. The teachers of the deaf are running an in-service training course on deafness and they want me to do a ten-minute spot on Total Communication. How laughable that is: looking for expert help, yet looked upon as experts in exactly the area where we are seeking help . . . and what a measure of our isolation. There is no one else they can think of to ask. There is no one else! What have I achieved, in my struggle for Total Communication? It seems I have won for myself a place in the front line, and I have gained for myself a reputation as an expert. But what good has it done Ben? How much better off is he, really, than before the struggle began? There are still no children he can sign to; his teacher is still attempting to teach him orally; he is still getting signing only in direct conversation with Ray and me, and our signing is still limited.

What has gone wrong? I was supposed to sort things out for us, bring about some changes . . . I have made changes—lots of changes—but they have been the wrong ones. I have allowed myself to be sidetracked by the philosophy of deaf education whilst shying away from the practicalities; the ways I have discovered to help Ben—and myself—have been wide of the mark—long-term plans, not short-term solutions . . . It is time to take stock.

Notes

1 PLAY MATTERS/The Toy Libraries Association for Handicapped Children, 68 Churchway, London NW1 1LT.
2 British Sign Language.
3 The British Deaf Association, 38 Victoria Place, Carlisle, Cumbria, CA1 1HU.

Mentally, I list my commitments, new and old: with Ben, speech and auditory training, John Tracy work, hearing aid maintenance and daily care, signing, contact with ordinary children through toddler group, contact with deaf children through NDCS, hospital visits for hearing tests, earmould impressions, examination by the consultant, general health check-ups. With NDCS: library organisation, fund-raising events, monthly meetings, social contact with other parents, helping with social events for the children (Christmas party, visits, carnival float), contact point for new parents, hotline for the computers. To improve signing: signing courses, constant search for information about sign language courses, manuals, videos, workshops, television programmes. To remain up to date with information: reading, making contact with 'useful' people and organisations . . .

Add the outside commitments I have taken on: CND, Labour Party, women's discussion group; add a weekly driving lesson and a full social and family life with all its associated events: Ray's school, nursery and toddler socials and fund-raising events, birthday parties, visits to and from relatives and friends; add broken nights—every night, difficult bedtimes with both children and the ongoing physical work involved in maintaining a house and feeding and clothing a family; add the mental strain of bringing up two children under five who cannot communicate with each other except at a very basic level; add a husband whose job is exhausting, whose hobby is precious to him but a source of anger for me; add isolated pursuit of an educational ideal . . . and you have too much for an ordinary person to handle. And this is what I am, just an ordinary person, with an ordinary person's limitations.

The women's group has spawned a small offshoot, a 'therapy group'. We meet every two weeks, and, working from a book,[1] we have been learning about self-help therapy by practising it. As I get to know the women in the group I realise how inaccurate my impression of them has been. Not one, it emerges, is exactly as she appears on the surface, not one feels that she has sorted out her life to her own satisfaction. One of the women maintains her Supermum status for longer than the rest, a free spirit, happy with herself and delighting in life . . . until a huge row with her husband proves after a while that she, too, is just like the rest of us, some of the time, that there are events even in her life with which she is ill-prepared to cope.

As I see the other women in the group go through observable stages in the emergence and the solution of problems I begin to see my own difficulties as a stage in my life, not as a permanent fixture. With their support, I find the courage to make changes, to be easier on myself. In a quiet time, alone, I set myself the task of red-inking some of my commitments. In cold blood, and deliberately ignoring feelings of guilt and responsibility for anyone other than immediate family, I start to cross things off.

Membership of a CND group involves more than wearing a badge; the local Labour Party expects more of its members than an annual subscription, and the nights off for meetings as often as not have resulted in a feeling that I am a passenger, that I should be supporting more events, that I should be more active, and I have come home feeling guilty, not refreshed, depressed rather than inspired, tired in body and mind. So I abandon them. I wear my badge, I pay my subs., but that's as far as it goes. My commitment stops there. At first it is hard to face other members of these groups, hard to say 'no' when asked for help, but eventually people stop asking. I feel slightly guilty, but I can handle that, now, and I turn to the list again.

I scan it carefully. Many of the commitments that remain were taken on with Ben in mind but are of questionable value to him, and are continued because of a sense of duty, a need to see things through which goes back to my schooldays, a horror of unfinished work, the disapproval incurred by abandoning projects or shirking responsibility. But a bigger responsibility has arisen now—a responsibility for myself. I owe it to myself and to the people I live with to sort myself out. It's time I came to terms with my own limitations, trusted my own judgement, made my own decisions.

The John Tracy course is the next to go. For a long time my main motivation in continuing has been conscience and a desire to prove to the John Tracy people that signing is a good idea. The more I read about the 'manual/oral' debate and the more I find out about deaf education in America (the John Tracy clinic is one of the few outposts of oralism left in the States) the clearer becomes the futility of my little effort to change their views. If they can hold out against the rest of America, the fact that Ben Fletcher signs *and* babbles is hardly going to persuade them to accept Total Communication. On that score the decision is easily made.

But can I be sure that Ben won't suffer if I give up the John Tracy course? Yes, of course I can. The exercises are designed for committed oralists and children who are being deprived of signing and therefore need all this extra stimulation. Our family doesn't fit that description at all. And my tutor is miles away; I do not have to face her every week—so I give up. I stop filling in reports and I give up my conscientious pursuit of the recommended routines, confining my activities instead to the ones I am sure Ben enjoys and to the ones which do not require hours of preparation. But my heart pounds when a letter arrives asking why I have stopped corresponding; it is so sympathetically written, and it appeals so subtly to that exaggerated sense of duty which I am trying so hard to rationalise that I blush to read it . . . so I fill in another report, to make myself feel better, and I send it off. But as I post it I vow to myself that this is the last. I have a complete course of baby lessons now; I have bought the pre-school section, complete, for the library. The information, the techniques, are there if I need them; there is no need for me to do any more. Having made the decision, I feel an enormous sense of relief. To be able to put away the instruction sheets, to be able to take

afternoons off to visit friends and do no training whatsoever, gives me a great sense of freedom and immediately
has the desired effect in terms of reduction of stress. 'Big
Brother' is no longer watching me—I can do as I like . . .
some of the time.

For there is still pressure. Ben's new teacher now visits
twice weekly; her work with Ben is similar to that
advocated by the John Tracy Clinic, but different enough
to make her want to establish her own programme for him,
and of course part of her job is to train us, as parents, to
continue the work when she is not there; it is understood
that even a twice-weekly visit by a teacher of the deaf is by
no means enough 'teaching' for a deaf child. Pre-school, the
parents must do the rest. I might have abandoned the John
Tracy programme; I am still expected to carry on with the
teacher's, much as I disagree with her methods and despite
her lack of success. But the real me doesn't want to do it. *I*
don't want to do it.

It takes a few weeks (and much easy talking with Ray,
who is in complete agreement with me over this) to pluck
up the courage to face the teacher with my opinion, but
eventually I manage to broach the subject. This is much
easier than I expected; I am surprised at the grace with
which she accepts my arguments. It is as if she, too, is
relieved at the prospect of change, and after some frank
talking and lateral thinking, we arrive, quickly and amicably,
at a plan of action which suits us both. I will not coerce Ben
any more into using the auditory trainer, nor will I try to
persuade Ray to do the coercing for me. If she wants to use
it during her sessions and can persuade Ben to tolerate it
without putting undue pressure on him, that's her affair
and I will not interfere. But I myself will not put pressure
on Ben to use his voice in situations where he does not do
so naturally.

As for the rest of our 'session' time, we decide to embark
upon a programme of 'environmental studies', in which we
work together at finding ways to help Ben become more
aware of and more knowledgeable about the world around
him. Since his level of communication, like that of all very
young deaf children of hearing parents, is inadequate for

him to gain very much information via language, we will engineer situations for him that will increase his experience, and hence his knowledge, and if I sign to him about what is happening, and interpret as best I can what the teacher wants to say, we hope that his use of language will progress—language via experience, perhaps, rather than knowledge via language.

The teacher really excels in this kind of work, and the contrast between these sessions and the formal training sessions could not be more marked. I actually enjoy her visits; I begin to see her as a friend rather than a problem. Instead of two hours of purgatory we now have trips out to look forward to: our first project is 'The Seasons' and we sally forth in the teacher's car to experience them first-hand, drawing Ben's attention to the features of a wintry landscape, the way mist forms on the windows of the car when it's cold outside, the way frost coats twigs and leaves in white, then turns to water when you breathe on it . . . Once we have a 'Nature Walk', just the three of us, through a nearby wood; the teacher goes in up to her ankles in a bog but she laughs it off and Ben chortles with delight. With her own camera, she takes photographs of our activities and has them developed; when the prints arrive we include them in collages with the things we have brought back from our travels, to remind Ben and so that we can talk about events which have happened in the past. She brings books with appropriate pictures; Ben is interested, for the first time expressing in sign that the pictures in the books are like the real world outside. When the snow falls we build a snowman; we cut out pictures from Christmas cards; Ben's vocabulary of 'winter words' increases.

Ben's signing and general awareness improve and, by wearing the radio transmitter and talking to Ben via the Phonic Ear, the teacher can ensure that she is giving him oral input as well. I am happy to continue working on themes when I have Ben to myself in the afternoons, because it does not involve tying either of us down, and I feel that by introducing him to new ideas and new experiences in this way we have found a way of educating him which is free from stress and has immediate and gratifying results. 'Copying' signs and strings of signs is now an everyday occurrence, and the time lag between Ben copying signs and using them spontaneously himself is getting shorter; by concentrating on the signs necessary for each 'theme', Ben is exposed to them often and regularly enough to incorporate them into his vocabulary. For a long time, he has wandered about with a puzzled expression on his face, signing 'Where?'; now he is able to understand my 'Where's what?', and soon 'What?' is added to the omnipresent 'Where?' and becomes one of his question words: he is able to ask many specific questions himself and communication takes on a new dimension as we have the beginnings of real conversation. He may not understand each reply, but he wants to know, he is able to tell us what he wants to know; he is initiating his own learning experiences. He is no longer the passive recipient of any information we choose to give him; he is gaining control, beginning to realise the power of language as a source of information.

As we continue to work in this way and to make progress, I find it easier to stand back and assess the value of all our experiences, weighing them up against the amount of time and energy they demand from me, deciding which of them are worth the effort and which are not. One visit to the consultant's clinic at the hospital results in the abandonment of yet another obligation. I have grown used to the travelling, to the idea that for Ben to see a doctor for five minutes the children and I have to be out of the house for a whole day and spend a fair amount of time waiting. But when that wait extends to two-and-a-half hours, in a bare, unpleasant room equipped with only a blackboard, a rocking horse and a decrepit old pram with two naked and virtually limbless dollies by way of play equipment, and when that wait precedes a two-minute 'consultation' with a junior doctor with no social skills, and a seeming inability even to read the notes laid out in front of him, I have no hesitation in deciding that enough is enough. Each visit is the same: a quick look in the ears, come back in six months. Never have I received a straight answer to a straight question; never have I been treated like an individual with an ounce of brain; never have I left feeling satisfied. Another obligation bites the dust.

When the health visitor arrives a few weeks after our first missed appointment to see why we haven't been, we talk about my depression, my new way of coping. She is sympathetic, very concerned. She had no idea that I was going through such a bad time. 'You always seem so cheerful,' she says . . . And I realise that this, too, is something I need to change. Not the cheerfulness—I hope I can keep that—but the covering-up. I have seen how much other people can help—but if they do not know what is wrong, how can they help? Apart from creating in me an enormous amount of tension, my determination—no, my lifetime's habit—of 'covering up', of 'putting on a brave face', is unfair on others, who might like to help but who are shut out.

Talking to my mother, who has waited and worried while we have become more and more unhappy, I uncover an enormous amount of sympathy, but also a lot of confusion . . . Why haven't I told her what's been going on? Why have I kept all this to myself?

So I open up to her, and to Ray's parents. Everyone wants to help; it is as if the floodgates have been opened. Offers to babysit become more and more frequent, and Ray and I accept them. At first, typically, I am guilty at this lust for freedom and guilty at enjoying the freedom so much when I have it. After all, we had our children because we were sure we wanted them, and wanting to escape now seems wrong. When the children go to their grandparents it is distressing at first to think of Ben having to cope without his night-time breast-feeds and without sign language. But these worries are short-lived. Both of Ray's parents—like Ray himself—have very expressive faces and very lively personalities; Ben 'reads' their faces and their gestures easily, as he did when he was a baby. Ben and his grandfather greet each other like long lost buddies each time they meet; in addition to a second name—both are called Joseph—they seem to share a second sense, a quality of communication which is indefinable, but ever present, and both get a great deal of pleasure from each other's company. When I am not there, Ben is happy to accept a bottle at bedtime; there are never any problems. Sarah and her Nannan are cementing a bond which began to form when we lived with them, when Ben was a baby and Sarah's Nannan gave her the attention I was unable to give. Both children enjoy their visits and gain from them. There is no need for worry and no cause for guilt.

Soon, the grandparents are so well accustomed to looking after both children at once that Ray and I are able to take whole weekends off, with spectacular results in terms of relaxation and improved communication. We had really forgotten what it was like to be on our own, how much time we could give to each other, how little work there is when there are only two adults to look after. Even if we don't actually go anywhere, just having the house to ourselves, being able to take off in the middle of the day for a proper hike or a drink at the pub, being able to lie in on Sunday and read the papers in bed . . . just being able to talk without interruption . . . all these joys we had forgotten. How little we appreciated them, too, when we had them, and how much more we appreciate them now. We go swimming, we play around in the baths like a couple of teenagers; we rediscover a joy in each other's company which we thought we had lost forever.

My mother comes over and looks after the children for a weekend so that Ray can compete in a fell race and we can camp overnight in the Lakes; this is the first of many such weekends. My mother loves to practise her signing and the children love her company . . . She even manages to do some housework! Returning home from a weekend away, feeling close to Ray, and being greeted by my own mother and two happy children in a clean and tidy house, I feel a deep sense of inner contentment. My batteries have been recharged; I can take over with confidence; every time, it is as if I have been given a fresh start. The weekends off are like peaceful little islands in a sea of chaos. Just by being there they make the chaos more bearable, and each time I return from one of those islands, I bring a little bit of peace back with me. It is amazing how many people are ready to help once they realise that there is a need.

Ben's teacher has arranged for us to attend a second toddler session, with a different group of women and children. Still nervous in large groups such as this, I gravitate towards Julie, who is mapping out posters in a corner, and allow Ben to make his own way. This is Julie's account.

When Ben and Lorraine first came into the room Ben was obviously deaf. He'd got the hearing aid and the amplifier on and I'd seen him in the village and never met him at all. He wandered about approaching different mums as all the new children do. And instead of the normal reaction from the mums of 'Hello, have you come to play?', etc., that we usually try to give these new children, Ben just got a sort of embarrassed smile or a look of pity or a very exaggerated hello, and nothing else. There was no interaction between Ben and all these other mums, because nobody knew how to communicate with him at all. It was very much Ben in his own world . . . a lot of the girls here are very well educated and yet nobody knew how to speak to him or talk to him or make him feel welcome in our group . . . So although watching Lorraine was very fascinating seeing her do the sign language, which I'd never seen before . . . it was Ben and his lack of reaction from us that really made me think for a long time about doing something constructive in order to reach him. And help him to reach us.

For a week I thought about him and dreamt about him. I couldn't bear to think of him not being able to communicate with us. And the following week I asked Lorraine very sheepishly and quite embarrassed, if it would be of any use if I learned to sign, would it help Ben. And I honestly expected her to say no or it doesn't matter or something like that . . . but of course she didn't, she nearly jumped up and kissed me on the spot. And she gave me her little Sign and Say[2] *manual and a fingerspelling chart.And I just went away with that, basically, for the first week, and pored over it and learned a few signs and came back the next week and put them all into practice. I felt very, very pleased with myself to be honest. And got a little—a little spark from Ben. And I just kept following, learning more signs each week with Lorraine's help and eventually, as soon as he saw me come into the room, Ben would come and take my hand and to whichever game he wanted to play with, whatever he wanted to do. And we would just play together and I would sign as much as I could at the time. And when I got stuck Lorraine would be behind Ben doing all the signs which I could copy and do for Ben . . . Eventually, after several weeks had passed and I could sort of cope with the sign language on my own, Lorraine would take my little girl away. And then I would just spend the session playing with Ben. And gradually, of course, other ladies started to notice that I was signing to him and he would begin to sign back, which was lovely . . . There were enquiries, why was I doing it, and one or two said yes, I would really like to learn, so we decided that we ought to do something positive. We made a date for Mondays and we would meet and begin our sign language which was very slow because it was me teaching the others and I really was very, very limited at the time. I did attend part of a course at a teaching centre, but again it was basic words; the building up sentences was very hard. We just concentrated on the things we thought Ben would need from day to day, what we could teach him, what we could communicate with him about the toys and the cars and what was he doing. Very basic sentences. Eventually there were five of us meeting. A lot of mums had just learned, 'Hello Ben, how are you, you OK?' and 'Where's Mummy?'—things like that; but the five of us really wanted to learn the language properly.*[3]

Gradually, thanks to Julie and her friends, Ben's horizons have begun to widen. Now, there are people he meets in the village who can do more than just say 'Hello'; Ben can go and play at people's houses without me and without Sarah, because there is a core of people who have established basic communication with him. Annette was quickly drawn in; she joined Julie's group and has made rapid progress; she enjoys the fact that Ben will now visit her of his own accord and not just as Sarah's little brother.

Now, indisputably, I am no longer alone. My faith in human nature takes another quantum leap: the attitude to women which has begun to evolve through the women's group receives another boost—they have come up trumps again. Even though all have young families, each is prepared to give up a couple of hours a week and struggle to learn another language for Ben's sake. I feel that I have found more good friends and that, thanks to Julie, Ben's position, as the only deaf person in a hearing community, has been eased considerably.

The toddler group establishes a Wednesday morning session without mothers for children who are approaching nursery age; Ben's teacher recommends that he go; Sarah, confident now after over a year at nursery, offers to go, too, 'to look after him'. Her willingness to take responsibility for her little brother during this session marks a big step in her development; being the oldest child in the group and 'big sister' to a group of little children increases the self-confidence she has already shown by choosing to go, and Ben, the staff assure me, quickly leaves her protection to explore the possibilities of the session on his own; he, too, is developing his independence in a situation which is relatively free of stress. The staff are pleased to report also that communication with Ben is much easier than they had expected; he seems to understand quickly what is required of him and, if he doesn't, a single demonstration is usually all that is required to put him straight. There are far fewer problems with other children than I had anticipated: when no longer under mother's watchful eye many children behave better rather than worse, and Ben is no exception. So I have Wednesday mornings completely free!

Annette also has more time on her hands now; Paul has started school and she and Little Sarah are on their own all day, so instead of restricting my children's visits to times when I can go with them, I let both Sarah and Ben go on their own and try not to feel guilty that at these times Annette sometimes has three to look after: she assures me that she doesn't mind, despite the fact that the two youngest are at a stage now when battles over toys are frequent and adult interference essential for much of the time. We arrange a sort of 'child-swap' so that Ben can have uninterrupted morning sessions with his teacher: Annette looks after my Sarah in the morning and I have her Sarah in the afternoon in return.

Gradually, as all these measures swing into play, life slows its pace perceptibly. And slowly there is room for a new commitment, taken on this time for the right reason: a very real need, felt by all involved with Ben: his teacher, Ray, myself and the women who now know him.

The language we are able to give to Ben, between us, is still limited. Reducing the amount of speech training has enabled me to concentrate on signing—and Ben continues to 'talk' more as he signs more—but now our signing is beginning to feel limited again. There is lots we want to tell

Ben; if we were more fluent it would be easier. We have to get back to the town deaf club. We have to see more of Ken. But there is no prospect of another course just yet, and we are shy of simply going to the club: we are not members, we have not been invited and we are not sure whether we would be welcome as visitors. Elspeth asks around for us. Ken will sign us in, she says. She is hoping to be accepted as a member herself; she has been doing a BSL course in Bristol and is far more confident in her signing and very keen to establish firm links with the club—so maybe in future she could sign us in. Ken promises to be there one Wednesday night; accordingly, we arrange for my mother to come and babysit, and we drive over.

This visit feels very different from those we have made before for the classes. Extremely nervous and unsure of ourselves, we sidle in, sitting for a while by the door trying not to look conspicuous, peering anxiously around for Ken, worried that we might be approached by an official and that there might be . . . horrors . . . *misunderstandings!* But our nerves are calmed by a partially hearing woman who remembers us from the signing classes; she comes over and talks to us until Ken arrives; at last, we are signed in and legally present. Ken talks to us for a while; when he disappears on club business Ray and I stick together like the shells of a clam, wanting to talk to people but nervous after all this time . . . We force ourselves to move around: to stand at the bar, to watch the snooker or the dominoes. And eventually we are drawn into conversation. If not actually conversing, we also learn a lot from watching, once we have made sure that in general deaf people don't mind being 'overheard' and that they do have ways of making their conversations private if necessary. Each time, the visits get easier; there are more people we can talk to and we feel more at home.

One week we are able to visit on a Saturday. We are surprised to see that there are several children around. No one seems to mind; the children wander around freely while their parents enjoy a drink and a chat. It is all very informal and relaxed. Here, we realise, is the situation we were looking for all those months ago: a signing environment for people of all ages. Would it be possible to bring Ben here? Ken suggests that we apply for membership; if we are members there should be no problem. So we apply, and we are accepted—a great thrill for us and something that we had hardly dared hope for. After all, deaf people come to a deaf club to relax; for the most part they have to associate with hearing people all day at work and sometimes at home; they come to the club to escape us and there are, understandably, rules restricting the number of hearing people who may join or be signed in at any one time. But they have accepted us, because we are Ben's parents, and now we can bring Ben.

With mounting excitement, we bundle him into the van early one Saturday evening. Sarah is excited, too; one of her favourite treats is to have crisps and a fizzy drink in the children's room at a pub or to visit the working men's club with her grandparents. She settles in straight away, at a table with her crisps and drink; it is a situation she has enjoyed many times before and she is happy.

But Ben is amazed. For a long time he sits close to Ray and me and he watches. His eyes flit from group to group, coming to rest every so often as, fascinated, he watches signed conversations taking place. Then he begins to circulate. He does quite naturally what Ray and I had to summon up enormous courage to do. He chooses himself a conversation from the many that are taking place, then he homes in and treats himself to a close-up, standing almost between couples as they sign, insinuating himself in a way that we would never dare. And Ray and I are able to relax. This is like no other social situation we have ever been in with Ben. It is completely free of stress. We are no longer the sole communicators, under pressure to talk to our child or to interpret for him. Here, Ben is interacting at his own pace, at his own level, with people whose communication he can see and who have no difficulty communicating with him. He does not converse; his own signing is still at a very functional level and polite conversation is not within his experience, but here no conversation is closed to him; here Ben is in a normal environment and we and Sarah are the odd ones out.

Watching Ben, observing the way the adults here include and encourage him, really highlights for us how strange and isolated and cut off he must feel for the rest of the time. How can he be so happy—for he is a happy child—when he spends most of his time in a world of strangers, a world of people whose communication he cannot see? What resilience he must have, what inner strength! And what right have we to put extra pressure on a child who already has so much to cope with? What right have we to demand speech from someone who might prefer to manage without it, as Ken does—as many of these people do? The language in use among the deaf people here is a silent one; they only use their voices when they talk to us. Obviously, we all need more time at the deaf club. At home,we must sign more, with Ben and with each other.

And now the decision is not an empty one. Between us, we really make an effort. Thanks to the visits to the club, my signing is now more natural, more relaxed, more fluid; I am quite at home now with everyday conversation; I can fit more signs into the amount of time Ben's attention span allows, so he is receiving more signed input from me during the day. In the evenings and at weekends Ben follows Ray about and I can stand back and see progress in their communication also; their natural exchanges are becoming more complex and I can see more specific signs in Ben's contributions. For a long time, as a hearing baby uses single words, Ben used single signs: the sign for 'Daddy' could be a statement, a question or a request. By the expression on his face he conveyed what hearing children convey by tone of voice, and the degree of understanding achieved depended to a large extent on how receptive was the other partner in the conversation. Now, Ben has reached the equivalent of the 'two-word stage'; he can convey much more information more accurately. Sarah, too, is now making efforts to communicate other than by gesture: she is proud of being able to use 'real' sign language with the deaf people in the club; she is beginning to make a connection between them and her brother and to see the advantages in effective communication there, at home and at the toddler session, where her skill as an interpreter is sometimes required—

and always admired. In Ben's signing there is more and more 'baby babble', especially after visits to the club; he plays with his hands and produces approximations of signs, highly delighted with his own performance. Concepts like 'more', 'difficult', 'mine/yours' appear, and the very useful 'dangerous', which he uses to describe anything he doesn't want you to do. The improvement in his signing does not mark a deterioration in his speech; many of the new signs are accompanied by speech and the old signs continue to be so. The sign for 'warm' is always accompanied by 'om', 'hot' by 'o', 'mummy' by 'mmmm'; we now also have 'more' ('mo'). The signs are indispensable because it is the signs which actually prove to us that Ben is making approximations of words. He said 'mum-mum-mum' for ages before he learned the sign, and on lots of different occasions. Only when he learned the sign could I tell when his 'mum-mum' actually referred to me.

Now, I am beginning to feel that we really do have 'Total Communication', and I am confident that it is right for Ben. The advantages are obvious; at last we feel that we have reached the 'pay-off'. It is only a year since we started to sign, but that year has been so full of doubts, of fears, of debate and discussion about what is best for Ben, and the family has been through so much in that year in terms of psychological change and upheaval, that it feels as though six years have passed. But at least we have come out of that year together, and with a firm idea of what we want, and we are starting to gain encouragement from what we can actually see happening. We have finally arrived at a plan which suits us all. We can be content.

I have reduced my list of commitments to a list of priorities, and the new list is very short: one, I must sort myself out; two, I must do all I can to improve my signing and hence Ben's. Already, life is much, much easier. There are still problems, difficulties in communication both with Ben and between ourselves as a family, but they seem to have taken on a healthier perspective. I have learned to say 'No' when necessary to avoid taking on too much, and I have learned to say 'Yes' to help, rather than feeling I should be able to manage without it. I am starting to get to know what I really want, for myself, for the family and particularly for Ben, and to base my actions on that knowledge, not on what other people want or expect me to do. I am starting to build up a firm base of confidence in myself, from which I can work towards what I feel is right.

Some of the decisions have been and might still be difficult, some might earn me the kind of disapproval which has so distressed me in the past, but I can take it. I have found out that disapproval of oneself is far more harmful in the long term than the disapproval of others, and I am happier now that, basically, I approve of what I am doing with and for Ben. Free of obligations and commitments taken on for entirely the wrong reasons, my mind is free to move, free to move on. In the process Ray and I have become closer again. We can talk about education as we used to do in the past, we can see educating Ben as a challenge we can face together, pooling ideas, sure of our motives and confident in our methods. Now that I have wrenched myself free of the line I felt obliged to follow in my pursuit of what everyone else assured me was right, I can join wholeheartedly with him and we can find our own way, together, without compromising our ideals. And this time the decision is a firm and lasting one. Very conscious —but not ashamed—now of my own limitations, I intend to work within them, for my own good and Ben's, and with the support of those I love. My nightmare is over.

Notes

1 ERNST, S., and GOODISON, L. *In Our Own Hands: A Book of Self-Help Therapy*, London: The Women's Press (1981).

2 *Sign and Say*, a small manual of signs produced by the Royal National Institute for the Deaf, 105 Gower Street, London WC1.

3 This quotation, and subsequent ones, are taken from interviews conducted by Tyne-Tees Television during the year July 1984 to July 1985, in the course of filming for their documentary *A Language for Ben*, and are reprinted here by kind permission of the company.

As you walk into the nursery at the Dale, the sound of children's voices—chatting, laughing, screeching with pleasure or excitement, greets you. There are children everywhere, busy, active, totally involved . . . There is plenty of large apparatus: things to climb on, things to climb over and crawl through, things to jump on and things to jump off, a huge slide by one wall. Children are building, hiding, jumping, riding.

The building is large, high-ceilinged, bright, full of colour and life. The walls display interesting pictures, obviously lovingly collected over years, in a variety of sizes and textures and at different levels. There are rugs on the walls, tea-towels, swathes of material with fascinating designs. At child level there are many things to look at, touch and explore: wooden things, bits of machinery, books and plants. In fact there are plants everywhere—in pots and vases on shelves and window-sills, in tubs and baskets on the floor. A pot of daffodils is accentuated by folds of material draped around it in similar colours: the yellow and new leaf green of Spring. A child whizzes past on a bike, wearing a hat in the shape of a dog's head, his own head bowed to disguise his face, looking up every so often to check direction. More children have made a train by tying some wooden trucks together with string. With the help of a nursery nurse they are completing the job, one child at the front on a tractor patiently waiting to drive the convoy away. On a child-level couch in a corner a teacher sits, telling a story to a group of children. She finishes one story, gets up to choose another book; the children follow in a little huddle and begin to argue over which book next; the teacher suggests they bring one each; armed with their books, the children return to the couch; the teacher resumes her place and begins to read again.

To the left of the main hall is a carpeted area: the 'Quiet Room'. It is here that the rocking-horse is situated, a beautiful dapple-grey, so large that a set of steps is needed to mount it. A child rocks on it, arms around the broad, strong neck, gazing into space, dreaming, every so often looking up, staring at something, then returning to the dream, the rhythmic rocking. In a corner, a wooden track is laid out on the floor; a teacher and a teenager from a local school are playing trains with a group of children. In another corner, three little boys are setting up a doll's house; their 'people' slide down the roof; the boys shriek with excitement. A little girl crawls into and around the carpeted area, pretending to be a dog. A boy stands at a little table working out with intense concentration how to fit a wooden jigsaw back into its frame.

The teacher on the floor is now constructing vehicles with a small group. As they play, she talks to them, encouraging them to talk, too; they tell her all kinds of things, connected and unconnected with their play, as they catch on to the joys of conversation. A boy dressed in a long nightie arrives at the 'maths' table; casually he completes a shape-matching puzzle, almost in passing. He has no shoes on—he has probably just got out of bed . . . For there are beds in the nursery—not the camp cots regimentally laid out in some nurseries at 'afternoon nap time'—but a set of real bunk beds, always made up, ready for any child who feels tired to snuggle down for a rest. These beds are part of the Wendy House corner—a whole section of the hall, equipped with full-size beds, cot and cradle.

In the 'kitchen' there is a full-size fridge, and a sink unit at child height; on a low table there are real mixing bowls and utensils, and around the periphery a 'café' has been set up, where realistic 'food' is available for sale: customers eat from real crockery at tables with gingham tablecloths and matching napkins. One orders a boiled egg from the menu; a waiter brings it, followed by sausage and chips. 'I'll bring you a knife and fork,' he says, as the customer begins to tackle his chips with his fingers. A lady at another table is trying to balance two life-size babies on her knee and feed them spaghetti on toast. The babies keep falling off; in desperation she dumps one in front of her on the table, the other into a nearby shopping trolley, and eats the spaghetti herself. 'Come on now,' she says to the one on the table, 'your turn now.' The over-zealous waiter brings a huge plate of fish fingers and mash; rolling her eyes, the lady takes her baby in one hand, the food in the other, and resolutely follows the waiter to the kitchen. 'We've already got some.' Close by, someone's mum is serving milk and biscuits; the children take their milk break when they are ready, sitting at little tables, alone or with friends; they can choose a cup or a straw; they are encouraged to clear up after themselves, but no one nags.

Through an archway is the 'wet area'. This is a very noisy place: children hammer and saw at a low workbench, and they use real tools. Only minimally supervised, they work on constructions using wood, nails and bits of plastic. In one corner there is an enormous round sandpit; in addition to the usual buckets and spades and trucks there are huge pieces of plastic piping and tubing and guttering, enabling elaborate constructions to be made; this is real building, not pretend. A row of easels is in constant use, the paper of different shapes and sizes, the colours bright and fresh, ready mixed one side, in powder at the other, for mixing by the children. On a table are huge pieces of home-made playdough in the same spring green and yellow as the display of daffodils. On another table simple techniques for printing are being demonstrated, and copied by successive children. A teacher and a nursery nurse circulate, replacing and replenishing materials, talking to the children, asking questions, commenting, simply conversing. In islands of quietness, birds twitter: in a corner there is an aviary; the budgies for whom this is home can fly around inside it and there is a 'private' section for nesting and sleeping—or just escaping! Just at the entrance is a low box with guinea pigs in it; next to this are two little chairs with cloths neatly folded over the backs, and every so often a child goes and sits down, placing the cloth carefully over his knees, looking around expectantly or calling for someone to take out a guinea pig and put it in his lap for him to stroke. The guinea pigs are tame; the children have learned to be gentle.

It is obvious that the nursery is extremely well-organised, but the organisation is not obvious; it is subtle and underlying, not rigid or restrictive. Between the staff there is an air of mutual appreciation, respect—and enjoyment; they laugh and joke between themselves; they are obviously happy in their work, and the children must feel this and benefit from an atmosphere in which the staff have plenty of time for them, but also can be seen to care about each other and the mums who come in to help. Everyone feels welcome; everyone feels wanted and appreciated and approved of . . .

During her time here Sarah has grown from a nervous little newcomer into a stable and confident resident; she knows where everything is and how to use it; she has been able to discover talents and build on them; she gains praise and encouragement from teachers who know her well, are aware of the unusual nature of her situation at home with Ben and of the need to compensate her a little—but without stifling her growing independence.

I have no doubt that if such a nursery had existed in the area where I completed my teacher training course it would have been pointed out to us all as an excellent example of good nursery practice. Every idea, every principle, every attitude which was considered desirable when I was training can be seen in operation here, and the children are thriving.

Every school day, Ben and I deliver Sarah to this nursery. At first, he would stay quietly in his buggy and look around, fascinated by the bustling crowds of children, just watching. Now, however, he insists on getting out of the buggy; no longer content just to watch, he wants to use the apparatus, to handle the materials, to get a closer look at things. Actually getting him back into the buggy to go home requires an increasing amount of skilful persuasion. Some afternoons I give up the struggle and stay to help—as do many mums with toddlers: with one watchful eye on our younger offspring, we make ourselves useful around the nursery, maybe taking the opportunity to play with or to talk to our older children while the younger ones are happily occupied.

At these times Ben is no more and no less difficult than the other two-year-olds who stay; like them, he learns the rules by a process of trial and error; if any behaviour is unacceptable, there is always someone around to gently redirect him.

It is Spring, 1983. In November Ben will be three. It is time to start thinking about nursery education for him. It is impossible to visit this nursery every day and not want what it offers for Ben, despite his deafness. Encouraged by the apparent ease with which he fits in, one afternoon I take a deep breath and ask Mrs Davidson, the head teacher at the nursery, if there would be any possibility of her taking Ben when he was three.

'We would have a go,' she says, instantly.

'What, even if he has no spoken language?' This is not a rhetorical question: I genuinely want to know what she thinks—whether Ben would gain anything from the nursery without the benefit of communication, the language that is so obviously being used and extended everywhere in this place. Mrs Davidson thinks back to the only other deaf child she knows, a partially hearing little girl who has recently left the nursery to start full-time school at a unit for the partially hearing in the town. This girl, she says, could say very little when she first arrived, but by the time she left her speech had improved tremendously and everyone was very pleased with her progress. She could make herself understood and the staff—with the help of her Phonic Ear—had no problem getting her to understand them. Perhaps it would be the same with Ben as he got a bit older.

Knowing the difference between a partially deaf person's expectations in terms of speech, and a profoundly deaf one's, I have my doubts, but having sown the seeds of an idea I do not persist. Mrs Davidson needs time to think now and so do we.

We know that, ideally, Ben should have the kind of nursery education offered at Dale, but in a signing environment, where he can gather information in the same situations and at the same level as hearing children, in a language he can understand and alongside children with whom he can communicate as easily as these hearing children do with each other. So we leave the idea of Dale Nursery in abeyance whilst, along with Ben's peripatetic teacher, we set out to find such an environment.

Knowing, as we do, exactly what we want for Ben and then setting out to find it, is a bit like deciding that you want a pink pair of trousers with blue piping, concealed pockets to the front and patch pockets with roses on them to the back—then setting out to find such a pair in the shops. But set out we do. Ben's teacher takes this aspect of her job very seriously. She finds out about all the existing provision in about a thirty-mile radius of where we live and she sets about investigating it with us. There are three schools for the deaf, two of which use Total Communication, and several Partially Hearing Units, none of which use sign at all. We decide to visit the two Total Communication schools and the nearest PHU.

I remember listening to a talk given by the head of this PHU at a NDCS meeting shortly after Ray and I joined, and being very impressed with the caring attitude she expressed towards her pupils, and the success she had achieved, both educationally and with speech. I remember how hesitantly, after her talk, I asked her the question which had been on my mind throughout: 'What's the deafest child you would take?' and her answer, that it would depend very much on the child, what progress he or she was making orally and what prospect there was of later integration into the main school. Then, my response was to hope that Ben would manage well enough orally to be able to attend the unit. Now, our ideas have changed. We know Ben better, and we are far more aware of the issues involved in educating the deaf. When we visit the unit, it is obvious to us that Ben would not cope there. How easy it is simply to be able to accept that now, rather than to suffer the disappointment which would have ensued had we kept that goal in mind and consciously aimed for it. This is a unit for partially hearing children, not deaf ones. All the teaching here is still done orally; Ben would be lost without the support of signs. However, the unit does reserve a number of places in the nursery attached to the main school; the arrangement is that any deaf child who attended the nursery (there are none at present) would be under the supervision of the unit staff, receive specialist teaching from them and have the benefit of an extra classroom assistant in the nursery, employed specifically to work with the handicapped children. This nursery is very small, but bright, cheerful, well organised and well run; there is lots going on and the atmosphere is warm and friendly. Ray and I spend a morning there, with Ben, who enjoys himself playing on the tricycles and push toys outside. One of the staff there remembers us—from signing class, which she has been attending 'just out of interest', and she tells us that if we want her to she will continue with her signing and use it with Ben if he comes to this nursery. This sounds hopeful—but we realise that this one person's efforts would by no means transform this nursery into the signing environment we had envisaged, and it looks as if Ben would be the only deaf child there . . . So we reserve a place, provisionally (this nursery is much in demand), and we reserve judgement.

Next, Ben's teacher and I visit the schools for the deaf with Ben. Each school is over an hour's journey by car from our house. As I sit in the back with Ben, attempting to interest him in the scenery, all he wants to do is sleep, and I wonder how he would cope with two journeys like this every day, whether he would sleep through both of them and whether I would then be able to get him to bed at night. Bedtimes are our worst time of day as it is. We try to avoid letting Ben sleep at teatime, because this results in another four or five hours awake before he is willing to go to bed proper. If this happened each schoolday, how would he manage then to wake up next morning at the early time such a journey would necessitate? He would be constantly tired—and so would we. Still, I push this worry into the back of my mind as we tour the nursery departments.

It soon becomes clear that, although both nurseries are situated in schools for the deaf, our notion of a signing environment for preschool children is very far removed from the reality experienced by the nursery-age deaf children in these schools. Talking to the teachers in charge we discover that *policies* on communication are very different: one school advocates Total Communication, the other an oral approach wherever possible—but, in fact, what goes on at nursery level is remarkably similar. Each nursery has a large population of local hearing children, integrated with the deaf children for the purpose of oral language input and socialisation. Each nursery is staffed by specialist teachers of the deaf, who are very involved in their work, totally dedicated to the children in their care, extremely concerned about the deaf child's acquisition of spoken and written language: at each school we are shown 'language areas' equipped with group hearing aids, where a semi-circle of little chairs with headphones on standby faces a large chair for teacher, the walls are covered with words and pictures—and there is a bank of buttons and levers and dials and switches 'so that each child's input can be controlled individually'. Language work goes on here, we are told; daily, the deaf children have speech and auditory training with the teacher—about half an hour, sometimes more, sometimes less . . . I listen as the teachers wax eloquent about the acoustics of the rooms and the superior quality of the sound input . . . and the amount of language that 'can be got in' here—and I think how much Ben hates the auditory trainer, how much he resists speech training, how 'language' for Ben means anything but oral input from a teacher . . . and how language at Dale Nursery, between the hearing children and their carers, arose naturally as they played, not in an artificial situation such as this . . . And where are the large toys, equipment for physical play, places to hide, things to climb on and slide down? There is some equipment outside—but what about the winter? How do the children work off their energy when it is too cold or wet to play outside? These are quiet thoughts, kept to myself—because these teachers do not mention play very much; they assume that what we are really interested in is how they will go about teaching Ben to talk.

In the oral nursery, I watch as children attempting to

communicate by gesture are gently but firmly reminded to use their voices, or are given, very clearly and distinctly, a spoken version of what they have just gestured, and rewarded by distinct approval when they copy it. I watch the praise and attention lavished upon children who attempt to communicate using their voices, the delight with which even a 'Hello' is greeted if it is attempted orally. I see Ben's eyes glaze over as the staff talk to him; I notice other bright, active children automatically repeating what is said to them with their mouths, while their eyes indicate that their minds are somewhere else altogether. Ben's behaviour would be deviant here; his signing, the signing that we have worked so hard to establish, and which is becoming his working language, would be, at best, ignored, at worst, actively discouraged. If he wanted to get on here, he would have to be oral.

'How can you teach reading without language?' I ask as we tour the primary department; the reply leads me to assume that, for deaf children, the written word itself forms the basis of language. A hearing child learns, first, what something is, that is, he recognises it in his mind as a definite entity. Then he recognises the word which describes it, then he begins to use that word himself. Only much later, after much practice, does he learn the written form of the word. For these deaf children, especially the profoundly deaf ones whose oral language is very slow to develop, the middle two stages are apparently missed out: they are presented with the written form of English before they can have any idea at all what the English language is. My mind boggles at the thought. How difficult that must make the teacher's job! How much easier signing would make it! Yet they resist it. Here, they are trying to teach children to read who are language deprived in the truest sense—yet they insist that this is the best way.

The other school is committed to Total Communication throughout; the head's views about signing and education are similar to ours; he is convinced of the damage a rigidly oral approach can do; his staff often have to face the unenviable task of trying to pick up the pieces when children who have failed in oral schools or units are passed on to them as a last resort. But the practical application of his philosophy seems to be diluted the further down the school we look. The older children do indeed have the benefit of a signing environment; they are bright, articulate, a delight to watch as they participate actively in their lessons and converse in groups in the corridors or at lunch . . . but apart from the specialist 'language' teaching for the deaf children, the nursery might just as well be situated in a hearing school. The teacher is learning to sign, so is a classroom assistant, but the wealth of language observable further up the school is nowhere in evidence here. By language, the staff here still mean English; the acquisition of spoken language by their pupils is uppermost in their minds, and this is where most of their energies are directed. Thinking of the philosophy of the school, I expected to find teenagers in this nursery, fluent deaf communicators from the senior department, playing with the children and encouraging development of their signing, whilst at the same time gaining for themselves valuable insights into life with little children . . . but there are none. And there are very few deaf children, so that the dominant language anyway is the spoken English of the hearing children who are integrating. So, the signing environment we thought we could find for Ben does not exist at nursery level even in a school for the deaf. And proper nursery education does not exist there either.

Dale Nursery School has a constitution, a list of aims and objectives, pinned up on a noticeboard in the entrance hall. It reads:

Into our environment, each child brings with him his own unique experiences, character, personality, innate abilities, tendencies, traits and potential—and he plays. This play is the supreme physiological need of the young child, necessary for mental health and full growth. It is hard work, demanding of the child concentration, perseverance, mental and physical effort, self-organisation and responsibility. It is a vehicle through which a child pursues his own personal interests and desires.

The environment we provide is warm, stable and caring, so the child can feel emotionally and socially secure, be accepted for himself at all times, and in which he is free to explore, experiment, discover and

learn—aided at the right moment by a sensitive adult. It is a wide, rich,
free saying environment which allows time for the child to do his own
thinking and learning at his own pace, either inside or out.

The day itself is 'fluid', flexible and adaptable—is subtly directed,
presenting to the child a stimulating environment in which he can enjoy
self-selected activities, enabling him to experiment and discover the world
as he sees it—come to terms with his findings, and gain control over
them.

We are completely accepting of the children and what they do, and
have a non-directed attitude. With this approach to children's learning
we can, being with the child, capitalise on what he offers in his
play—that is, the learning he has already achieved—take it—enjoy
it—reinforce it, and then develop it.

The contrast between this attitude to and philosophy of
education and the one we have encountered in the schools
for the deaf is very marked. From educators specifically
concerned with the deaf, even at nursery level and before,
we have heard more about training than experiment, more
about imitation than discovery, more about structure than
freedom, more about work than play, more about directed
activities than non-directed, more about discipline imposed
from outside than self-organisation, more about changing
than accepting, more about using time than allowing time.
'Play is the supreme physiological need of the young child,'
says the nursery. 'Speech is the supreme physiological need
of the young deaf child,' I hear the deaf educators retort.

Ray and I are intensely disappointed. We have, indeed,
arrived at the end of our shopping trip without finding
anything remotely like what we wanted. We have to think
again in the light of what we have just seen and reconsider
our options. In a sense, the task is easier now, since the one
criterion we had firmly lodged in our minds as most
desirable in finding a suitable nursery for Ben has proved
impossible to satisfy, locally at least. Since a signing
environment does not exist at nursery level in our area, we
can consider the four options on their merits. The choice
now is a simple one. Do we want a first class nursery
education for Ben, or will we opt for a second-rate nursery
experience but one backed up by specialist teachers and

teaching? At this stage, do we want Ben to be educated by specialists in nursery education or by specialists in deaf education?

On the surface, the decision, put like this, should be easily made. My training, our views on the education of the deaf, plus our personal experience both of nursery education and of deaf education, make Dale the obvious choice. Apart from getting an excellent introduction to 'formal' education there, Ben would be able to remain within the community, build on friendships he has started to establish in the toddler group and at home, start his school career in exactly the same way Sarah did in a place he has shown that he likes, and without the strain imposed by a long car journey each morning and evening.

But—and it is a very big but—if Ben went to Dale Nursery he would not be able to communicate properly with anyone there. Each of the 'special' placements would offer something in terms of communication: the PHU nursery, though without other deaf children, does have a classroom assistant who is learning to sign; the Total Communication nursery has one or two deaf children and staff who are learning to sign, and even the totally oral nursery has enough deaf children for them to begin to establish some form of signing between themselves, if only in the playground. Dale has none of this . . . but it is terribly hard for us to reject it.

Ben's peripatetic teacher is extremely helpful and supportive; she, too, has seen all the options and she knows from her experience of us that Dale has a lot to offer us—and indeed the policy of the LEA towards profoundly deaf preschool children is to recommend local nursery school provision with peripatetic support. But she, too, perhaps conscious of her own limitations—is concerned that Ben would miss out on a lot of communication if he went there. So she starts to put out a few gentle feelers. On a visit to the nursery she talks to Mrs Davidson about Total Communication; in turn, the staff there question me about it; I lend them suitable pamphlets to look through, and, as luck would have it, *See Hear* put out a programme about a Total Communication preschool playgroup which has just been established in Northern Ireland. (This is Susan Phoenix's brainchild. It was highly successful but, because Total Communication is not widely accepted in Northern Ireland, particularly by the education boards, the playgroup had to be funded privately and has since collapsed because of lack of finance.)

In this programme the hearing mother of a two-year-old deaf girl eloquently puts over her views on the state of deaf education in general, her fears for her daughter, her hopes now that a proper means of education has been established in her area . . . I watch the programme one Sunday and am able to ask Ben's teacher to recommend the Monday repeat to the nursery staff. The programme puts forward our point of view much better than I could, and the fact that it is a second person expressing these views means that I do not have to be involved at all. The nursery staff can discuss the programme and how they feel about Total Communication without the sense of obligation they might feel if I were presenting the arguments. Ben's teacher and I entertain a vague hope that one or two of the staff might be moved to learn to sign, but we want to give them the option; we do not want to pressurise them.

When there is no immediate comeback, though, I can't resist asking, very soon afterwards, what they thought about the programme, and I am a little shocked by Mrs Davidson's non-committal reply; it seems so out of character. All she will give me is a rather vague 'Very interesting, dear.'

At the signing course, we more experienced signers have progressed now into an 'advanced' group, which meets separately and does slightly different exercises, but half-way through each session the whole class comes together for coffee. One Monday evening, as I make my way towards the coffee bar, I hear a voice I know—and for a while I can't place it. I am used to hearing that voice somewhere else. But then, through an open door, like a scene from a film or a dream, I see, not a familiar face—not one, but six, or seven. I can't believe it. Emotions crowd in on me—amazement, joy . . . and an overpowering sense of relief. *The whole of the staff of Dale Nursery is here, learning to sign!*

For a minute or so I am too choked to speak. When I do, the words I say are unintelligible; my mind is full of babble. All those faces, smiling out at me. We care, they are saying. We care about Ben. We care enough about him to give up our Monday evenings to learn to sign for him. I feel like hugging them, but I can't. I just stand there, my eyes full of tears, until Mrs Davidson says something funny and the tension is broken. My heart is full, but my mind is quiet. Now I can have what I want for Ben: an excellent nursery education, with people who can sign, without him having to travel.

I can't wait to tell Ray. I couldn't hug the nursery staff but I can hug him. We sit together in front of the fire until well into the night, with happy little smiles on our faces and hope in our hearts.

*   *   *

'It's all very well learning signs,' says Mrs Davidson in a familiar plea a few weeks later, 'but we can't put them together.' So another informal signing class begins. As Julie is teaching her friends, I am teaching the nursery staff; useful little phrases like 'Be careful!!!' 'What are you doing?' 'Do you need the toilet?' Ben's progress out of nappies and into pants has been a very puddleful one. Sarah would 'puddle' on purpose sometimes . . . How long ago that seems now! Now, she looks on piously as, on a bad day, Ben appears to have no control at all: 'EEEEK! Mummy! He's done a wee! MUMMY!!! He's doing a wee on the BED!!!' Sarah is really the big girl now. Moonbeam, I call her, light of my nights. My fears for her have—so far—proved groundless. She has grown sensible, tolerant, very loving and lovable, a real friend to me. She reassures me about Ben's impending entrance to nursery: 'Don't worry, Mummy, he'll be all right with me, I'll look after him.' And so that she can help to integrate him (for when he officially starts nursery she will officially start school) Mrs Davidson agrees to take Ben for a couple of weeks before school closes in the summer. Sarah feels very important as she, too, begins to 'prepare' the staff by teaching them the signs she knows. Preparation of the staff intensifies as the day of Ben's admission approaches; I make up a little file of the signs that he understands and those he uses himself, and I go through this with the staff, to make sure that they are able to understand him as well as possible, as well as being able to make themselves understood. The staff's determination to learn, and their seeming enjoyment of the task—is wonderful to see. They are nervous—but excited as well.

The big day dawns: on a fine, warm, July afternoon I take both my children down to Nursery. For reasons of insurance I have to stay on the premises, but I keep out of Ben's way and, though he knows I am there, he hardly ever seeks me out. To him, this is bliss. He doesn't have to go home after delivering Sarah, he can stay; he can build, climb, ride around, do all the things he enjoys doing, all afternoon. And the staff cope admirably. Although I am technically available as a sort of 'walking dictionary', they don't often use me; they appear to get through to Ben with little difficulty, using the signs they know and the mime and gesture they are accustomed to using anyway with the little children. Sarah is anxious to help and is pleased when asked; she feels proud of her developing ability to sign and they encourage her and give her lots of praise.

'Well?' I ask Mrs Davidson at the end of term. 'Are you reasonably happy about September?'

'Yes,' she says, 'we shall be sorry to lose Sarah, but we shall be happy to have Ben.'

*   *   *

As the summer break begins, Ben's Phonic Ear breaks down. We drop it in at the hospital to be repaired, and we go off camping. Soon after we return, I pass my driving test. Soon after that, it is time for Sarah to start school and Ben to return to nursery. Before the holiday I had two children at home for most of the time. Now, I have every afternoon free.

Afternoons off! With great determination I designate these afternoons 'my' time. If I have had a bad night—or just a busy one—I can have an hour's sleep—or I can spend an afternoon with a friend—or I can read. Sometimes I use the time to prepare teaching materials for Ben—for his peripatetic teacher is still working with us—but the decision is mine now. If I do it, it is because I have chosen to, not because someone else has issued instructions which I would feel guilty if I ignored. Sometimes I do some housework or prepare a special meal because that's what I want to do, not because that's what Supermum would do. I run down to fetch Ben at the end of the day not because I am late but because I am happy. Ben and I enjoy our mornings together: one child is so very much easier than two. I can follow his lead without neglecting Sarah; I can play with him all morning if I want to. I feel as I used to do with Sarah before Ben was born; it is easy to plan nice little routines which suit us both; alone with one child I can thoroughly enjoy his company: I feel contented, patient and affectionate. And now, because I can sleep in the afternoon if I need to, broken nights are no longer so significant. Ben is busy at Nursery; both his body and his mind are kept active; if we can prevent him from falling asleep on the way home (he is so tired after a session at Nursery that he prefers to ride home in the buggy) he will accept quite an early bedtime. He hasn't yet given up his bedtime feed, but he has changed to a bottle, so, although I still have to do the night shift, Ray has been able to take over Ben's bedtime routine and I can have more time with Sarah. I am determined to give her more attention, and am now less tired and irritable at the end of the day, so we can use that time well; I can really concentrate on what she wants to do. Life is considerably calmer and easier, and I am making a conscious effort to keep it that way, so that the rest of the family does actually derive some benefit from my time off.

I can remember being asked what I would do with myself once Ben was at nursery.

'I shall sit in the armchair with my feet up eating chocolates,' was the quick, if slightly ungrammatical reply. Now, though not exactly eating chocolates with my feet, I am achieving the state of mind which that reply anticipated.

I have time during which I can relax, during which I can think things through at my own pace, indulging my body and mind in peace and quiet. This is a kind of lull, a breathing-space . . .

Which is fortunate, really, because now, another decision is asked of me which, a few months ago, would have driven me to despair.

When we collected Ben's Phonic Ear from the hospital at the end of the holiday his attitude to it had changed. Rather then putting it on straight away, as usual, he indicated that he wanted to leave it in its box. He refused it again when we got home, and again the following morning. As before, we persevered . . . But Ben is older now, stronger, and more resourceful. The harness for the aid was babyproof, but it is not childproof. With a little practice Ben could wriggle out of it; the whistle of feedback told us that we would find it lying abandoned somewhere in the house. Each morning, the battle to persuade Ben to put on the aid became more protracted. He did eventually comply, but there was no guarantee that he would leave it on. As the days went by, we became less and less diligent about replacing it: Ray was on holiday, we were busy, there were many occasions when it was easier to leave it off. Ben had got used to running around in just a pair of shorts while we were camping; no wonder he was reluctant to go back to T-shirt and hearing aid. But my conscience and the voices of a thousand teachers of the deaf combined to insist that I should be consistent and replace the aid *every time* he took it off, as we did when he was a baby—and I suppose, if I felt, as I did then, that the aid would make any difference to his responses, I would have done just that . . . But over the holiday we noticed that Ben's responses had not in fact changed: he was still using his voice, still 'chatting', and his 'hearing' without the aid was just as erratic as with it: sometimes he responded, sometimes not.

When term began again, Ben seemed to accept that the routine had to change, and was happy to wear the hearing aid for nursery and for the peripatetic teacher's visits. The teachers at nursery were familiar with it, willingly wore the transmitter and competently replaced straying earmoulds, and at first there must have been so much going on at nursery that Ben forgot about the aid while he was there.

But now, he has started to resist the aid every day. The daily battle is exhausting, and reminds me of times I thought were gone for good. As soon as he sees me approaching with the aid now Ben begins to back away, shaking his head. If I haven't got him cornered he runs and hides, slamming his bedroom door and leaning against it from behind. I have to literally force him into the harness and tie it very tightly and in double knots so that he can't undo it or wriggle out of it. If he is thwarted in this way he sometimes now systematically dismantles those parts of the aid which are detachable, separating the cords from the amplifier, the receivers from the cords and the earmoulds from the receivers, then distributing the pieces around the house. He could not make it clearer that he does not want to wear his hearing aid.

One morning, my mother is with us as the daily struggle begins in preparation for the peripatetic teacher's visit. She sees the tension mounting, she watches in disbelief as I manhandle Ben, trying to get his wriggling little body into the harness. She looks on for a while at the fuss, the tears, the anger, then she asks the obvious, innocent question.

'*Of course he has to wear it!!!*' I scream at her in reply.

'Is it really worth all that fuss?' I ignore my mother, totally bound up in my own frustration.

Eventually, the hearing aid in position, Ben occupied once more in play, I calm down enough to talk to her, to tell her about the pressure there is on me, as his mother, to make sure that Ben wears his aid: Ben's teacher, the audiologist, the consultant . . . I simply cannot make the decision to abandon the aid altogether.

'Why don't you just ask Ben, then?' my mother suggests simply. 'Then it won't be your responsibility, it'll be his.'

Next morning, I do just that. I approach Ben slowly, like one does a pony for breaking, the aid in its harness held loosely in one hand, like a bridle. With my free hand, I sign, 'Do you want to wear this?' My heart is beating so hard I can hear it. We have reached a turning point. I am about to allow Ben to make his own decision, and when he has made it, I will respect it and defend it. He shakes his head and looks warily at me, ready to run. But something in my face tells him he needn't run, this time. He watches me intently as I remove the aid from its harness and pack it away in its box. The analogy with a wild horse is irresistible. This pony wants to run free. I give it a pat on the rump, and I let it go. In my mind, it gallops off into the distance, scattering my fears behind it, like clouds of sand.

'What am I supposed to do with him now?' asks Ben's teacher incredulously when she comes and finds him without his aid. Now that the decision is made, I find her attitude amusing. With Ben in his hearing aid, even though she was getting no response, she must have been working on the assumption that her talking was getting through. Would she have carried on indefinitely? How long would she have talked to him before she began to worry that he was not talking back, before she interpreted his lack of interest in the spoken word as a lack of hearing rather than a lack of concentration? For her, the wearing of a hearing aid meant that Ben could be treated as someone who could hear. She didn't have to make any great effort with her signing because she was relying, really, on the spoken word. Even though all her own experience of Ben points to a profound hearing loss, she has been basing her treatment of him on the idea that, through his Phonic Ear, he might hear enough to enable him to learn to speak. Ben's hospital notes call his hearing loss 'severe'; Jan's notes say that he has responded to sound, so, even though she herself has seen no proof that he hears anything at all, his teacher has continued to rely on their opinions entirely in her approach to communication. Without the aid, she is completely lost. I find it unbelievable that the change from 'almost no hearing' to 'no hearing' should make such a difference to this teacher's confidence in dealing with Ben. But it does. Now, she has to admit to herself that she is dealing with a child who is almost totally deaf. Now, there can be no talk of 'residual hearing'. She has to rethink her strategy entirely.

At nursery, and in general, life for Ben changes when he abandons his aid. At first, the children are confused: one, delighted, tells his mother, 'Ben isn't deaf any more, he doesn't have to wear that thing now!'—but the fact that he no longer wears an aid means that lots of people approach Ben and his deafness differently. For strangers, it means that his deafness is no longer immediately obvious, and for a while I debate the question of making Ben a little badge saying 'I AM DEAF'. For people we know, the effect of abandoning the aid is to start them thinking again about how best to communicate with Ben.

Ray: *There was a change in the reaction of other people once he didn't have his hearing aid on. With his hearing aid on, everybody quite naturally assumes that he can hear something, so they shout and talk to him. Once the hearing aid's off people started to use more than just talking. And they started trying to use sort of natural forms of sign language, making up their own gestures. And I think that seemed to me something very important, that people were trying to communicate, and more successfully than they had been with the hearing aid.*[1]

Throughout the community, especially in people who see Ben daily, as at Nursery, the effect is marked. There is more interest in signing, more discussion in general about deafness. Controversial issues are raised and thrashed out in the street, in people's houses over coffee, in the corridor at Nursery. People's embarrassment changes to fascination as they learn about deaf education; incredulous at the philosophy and the teaching methods of the oralists, they make the connection between the oralists' insistence that deaf people must learn to speak in order to be accepted by the 'hearing world', and their own complacency. Without prompting, people reach the conclusion that it is infinitely easier for a hearing person to learn to sign than it is for a deaf person to learn to speak. For some, this results in a decision to learn to sign—now, or at some point in the future—not only for Ben's sake, but for the sake of all deaf people. Not one questions Ben's need to sign; one likens the deaf child's right to sign language in education to the blind person's right to use braille. For me, it is comforting to have found a group of people who believe that what we are doing is right for Ben, who have thought his situation out for themselves and who have reached the same conclusions as Ray and I, independently.

At about this time we meet some other people whose views correspond with ours: Jim Kyle, a researcher from the School of Education in Bristol University who has been working on sign language. He is committed, not just to signing, but to BSL, the true language of deaf people, that silent language we have observed at the deaf club. There are deaf people on his team, including Lorna Allsop, who is with him when he comes to carry out a sign language assessment on one of his students and to give a talk at the deaf club.

Later, when we meet the two Bristol people in the pub, the inevitable discussion about 'issues' arises, and it is Lorna's view which stays with us. Lorna—another deaf child of deaf parents—has learned to speak, but she chooses to sign. She loves her native language and she is determined to make a place for it in hearing people's lives. For Ray and me, listening to—or watching—her, is like listening to the voice of our own conscience. For me in particular, her expressed opinions open up an old wound. I am the one who has always insisted on speech for Ben; I am the one who is starting to do without speech in my conversations with adult deaf people but still insisting on it when talking to Ben; I am the one who advises the Nursery staff, 'Speak clearly and add signs.' I am the one who is still uneasy about Ray's inability to speak and sign, even though I can see that Ben loves conversations with his father; really, I am the parent who is holding on to English. The Bristol people are very broad-minded—for them, the important thing is that we continue to sign. 'Keep up the good work,' says Jim, as he leaves, 'With or without speech. Do what feels right. Don't worry about it.'

A journey home, thank goodness, to talk, a period of reflection for me, during which pictures keep surfacing of Ken, and now Lorna, articulate without speech, socially acceptable without hearing. Ken and Lorna choose not to wear hearing aids, so does Ben. He wants to be like them. He wants to stay deaf. I must have more respect for his language—not my version of it, which is neither proper English nor proper sign language, but Lorna's and Ken's. BSL. Proper sign language. The silent language of the deaf.

Ben has only been at nursery for a month when a letter arrives for me. I am invited to a workshop[2]; some teachers of the deaf are meeting to discuss sign language in education; Elspeth is involved and has asked if I can go, knowing that I would be interested.

'Although the workshop is really just for teachers, you will be very welcome,' the letter says. 'We hope to be covering some things which you may find useful. Best wishes, Miranda.'

October 14th finds me en route to the Midlands, in Elspeth's car, feeling the kind of nervous and excited anticipation I felt on our first trip to the signing classes with Jan. It is Friday evening; Ray and the children have gone to spend the weekend with his parents; I feel I am on a voyage of discovery. Sign language in education! After the meeting with Lorna and Jim, this is what has been on my mind the most. Elspeth has lots to say; she has just completed a course in advanced communication skills with deaf people, run by the University of Bristol in conjunction with the deaf community there; she has been working closely with Jim and Lorna, and many of the people who will be at the workshop also followed the course. Teachers of the deaf with advanced signing skills . . . teachers of the deaf who are interested in 'proper' sign language! How will they manage to combine BSL with speech training? How will they manage to teach English if they use Sign? Elspeth can answer some of my many questions—but she, too, is looking forward to some practical discussion with other, like-minded teachers. This is the first workshop; the teachers will have finished their course and gone back to their classrooms; all will have been trying to implement their new knowledge. I will have much to learn from them because we shall all have been struggling with the same dilemma—they, at school, me, at home. I can't wait to meet them.

The course is to be held in Miranda's unit; after some wrong turns, we arrive at last, late, emerging from the darkness into a room full of light, packed with people, seated seminar-style at tables arranged in a circle around a bank of electronic equipment—not the group aid I am so used to seeing in this sort of place—but a video, a computer, two TV screens. An enormously energetic woman is bounding around in the centre, talking ten to the dozen, signing as she speaks for the benefit of the deaf people present. I can see Lorna; there must be more. Everything stops to accommodate our arrival; Elspeth introduces herself; I tell them a little bit about myself and Ben, then, relieved that my signing didn't let me down at the last minute, I find a seat next to Elspeth, and a plate of food and a sheaf of notes is placed in front of me. Thankful for the diversion I concentrate on the food and the show goes on. For it feels like a show! Here is Miranda, a teacher of the deaf who is lively, entertaining, full of life and fun. I'm amazed at the amount of energy and enthusiasm this teacher gives out. Oh! If only Ben could come here, I find myself thinking, then I give myself a mental slap on the hand. This is what I am coming to recognise as the 'deaf child's parent' syndrome—never satisfied, always on the lookout for something better . . .

The ideas being floated around are way above my head; even with the benefit of a summing-up I am none the wiser. Gradually I become aware that what is being discussed is linguistics, but the brief introduction to linguistics which I followed at university was no preparation for this, and I find myself watching this teacher instead, trying to isolate signs as she speaks, treating this as an opportunity to learn some new signs rather then attempting to follow the written notes to which everyone else keeps referring. This must be signs supporting English, that is, what I am trying to use with Ben . . . but how much more able this teacher is than anyone I have seen before!

I make no contribution to the linguistics discussion, but by the end of it the purpose of it has become clear: using BSL in educating the deaf means that traditional assessment procedures are inappropriate because they are based on the English language, not on sign language. The more experienced members of the workshop have been trying to arrive at a system for assessing deaf children's progress in BSL, using LARSP, a complex linguistic analysis.[3] It seems that they have not got very far. Systems based on English are very difficult to convert for use with a language which is so different.

After coffee, the discussion becomes more general; people recount their experiences of BSL in the classroom. It is understood and accepted by everyone there that BSL and English are two languages as different from each other as, say, French and German, and that they cannot be combined. Signed English and signs supporting English, the systems used in all British schools that are using Total Communication, each have their uses, but they are different from, and ideally should be taught separately from, British Sign Language. In trying to do this, some of the teachers at the workshop have met with outright opposition at their schools and have not been allowed even to mention BSL as a teaching language. Others have arrived at a compromise by, for example, using signed English or signs supporting English in the mornings and BSL in the afternoons.

Having decided that I am too inexperienced to make any contribution to this discussion, feeling very much the outsider and extremely short of confidence, I listen to what people have to say. The problems being thrashed out are very familiar; they are the ones Ray and I have thrashed out together recently: dare one abandon speech? Can hearing people ever reach proficiency in BSL? How can teachers maintain their credibility in schools whose main aim is to encourage speech, if they do not use their voices in communicating with the children?

Teachers recount how much more relaxed the children are when they are allowed to forget about speech for a while; how much more complex discussions can be if they are conducted in the language which the children use amongst themselves rather than in 'classroom English', how thrilled the children are when their teachers accept their way of signing without correcting it or trying to convert it to English, how children who had gained a reputation for non-participation have suddenly gained confidence and begun to contribute to lessons. Then those same teachers recount their difficulties, the criticism they have had to cope with from other staff, their decision—

sometimes—to conceal their knowledge of BSL, only to use it behind closed doors. I am reminded of tales I have heard about 'oral' schools, of children signing in toilets; clandestine signing, to avoid punishment. Total Communication is gaining ground, slowly, but it seems that it has to be English-biased in order to be accepted. Sign without speech—at least from teachers—is still taboo.

As the discussion progresses, so my discomfort grows. In our house, the same problems have been encountered that these teachers are now meeting in their schools, and it hurts to realise whose side I have been on. Ray is the one who has accepted—even emulated—Ben's language. I am the one who has carried on speaking, even when it was obvious that my signing was suffering as a result.

At night, in Miranda's house, sharing bunk beds with Elspeth, I feel a great need to talk. I feel as if I have reached a turning point; listening to those teachers, it came home to me that I still had a decision to make, that deciding to sign—that step which seemed so crucial and so final eighteen months ago—was really only a first step; that now, there was another choice to be made, and I haven't yet made it. Elspeth can't help; she is still struggling with the problem herself and she is reluctant to give advice. I think about home, I picture Ben with me, Ben with Ray—how, since Ben was a baby, Ray has known how to communicate with him in appropriate ways, while I have persisted in following instructions, other people's recommendations; how Ray could communicate easily with grown-up deaf people while I was still struggling . . . because he was, naturally and without really thinking about it, accepting their language and using it himself. I think about Sarah. *Could* we now be a signing family? Does Ben really need English at this stage? Should we go for BSL, and teach speech separately and English later? Sleep is a long time coming, but I don't reach any conclusions.

Next day, the workshop gets under way again: everyone gathers at the unit in preparation for the morning session. Suddenly, Miranda's voice—a mixture of relief and—is it pride?—calls: 'Here's Syd!'—and she stops talking and addresses herself, in sign, in silent, flowing BSL, to the man who has just come in. He is tall, dressed in dull colours; a brownish face, greying hair—and a sort of stillness, an immense calm; steady, steady eyes, a slow, rather shy smile which, as he is introduced, seems to spread, to include us all, to greet us all. He radiates loving kindness, this man. He and Miranda engage in a silent conversation; I am talking to someone else, but I can't concentrate. Almost instinctively, I know where he is, and I watch him. This is like falling in love.

Miranda shows videos: Syd signing. Syd with a teenage boy. Two cameras have recorded their conversations; the child is animated, eager to tell Syd things. He watches, his attention complete; gently, he extends the conversation. His timing is faultless; at first it appears that he is interrupting the child, but then I notice that he is responding to very subtle invitations to comment: he is tuned in to this boy, it is almost as if he can read the child's mind, and the child is happy, relaxed, totally involved. This is a deaf man and a deaf child in conversation, in conversation as enjoyable and intimate as any I have ever seen. They are like father and son, or like brothers. Syd watches, reliving the conversation, smiling to himself at the funny bits. All I can think of is the teachers of the deaf I have seen in similar situations: their apparent allergy to silence, their dread of pauses, their need to fill each moment with sound. Here, the pauses are all-important; Syd waits, without embarrassment; he knows when the child needs time to think; he maintains eye-contact during that time and he watches for a call for help; if it comes, he helps, if not, he holds back, not agitated, but calm, waiting for the child's next move—yes, with the concentration of a chess master.

When does Ben get this? I wonder. Not with me. Certainly not with his teacher. With Ray, sometimes. Ray will wait, quietly. Ray is not always anxious to get the next bit of information in, or out. Ray is not teaching, not pace-conscious—he is game-conscious: move, wait, move, wait; he takes his cue from Ben in conversation as he used to in their little play routines. His technique is closer to Syd's than mine is, and closer than any teacher of the deaf I have

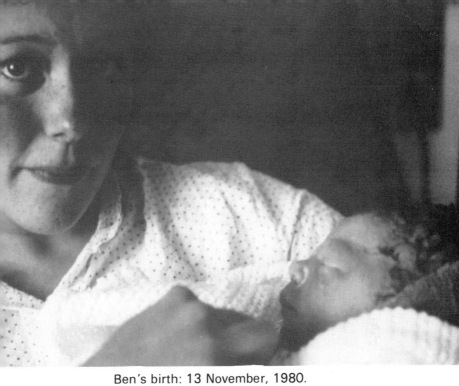

Ben's birth: 13 November, 1980.

Autumn 1981.

Autumn 1982.

At the NDCS Christmas party, 1982. *Photo: Huddersfield Daily Examiner*

Spring 1984.

With Sarah, Summer 1984

With Judith, Summer 1984. *Photo: Tyne-Tees Television*

At Nursery School, Autumn 1984. *Photo: K. Holt, Daily Mail, Manchester*

With Judith, Autumn 1984
Photo: K. Holt,
Daily Mail, Manchester

Autumn 1984.
Photo: K. Holt,
Daily Mail, Manchester

With his grandad, Winter 1984–5.

With Sarah, Winter 1984–5.

With Roland, Winter 1984–5.

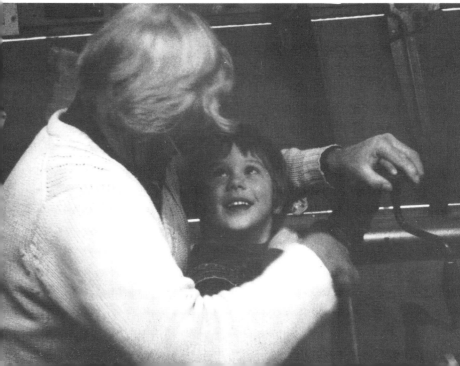

With Lorraine, Ray and Sarah, Summer 1985. *Photo: Tyne-Tees Television*

With Judith, Summer 1985. *Photo: Tyne-Tees Television*

Above and below: With Judith and Little Sarah, Summer 1985.
Photos: Tyne-Tees Television

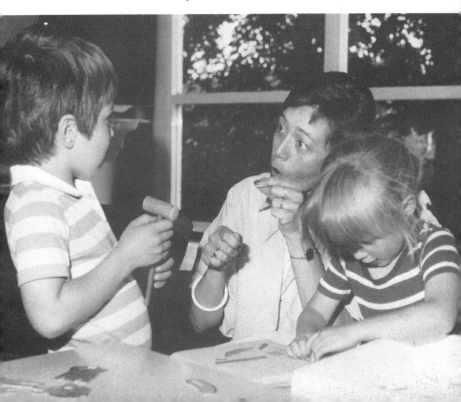

With Lorraine, Summer 1985. *Photo: Tyne-Tees Television*

With Ray.

seen in action. Watching Syd, the difference becomes clear to me. We are in far too much of a hurry, we hearing people. In our determination to get our deaf children communicating, we do not allow them the time to contribute in their own way. We ask questions that require specific answers; we assume responsibility for exchanges; we initiate them—and we end them, by looking away. Syd does not look away until he is sure that the conversation is over; he follows the child's lead, he allows the child control; interference, if any, is subtle and unobtrusive. No repeated questions, just gentle probing. No breakdowns in communication, no abrupt changes of topic 'to keep the conversation going'. No rush, no hurry—real learning, at the child's pace. For these children are learning. These conversations are not an 'extra', not a 'filler-in' before the real work starts. They are the work. And they are conducted in BSL, in the language these boys share with Syd, in their own language, not hearing people's English.

Miranda explains. When the children at the unit arrived there they had almost no communication. From oral schools, they had reached their teens without speech and with only the rudiments of 'playground signing'. They could not read; their writing was restricted to copying. They had no confidence, in teachers or in themselves. They had failed, and they knew it. They were isolated, from their families and from each other, completely lacking in self-esteem, ashamed of their deafness and of themselves. Because each had an additional handicap, an excuse could be found to set up this special unit for them. The oralists felt safe; this would not be admitting that their methods had failed: these children were not too deaf to benefit from an oral approach; they simply had severe learning difficulties because of their additional handicaps. Miranda and Syd were under no such illusions, and the children's progress since they came to the unit is proving them right. Thanks to Syd, they have learned to communicate in Sign; because they are not restricted to English they are able to find outlets for their talents and to demonstrate their undoubted intelligence. Using a computer program invented at the unit they are able to learn to read and write, first, in sign language, (the program has Sign graphics), then in English. It is not their IQs which have held them back, nor is it their additional handicaps. The biggest impediment to their learning has been lack of access to their natural language.

Apart from helping them to extend their use of Sign, however, it becomes clear that Syd's presence has had another very significant effect on the boys. They are starting to develop a group identity which is positive: they are no longer ashamed of their deafness. Syd is deaf, like them. They respect him, and they can relate to him; in him, they can see themselves as adults, and they like what they see. Syd is no failure; the teacher respects him, and, very importantly, she is seen to respect his language; she uses it; she does not expect him to use hers. How lucky these children are and, Miranda makes it clear, how lucky she is, as a teacher, to have Syd's example to learn from.

Syd sits through all this, quiet pride shining out of him. It is obvious that he, too, is enjoying and benefiting from the work. He loves the job; he loves the children; he enjoys seeing the progress they make. His own education was dominated by English; it took a while for him really to believe that this teacher was genuinely more interested in his language than her own, but now, he is confident in his own rôle: in that classroom, he is the expert, and everybody knows that.

It is late in the afternoon, when the workshop is drawing to a close, that the idea hits me. Not the 'deaf child's parent syndrome', but a realisation, as clear as the light of day, that Ben needs a Syd. Not in twelve years' time when the system has failed him and the powers that be are getting desperate, but *now*. As soon as possible. Maybe at infant school. Ben needs to develop his language. He needs to know that growing up deaf is not a disaster. There needs to be a deaf adult at school with him, someone like Syd, someone Ben can learn to love, to trust, to relate to in the way I watched happening on video. If Ben had daily contact with someone like Syd, I would not need to worry so much about the quality of my signing and Ben's consequent lack of access to BSL. In fact, watching Syd, I feel that I would have no need to worry full stop. This man is deaf—and he is wonderful!

Not surprisingly, other people at the workshop have reached the same conclusion. Syd has impressed them all. Obviously, if you are going to make BSL available to young deaf children at school you need a fluent signer in the classroom—and that means a deaf, preferably a native (i.e. with deaf parents) signer. There is some discussion of how this can be achieved. Some of the teachers are hopeful; some have to admit that such a plan would be impossible to implement in their present situations. The education officer from the BDA offers support, but warns everyone that changes such as we envisage take a long time: anyone seriously considering the possibility should start now. I don't need any encouragement. My mind is buzzing. I can't wait to talk to Ray.

Ray is impressed with the idea in principle but, as ever, he is cautious. Where, for example, would we find 'someone like Syd'? He remainds me that we have tried to discover the whereabouts of the deaf community locally and have had to concede that it doesn't exist: local deaf people tend to migrate. And he sees persuading the LEA as a daunting task. But visions of Syd Stone spur me on: I keep seeing him with those children, imagining him with Ben. I know that we have to try, that we have to arrive at a strategy so that if we *can* find someone, the Authority will employ him, or her.

The Monday after the workshop Ben's peripatetic teacher visits. I put the idea to her. Possibly because her own methods have received such a knock recently, with our rejection of classic deaf education and Ben's rejection of the hearing aid fresh in her mind, she, too, is enthusiastic, and as open-minded as ever despite the setbacks. 'I'll support you,' she promises, 'but I don't know how you're going to manage it!'

The next step is to talk to someone higher up in the power structure of the LEA whom we feel might be sympathetic. Ray remembers the Authority's adviser for special education, the man who originally supported Jan when she asked to set up the signing course, and who actually attended some of the classes himself. I contact him and ask if we could meet him for a chat; he offers to come and see us at home.

Then a period of letter-writing begins. My first letters are to the Bristol research team and to the BDA, asking for their help, knowing that they will support in principle the idea of the employment of a deaf adult to work in school.

Then I visit the head of Sarah's school. When we were looking for a school for Sarah and we found and liked this one, I had already seen the provision for the deaf locally, and had been so shocked at the difference in quality of education, that I had mentioned—very vaguely, because our plans generally for Ben tend to be short-term and it was nursery education I was considering at that time—the prospect of Ben starting his full-time education here. The head seemed generally sympathetic then; now, he is still sympathetic, especially when I tell him that we would not consider sending Ben to his school without ancillary help of some kind. The prospect of having *deaf* ancillary help comes as something of a surprise to him, but he is not anti-, and I breathe a sigh of relief.

But he does ask me why I don't approach the schools and units for the deaf with the idea, and at first glance this seems a sensible suggestion—but I feel that I know the philosophies of the local establishments fairly well now, and I cannot see any of them agreeing to employ a deaf adult to work with infants, when none of them actually make use of their own teenage population in this way. From my own experience so far and from listening to the problems of the teachers at the BSL workshop, I am far more hopeful of ordinary teachers in an ordinary school having the courage to try something new than I am of the people in charge of deaf education. The headmaster takes my word for it, and wishes me luck.

Having started the ball rolling, clear in our own minds about why and how we want it to happen, reasonably sure of support from the people involved locally, we are now ready to outline our plan to the adviser. He comes to see us one evening and we put the idea to him. As we explain, his face lights up. His response is more positive than we could ever have hoped.

'Well!' he exclaims, 'Why on earth didn't I think of that?' The Authority's policy encourages 'integration', the education of handicapped children with ordinary children in mainstream schools. This is an easy way to integrate the deaf into their local schools without depriving them of access to sign language. He will support us, he says, but he can't promise anything until he has consulted with the Advisory Service—the teachers of the deaf. My heart sinks. Something tells me that, as a body, they will oppose. The adviser leaves us with a telephone number. A useful contact, he says. A local councillor very active in deaf work, very sympathetic to signing. It might be profitable to enlist her support. Give her a ring, he says.

Next day, I ring the councillor. Though not from a deaf family, she has grown up with deafness: some of her childhood friends were deaf and she has kept in touch with them and with the wider deaf community. She has vivid memories of their accounts of their experiences at oral schools: signing together at home, they had been forced during lessons to sit on their hands, and if they were discovered signing, even outside school, they were punished: they were made to stand up in front of the whole school while the head teacher admonished them; all their privileges were suspended for long periods of time: no games, no swimming, no visits, no social contact in the evenings. The whole school population was encouraged to ridicule them and to 'report' them if they signed; their manual communication was publicly derided and they themselves were made to feel like freaks. Even over the telephone I can hear the emotion behind her reaction: all her life, she says, she has been determined to do something about this injustice; she has kept herself informed of issues in deaf education, helping where she could, and recently she has been pleased to see some progress—but not enough. She will be delighted to help, she says, and will do all in her power to persuade people she knows 'on Education' to support us, too.

'I've been waiting for years for something like this to

crop up,' she says gleefully. 'It's a battle I've been waiting to fight, and now I've got the chance.'

She promises to let me have 'some information I've been collecting over the years'; she visits the nursery and gives me a wallet full of leaflets on the human rights of deaf people, including the right to signing in education. Some of them I have seen, but some are new to me. I can't believe our luck—or Ben's—to have found such an ally. Not only does she support us, but she is well-informed; she has knowledge to pass on. At home, I read the leaflets and as much other appropriate literature as I can lay my hands on. The free afternoons become a time for research, for telephone calls, for more letter-writing. When the time comes to present our case, I want it to be watertight.

Our next contact from the LEA is an educational psychologist, checking on Ben's progress at nursery and his general well-being: 'Really, I want to know what you want for Ben.' Ray and I are both home when she visits: this is our cue to put out more feelers: neither Ben's teacher nor the adviser has made any progress in general terms with the office; really, we have no way of finding out how much effort they are putting into their 'support'. Now, ideas come tumbling out. We know exactly what we want and why we want it; the educational psychologist listens as we explain; she genuinely wants to know how we feel. Her response, in the end, gives us yet more cause for hope.

'Do you know about the 1981 Education Act?' she asks innocently. She explains that all children with special needs, of which Ben is one, now have a legal right to be 'statemented', that is, they can be assessed by a body of people composed of medics, educators, psychologists and other interested professionals, and a policy for their education arrived at. The new Act states that parents have to be kept informed, and given the opportunity to be involved, at every level of the procedure, and that they have the right to make their views known and to challenge the decision arrived at by the professionals if they feel it is wrong. In theory, parents should always have had some measure of control of their children's education, but it hasn't always worked that way. Now, with 'special needs' children at least, that element of control has legal backing.

The implications for us are great: if we can prove that what we are asking for is what Ben needs, there should in theory be no barrier to our getting it. And the educational psychologist is encouraging. She thinks that our idea is a good one; it fits in with the Authority's general policy and would appear to be an ideal solution to Ben's need for exposure to sign language. She will put out some feelers and do a bit of research of her own, she says, and will keep us informed.

Now, we have to wait, and waiting is agony, because we are beginning to feel a new sense of urgency. We realise that planning for Ben to have the help of a signing deaf adult while at school means that valuable time is being wasted.

Down at Nursery, although Ben is happy and the staff feel that he has settled well and is making good use of the facilities provided, everyone is becoming aware that there is something missing. Preschool children need language, and lots of it: part of the function of nursery education is to encourage and develop a child's use of language; part of my disappointment with the deaf school nurseries was because of the low level of language in use there. Here, too, despite all our efforts, the level of language use available to Ben is low. We did anticipate the problem, but we have not gone very far towards solving it, and this is becoming more and more obvious. We have to speed up our search for help, but, in the meantime, we can't afford to be idle. He needs more input *now*.

On Miranda's bookshelf I saw a BSL teaching manual, written by a deaf woman, Dorothy Miles.[4] If I had access to this I could at least improve my own knowledge and practice of BSL, so I order a copy from the BDA and start to wade through it. It is full of photographs, and the course of ten lessons is well planned and uses the most modern teaching techniques. There is no learning of vocabulary lists: the course starts off with enjoyable exercises to encourage awareness of the non-verbal communication skills hearing people possess anyway, then progresses to very simple, but eminently useful 'points of grammar': how sign language works. Having digested the information in the manual, I feel far more confident that I know what BSL is, and far more capable of using what I know when signing to Ben and when deciphering what he is signing. It is a small improvement, but a significant one, I think.

The village signing group is still plodding determinedly on; Julie and her friends meet weekly, but my decision to limit commitments has so far kept me away. Now, however, I feel that I might have something positive to give, and I am acutely aware that the more people who develop BSL based signing skills, the better off Ben will be—so I offer to try and teach the course to the group. They welcome me with open arms; they make me feel as if I am doing them a favour, rather than that they are doing something for Ben's sake.

The sessions are great fun and we can see progress; this really feels like learning a different language, not just adding the odd sign to our own—but we are conscious that a very important resource is missing. The course was written to be taught jointly by a hearing teacher and a fluent deaf adult—and we have no deaf adult. Julie has enlisted the help of a partially hearing ex-social worker; she is only able to come occasionally but her presence makes a vast difference: we have an expert to refer to and we are prevented from lapsing into English. When she is not there the tone of the sessions is different: although determined to sign all the time it is all too easy to 'forget', and we get discouraged when a sign is needed for an exercise and none of us can think what it is. Ben needs the help of a deaf adult but, we realise, so do we.

The educational psychologist has been busy. Just a few weeks after talking to her, Ray and I are invited to a meeting at the Nursery. The assistant officer with responsibility for special services would like the opportunity of discussing our idea.

Ray's headmaster, always sympathetic, allows him time off; the meeting is informal and very amicable; we are given plenty of time to express our views, and the officer from the LEA is extremely receptive and open-minded. He expresses his worries frankly; we are able to reassure him.

At one point he asks, with suitable reticence: 'Would this not be a bit like—well, the blind leading the blind, shall we say?' I admire the man for voicing this opinion. It is one, I feel, which many teachers of the deaf have but dare not pronounce. I am pleased to have the opportunity to counter it, visions of Syd Stone spurring me on: how could anyone observe his relationship with those boys and conclude that because of his disability he was unfit to teach them?

The meeting ends on an optimistic note: although the officer cannot make any promises, he does feel that the idea is viable, and that we could profitably continue to pursue it 'as part of the statementing procedure'.

Now, we have to wait again, and as we wait, we gradually realise that assurances of support are not synonymous with instant action. I become more and more agitated. We can't afford to sit back until Ben starts school proper. We need help while Ben is still at Nursery. We must get things moving. Telephone calls to the people involved prove fruitless: in education, things move at their own pace, which is slow. Sitting at home, I cannot bear to leave the action to other people.

Just on cue, the opportunity actually to *do* something presents itself. The educational psychologist arrives with a letter from the LEA, informing us that the professionals will soon be preparing their reports in readiness for Ben's assessment, and that if we wish to make written representations about what we feel are our child's particular needs we have twenty-nine days in which to do so.

A quick calculation reveals that the twenty-nine days includes the February half-term. If Ray looks after the children I shall have time then to prepare a clear argument for the employment of a deaf adult to work with Ben as soon as possible. Immediately, preparation begins. I make more telephone calls, write more letters, read more research papers, speak to more people, this time looking for evidence. I want conclusive proof that BSL is the best language in which to educate a preschool deaf child. I need up-to-the-minute research and indisputable evidence. Our social worker lends me notes he has obtained while interpreting at recent conferences; the Bristol team sends photocopies of draft material for forthcoming books; the BDA sends leaflets. I pore over the information until I am so familiar with it that whole chunks of prose appear in my mind as I wake up, as they used to do when I was preparing for exams. In the afternoons, I digest information. In the evenings, I discuss it with Ray. I wake in the night thinking about it, and in the morning, as I wake up, my mind is already working on structure: how best to put the case, what to say first. For the whole of the half-term, I work solidly, absolutely determined to make the most of our chance to have some influence over the decision which is about to be made.

Having written the letter over a few days, I have to date it. Its 'gestation period' has included my birthday. Birthdays are lucky days, so this is the date I choose. Dated February 17th, 1984, the letter is posted to the educational psychologist, our 'named person' at the LEA. Then I cross my fingers and wait.

Notes

1 From the Tyne-Tees Television interviews.
2 Now LASER workshops: Language of
                        Sign as an
                        Educational
                        Resource
   23 Wellhouse Avenue, Oakwood, Leeds LS8 4BY
3 CRYSTAL, D., *et al. The Grammatical Analysis of Language Disability*, University of Reading.
4 MILES, D. *British Sign Language Teaching Manual*, British Deaf Association Publications (1982).

Representation re: proposed statement on Benjamin Joseph Fletcher.

Ben was diagnosed 'very severely deaf' at the age of ten months. At that time he registered no response to sound up to a level of 100dB. He was not tested above this level. Since then, successive tests have discovered no hearing whatsoever in either ear. Even with the best form of amplification available the specialist teacher allocated to him has elicited no response to any sound, let alone to the human voice. Our audiologist has told us that Ben's only perception of sound will be by tactile means. In other words, Ben is profoundly deaf.

Respected research indicates that a prelingually, profoundly deaf child has less than a five per cent chance of learning to speak intelligibly. At the time of diagnosis, the surgeon who had performed the investigatory tests told us that it was impossible to predict whether a child with such a severe hearing loss as Ben's would ever learn to talk.

My husband is a teacher. My degree is in languages and I am a trained nursery and infant teacher. When we began to think about the prospects for Ben's development during his childhood we were deeply concerned, for the following reasons.

It is generally agreed that a child's formative years are from nought to seven, at the latest. Language is learned effectively before the age of five; hearing children do this quite naturally and instinctively, without being taught, but it takes even a moderately deaf child much longer than this to acquire enough speech to function adequately as a language, and a profoundly deaf child is lucky if he can say a few words by then. Lipreading can only take place if there is comprehension—and, without language, how can one expect any degree of comprehension? Once the optimum period for language learning is over, the rest of the process must be done remedially, a long hard struggle for all involved, and during that struggle to acquire language COMMUNICATION, the raison d'être of any language, is of course severely restricted.

Given the degree of Ben's deafness, then, we faced the prospect of bringing up a child with whom we would not be able to communicate effectively for precisely those years which are generally agreed to be the most significant years of a child's life. The picture was bleak: baby years without lullabies and silly talk; nursery years without nursery rhymes and explanations, all those explanations; infant years without stories and poems and real conversations. These are years which must be fraught with anxiety for a deaf child, with bewilderment and the frustration involved in trying to sort out life entirely on your own, never being able to ask the how, the where, the why of things. Add this to the pressure on that same little child to learn, against all the odds and with no linguistic background, the intricacies of the English language WITH THE SOUND TURNED OFF and the difficulty which this must present in learning to read . . . A deaf child, deprived of language during his formative years, must spend the rest of his school career vainly trying to catch up on what he has missed, not just in language itself, but in those vast areas of learning which effective use of language permits, not least the development of social skills and the beginnings of self-discipline. It would be a miracle indeed if such a start did not affect him adversely for the rest of his life.

We have two children. Sarah is two years older than Ben and is not deaf. We could not accept that, just because he was deaf, Ben should be denied the sort of intellectual and emotional development which we had so carefully nurtured in his sister. Given the time factor, given the tremendous importance of the first years of life, we felt it essential that Ben should be given access to a language which he could assimilate easily during those years. We did some reading, we spoke to some professionals, but mostly we trusted our own common sense, and we settled on British Sign Language.

BSL is acknowledged by linguists to be a language in its own right. Used by native/fluent signers it ranks alongside English as an effective and totally adequate and efficient means of communication. For deaf people, it has the advantage over English of being a VISUAL language which, since it was devised and is used by deaf people, uses as its base structures which stem from the way the deaf perceive things: visually and spatially. It can include a wealth of detail, the intricacies of which are lost on any but the most experienced hearing observer.

It seemed perfectly logical to us that a person whose ears don't work too well should learn his first language via those parts of his sensory apparatus which do work, and that this language should be both visual and symbolic, a logical notation of the detailed pictures and sequences in which a deaf person thinks, a language which can be learned by a deaf child as easily and as quickly as a hearing child learns speech.

This is the schedule of development we envisaged for Ben: he would have his first language; he would have acquired it within the normal time span of four to five years. He would not have wasted those precious baby/toddler/preschool years struggling parrot-fashion through lists of words; he would have been communicating from the start, finding out for himself what language is really for, and using it to find out about his world. He would then have a tool with which he could continue to learn throughout his school career and from which he could progress to the learning of English as a second language, written and, if he proved to be an 'oral' child, spoken as well. He would learn to lipread more easily because he would possess that language base which is so essential in deciphering what other people are saying. Far from isolating Ben from users of English and from the English language itself, sign language would eventually bring him closer to them.

The most successful and confident group of deaf adults are the children of deaf parents, children who have had access to sign language since birth. If we used sign language it would give Ben every possible chance to develop as they do, to achieve his true potential. It would not ignore his obvious visual acuity and perception and his ability to express himself using bodily and facial expression. Above all, it would accept him for what he is and it would allow him to be himself. We felt in our hearts that it was right that we should sign with Ben and that we should accept and delight in every effort he made to communicate with us.

It had been made clear to us by many of the professionals involved that, logical as this solution to Ben's problem appeared to us, it might be difficult to implement. We found ourselves in a geographical location where the Local Education Authority, regardless of the degree of deafness of the children in its care, offered them a single means of access to language: spoken English. Now, two years later and despite rapid progress by neighbouring Authorities in what is called Total Communication (that is, sign language and fingerspelling combined with speech and amplification, mime, gesture, pictures, etc.), this Authority still only has the oral-auditory method to offer to preschool children. Not one of the teachers employed by the Authority is a fluent signer.

Fortunately for us and for Ben, the teacher offered to us two years ago was prepared to accept our decision and to support us. She introduced us to a signing class in our neighbouring town and then arranged a beginners' signing class locally, which was repeated a year later. The Authority agreed to fund this, but that is the only practical support we have received from the LEA to date. We asked the Social Services department to find us a deaf signer to make friends with; they could not. Subsequent progress in learning sign language has been entirely as a result of our own efforts in making other contacts, and it is only as a result of sheer dogged determination that we have managed to acquire a working knowledge of sign language for ourselves and, through us, for Ben. The members of our nearest Deaf Club have been extremely supportive; deaf people themselves approve wholeheartedly of what we are doing and are only too pleased to help. Ben is now producing whole phrases in British Sign Language, so that the specialist teacher employed by the Authority specifically to teach preschool deaf children can in no way match his fluency. Where else in education would it be accepted that a three-year-old's use of the language with which he will learn is more highly developed than that of a teacher specially selected to teach him?

Ben depends on sign language. It is his first and as yet his only means of communication. Thanks to sign language, Ben is having, as far as possible, a 'normal' upbringing, in that he can communicate with his parents. But despite all our efforts, the standard of that communication is quite low in terms of content. At best it can be termed 'functional' simply because we are not yet fluent and we are not deaf; we are not native users of his language. We are the models from which, in the main, Ben is learning his language, and at present his language can go no further than the level at which we are using it. Yet his potential for learning language is at its peak. He takes all that we can give him but he is ripe for more input.

We feel that it is now time for those in charge of his education to begin to make a contribution to his acquisition of language and provide him with extra input at his present place of education.

We asked for Ben to be admitted to Dale Nursery School for lots of reasons:

a   It is an excellent and well-equipped nursery with caring and dedicated staff.

b   It is a local nursery: Ben has his roots firmly entrenched in this community; he has friends here and gets a lot of loving support from local people, a number of whom are learning to sign.

c   When Ben started school his sister was still there and Ben was *accustomed to the routine; in this way we avoided the trauma often experienced by young children on starting school: Ben settled happily.*

d *The staff at the nursery were willing and enthusiastic to learn to communicate with Ben in his own language. They have attended sign language courses and have tried to keep up to date in their communication. They have, like us, achieved a functional level of communication with him and he is quite happy.*

We are perfectly satisfied with the calibre of education Ben is receiving at the Nursery, with the exception that language input is not adequate for a person with his intellectual capabilities or potential—as far as we can judge it at this time. Normally, when a young child is in nursery, he is surrounded by language: commentary is available about all he does, so his learning is reinforced; not only does he learn from his own experiences, but also from other people's comments on them. In that way both his understanding and his language improve, because of the availability of a sympathetic, communicative adult at the right time. The nursery staff are concerned that this very important aspect of Nursery education is only very rarely available to Ben, because of their lack of fluency in the language upon which he depends. They share our concern about the pace of his language development.

We ask that the Authority provide a model from which Ben can learn his language properly, that is, a native user of British Sign Language, to work with Ben at the nursery. We would argue that the employment of a deaf non-teaching auxiliary would be of immense benefit, not only to Ben but to his teachers, his friends and their parents. A deaf person in the nursery would be able to make available to Ben what the hearing children gain almost incidentally. A deaf person's perception of the world would be so much closer to Ben's; his or her communication would be natural, efficient, spontaneous as opposed to the slow, laboured, cumbersome efforts of the hearing signer, so that Ben would have the opportunity of picking up his language from a perfect, rather than a highly imperfect model. The signing capabilities of both staff and children would improve dramatically. Everyone would benefit indirectly from contact with a severely handicapped adult; maybe they might discover that deafness in itself is not such a severe handicap at all—it is just hearing people who make it so by refusing to accept the language of the deaf. For Ben, far from the blind leading the blind, it would lead to a better understanding of the world 'as it sounds through deaf eyes', and to

*a better chance of his functioning successfully alongside his hearing
contemporaries.*

*At the present time, in this Authority, Ben's educational progress is
being impeded. The help which we are requesting would cost less than the
establishment of a special unit or placement at any of the schools for the
deaf in surrounding areas. The step which we suggest would not be a leap
in the dark for the Authority, and it would enable Ben to gain from these
precious preschool years what any hearing child of normal intelligence
gains as a matter of course: his first language. Please give him this
chance NOW. In two years it will be too late.*

Lorraine Fletcher   *17th February, 1984*

'It will be too late.' Now, this is my worst fear. I cannot
bear to sit back and wait once again. I know only too well
that what is urgent to us, is just one of many documents to
a bureaucracy as extended as a Local Educational Authority,
and that it must wait to be processed along with the rest.
We know that each of the people involved with Ben will
receive a copy eventually, but we have no idea when. So I
have more copies made, one of which goes directly to our
sympathetic local councillor. Another goes to Ben's teacher
and, through her, to her superior. The effect is immediate,
and twofold. Firstly, we are offered a different peripatetic
teacher for Ben's next academic year, a very experienced
teacher and the Authority's best signer. Secondly, we are
given to understand that there will be some opposition to
our plan to introduce a native signer into Ben's nursery and
we are asked, politely but firmly, to keep our views to
ourselves 'because some of our parents are becoming quite
upset'.

This request comes as a shock to us. We are prepared to
admit that what we want for Ben might not be right for
other deaf children—but surely all parents should have the
right to know when something different is happening and
to make an informed choice?

We remain convinced that what we have found is what is
right for Ben—but will he get it now? Will opposition from
within the service mean that the other professionals who
have offered their support will have to back down?

Finishing my letter, I was optimistic. Now, I am not so sure. There has been some heated discussion. If the discussion is to become a widespread argument we cannot afford to be complacent. There is more which can—and must—be done.

It is time for all Ben's pre-assessment checks. Ray and I make sure we are both present at these. We must make everyone involved aware of Ben's needs as we see them; we must be clear and convincing. We become skilled at putting our case firmly and concisely. Ben's behaviour on these occasions supports our case: people expect to find a severely handicapped, disadvantaged child. Some have had some contact with young deaf children and expect little communication and much frustration. Ben is a surprise to them. Despite his deafness he is developing normally, except that he uses sign language to communicate. He is co-operative in tests; though questionable at other times, his behaviour on these occasions is excellent. It is as if he knows what is at stake. His progress proves that, so far, we must have been treating him in a manner appropriate to his needs. People are therefore inclined to respect our views about his subsequent education. At every meeting, we gain in confidence. We seem to be in control.

The date for Ben's review is duly fixed; the review is to be held at Nursery; everyone involved with Ben is invited to be present, so that together we can arrive at recommendations for his future education. As the date approaches, so I become more nervous. Everyone knows about it: the neighbours, the signing group, friends with children at Nursery, the women's group. Everyone also knows that, for me, emotionally, a lot depends on the outcome of this meeting. In many ways, Ray and I are confident: we have spoken to everyone who will be present and we have been assured of a great deal of support. Ben's own peripatetic teacher continues to support our case. But not everyone present at the meeting is convinced, and because of this there remains a nagging doubt. Throughout the meeting, I am almost holding my breath. The nearer the conclusion, the more remote the possibility of something going wrong. Our turn to speak comes and goes; really, by that time, all that remains for us to do is to agree with the many people who have supported us. Doubts have been voiced, but our argument has remained convincing. Nothing has gone wrong.

At the end of the meeting, the mood is one of co-oper-ation and optimism. Ben needs a native signer at nursery —official! The relief is almost tangible. Looking ahead, not wanting to waste time, Ray and I make noises about compiling an advertisement—and it is then that we are told that nothing can be done just yet. Yes, we have reached agreement, but no, it is not yet 'official'. The proposal has to go 'through Education'. After some discussion, however, and again probably thanks to the educational psychologist's sensitivity to our feelings, it is agreed that an advertisement should be compiled as soon as possible, so that as soon as 'Education' has reached agreement, the search for the right person can get under way. Another meeting is timetabled, specifically to arrive at a suitable format, and in view of the unusual nature of the appointment Ray and I are to be allowed to be present.

As soon as we get home, I ring Miranda, who is delighted to provide us with the job-description she prepared when advertising the post which Syd now holds; I also still have job descriptions, from Calderdale, for NTAs working with deaf children in ordinary classrooms. At the meeting, which takes place not long afterwards at Nursery, a format is agreed and a job description arrived at with the minimum of fuss; it feels as if people have realised both what this means to us and the amount of effort we are prepared to put in to make it work. All our proposals are agreed to. A friend copies a recent photograph of Ben in the top left-hand corner of a sheet of A4 and we compile a poster, which is sent to the LEA to accompany the advertisement. Also, as requested by the office, we send a list of places where we feel it might be profitable to place the advertisement: local schools for the deaf, deaf clubs and centres, social services departments, individuals we know personally and, of course, *British Deaf News*, the monthly journal delivered to deaf clubs all over the country. Now, all we can do is wait.

DIRECTORATE OF EDUCATIONAL SERVICES

Appointment of Part-Time Language Resource Assistant
Dale Nursery School

The Authority proposes to make a part-time appointment of a suitable person to work with Ben who is $3\frac{1}{2}$ years old. He is the profoundly deaf child of hearing parents with whom he communicates in sign language. He is fully integrated with hearing children into a mainstream nursery school where the teachers are learning to sign.

The successful candidate will work in co-operation with the nursery staff and be responsible to the Head Teacher. He or she will have special responsibility for communicating with Ben.

The appointment will extend during the period that Ben is in Nursery School, i.e. to 31.8.85.

Key tasks
1   To assist Ben by providing a model for his language needs in the areas of story, explanations, observations, descriptions etc.
2   To extend the use and understanding of sign language for Ben, his peers, teachers and helpers.
3   To encourage Ben's own expressive use of British Sign Language.
4   To assist in the training of parents and staff in the use of British Sign Language.

Candidates will be encouraged to visit Ben either at home or at school for further information before attending formal interview.

Late one Monday evening, Ray takes a telephone call from the vice-chairman of the Education Committee.

'I've just read your submission,' the man says. 'A local councillor gave it to me personally and told me I must read it. I just want to let you know that I shall be chairing the meeting tomorrow at which this matter will be discussed, and I shall be supporting you. I shall recommend that this appointment is made.'

So limited is our knowledge of local government that we had not realised that our friendly councillor's support could have any concrete results. Now that it has, we are relieved. But at the same time, the realisation sinks in that, even with the protection of the '81 Act, our control at this stage is limited. There are meetings going on at which we are not present: the cogs of the Education Department machinery are turning without our assistance. Discussions are being held over which we have no influence, other than by proxy. I find the knowledge that this is going on extremely unnerving.

Immediately, I want to know more about these meetings —where they are held, when and why. There are Education Committee meetings, Schools Sub-Committee meetings, full Council meetings, Resources and Planning (Manpower Services) Sub-Committee meetings—all of which bodies can influence what happens to Ben. Evidence that there is something happening behind the scenes is hard to come by: sometimes I get to know the date of a meeting from the councillor, sometimes the educational psychologist mentions one, and at these times I am beside myself with anxiety.

Other decisions about Ben's education have been arrived at painfully, after much thought and argument and discussion in my own mind and with Ray; I have gone through mental torment as I struggled to work out what was best, fought with my conscience to escape the trap of always doing what I was told, found the courage to do what I felt was right, came to terms with the limitations of what I could do. But they were *my* decisions, *our* decisions. Sometimes the gaining of control took an enormous effort, but it could be done. Recently, Ray and I have discovered that, if we present our case well, we have a good chance of gaining support; we can rely on our own powers of persuasion, and this knowledge has given us tremendous confidence. Now, I know what I want, I have done all I can to make it happen, but I still have no guarantee that it will happen. The situation is out of my control, and I find this new powerlessness intolerable. Having fought so hard to gain control, losing it again is worse than never having had it at all.

On days approaching meetings I chew my nails, I eat to excess, I ignore Ray and the children, I retreat into a little world which is peopled with imagined arguments with imagined people. My temper—which I have been so proud to have calmed—is like quicksilver, and I remain in this state of tension until I hear a result: one more stage has been gone through successfully, one more hurdle cleared.

At Easter we have a holiday—camping, supposedly to give us a break, for me to get away from it all. But I can't get away. The 'final' meeting is on the Wednesday, and in my mind I am there; I lie in my sleeping bag and eat chocolate biscuits while Ray plays football with the children; I pretend to sleep, so that I can worry undisturbed. I am lethargic, pathologically short of energy. After Wednesday, I can't wait to get home, to find out what has happened.

But the meeting goes well. On our return, a telephone call to our new friend on the Education Committee reveals that the full council has given its approval, and within a few days a letter from the office arrives to thank us for the poster and the information and to reassure us that the advertisement has now been sent off.

There is no celebration, no jubilant cries of 'We've done it', no real feeling of triumph. The process has been so fragmented, success has depended on so many factors outside our control, that any illusion of victory has vanished into dust. All we feel now is a sort of quiet relief, as if we have been reprieved. There is no 'high', just a slow draining away of months of tension, a feeling that, at last, we can relax; the worst is over. Now, all we have to do is await the deluge of replies.

But there is no deluge of replies. There is not even a trickle.

'I thought we might have this problem,' says Ray, reminding me of the doubts he expressed right at the beginning, thinking about how we had already looked for the 'deaf community' in our area and found none. I, too, have known this all along, but have pushed the knowledge aside as 'the least of our problems' throughout the process of gaining the LEA's agreement. Now, this 'least of our problems' has resurfaced and it proves to be far greater to overcome than even Ray had anticipated. True, all the deaf clubs within a twenty-five mile radius now carry the advertisement and display the poster. True, the FE departments with deaf students in local colleges are aware of the post—but we have no way of ensuring that news of the job has reached everyone who might be interested. After three or four weeks we begin to panic.

The advertisement has been placed in local newspapers, but we are only too aware that some deaf people—especially those profoundly deaf people we are hoping to attract—although they might have excellent signing skills, might also have quite a low level of literacy in English and may not even take a local paper. In recognition of this fact, I ring every social worker in the area, and visit some; they are helpful—but reticent. All express great admiration for the idea in principle, but some find our insistence that signing skills are more important than good speech or good English a little difficult to accept, considering Ben's placement in a hearing school. One social worker will not recommend anyone because none of her clients matches up to her own very strict criteria for 'the right person'. There is also the small matter of pay . . .

The job is part-time, fifteen hours per week, the pay is low (Non-Teaching Assistant grade 1), so anyone travelling any distance would find his or her pay eaten up by bus or train fares or by car running costs. The social workers who report an interest, also report concern about money. An excellent prospective candidate from our neighbouring town would be prepared to make three bus journeys each way to reach the nursery school—but the cost of travel would almost leave her in the red at the end of each week. Effectively, the level of pay offered restricts applicants to those who live nearby and, as we have said, 'local' deaf, as far as we know, are few and far between.

Our telephone is red hot at this time. The LEA will not consider increasing the level of pay, or providing travelling expenses, even in view of the unusual nature of the post, for fear of setting a precedent for the countless other non-teaching staff employed by the Authority, who might then discover good reasons why they, too, should be paid more. So we have to make sure that we leave no local stone unturned.

As I make telephone calls, make visits, write letters, the feeling of powerlessness which so disturbed me towards the end of the 'persuading' phase threatens to return. Gradually, I have to accept that there is nothing more I can do, no more sources to tap, no more leads to follow. And this time the frustration is doubled, because we have managed, against all the odds, to get this post established, and now it looks as if we shall not be able to fill it. The months and months of effort will have been wasted and Ben will be no better off than he was before this whole business started. In fact, he will be worse off, because my preoccupation with The Idea has meant that I have given him less time than I could have done, and made him—and the whole family—suffer while I awaited the outcome.

Where is the support team now? a little part of me is whining. What price audiologists, consultants, medical officers, teachers of the deaf now? What interest have they shown? What effort are they making? At a time when social workers in other towns are scouring their files, where is *our* social worker? This family is under pressure and she is nowhere to be found.

But now, the real support team swings into action. It is a team that has litle to do with the professional 'back-up' service. The real support team, as it always was, is in our village and in our own extended family. The teachers at Nursery really care; every day they ask if there is any progress, until the weariness they read in my eyes is all the information they need. The signing group battles on, making 'contingency plans': they will work hard on their BSL and take turns, voluntarily, to support Ben in nursery until a deaf adult is found. The women's group, as ever, listens, gives me time to talk. Ray's parents offer weekends away for the children; my mother comes and does the housework and the garden, to help to ease off the pressure. Annette and Julie and other friends play with my children, make coffee for me as I recount the latest disaster. They have been there all along, these friends, babysitting, childminding, collecting our children from school or giving them lunch while Ray and I attended meetings, always there if I wanted to talk, asking nothing in return, just wanting the best for Ben and for us as a family. Now, they join forces to pull us through, they give me the push I need to carry on trying, not to give up hope.

Thanks to a series of telephone calls, the BDA itself is aware now that an opportunity, albeit in a small way, to gain for the adult deaf a place in the education of deaf children, is about to be lost. At the beginning of June, the *British Deaf News* publishes a little article about the job with Ben. Whether because of that, or because news of the job has filtered through in other ways, applications begin to trickle in.

The deaf women who apply are pleased to have the opportunity to visit Ben at home and at Nursery in an informal way; on different days, three or four visit Nursery and then come home with me and Ben. As well as giving the deaf applicants a chance to see how they might fit in at Nursery and how they would get on with Ben, it gives the Nursery staff and myself a sort of informal preview, so that we have some idea about the suitability of each person before interviews are held.

But something is happening now which neither the Nursery staff nor myself are prepared to admit to outright. We do not wish to be unfair on the deaf people we see; we realise that the situation is stressful for them and that shyness and lack of experience might result in our gaining a misleading impression of their abilities—and we are desperate now to find someone to work with Ben—but none of them *feels* right. There is a lot of talk of 'faces fitting' amongst those who have a lot of experience of interviews, particularly in schools. It has always struck me as being rather unfair, especially as I was once, on paper, the most suitable applicant for a job which actually went to the person whose face fitted, but now, from the other side, I can see how it works. All the deaf women are very pleasant,

all manage to communicate with us at home and with the
Nursery staff either by using their voices or by signing, but
not one of them seems to fit in.

'Ben needs a Syd!' was the message in the beam of light
which hit me at the BSL workshop. I have made the
mistake of thinking that all deaf people are like Syd—but of
course, they are not. Few hearing people have natural
teaching ability. It is reasonable to assume that not many
deaf people have this skill either. At the deaf club, Ben picks
out people to watch. He does not just watch anybody; he
watches the people who interest him. And none of the
people who apply to work with him interest him . . .

Until Judith.

Judith arrives at the Nursery with her mother and they
stand in the wet area, conversing in sign. Judith's clothes
are bright; her smile can light up an entire room. B⌐
watches her. The other children watch her. The Nu·
staff watch her, with little, satisfied smiles. I talk to '
to her mother about Ben and what we want for
they agree with us completely. Her moth⌐
towards Judith. Look at her, she says. She h⌐
with BSL. Her education began long before
school, at home with her parents, becaus
communicate. Judith adds that, as she g
learned English, and now she has two langu
sign in English, but with Ben she would pre.
BSL—it's quicker; it will catch his attention better. I a⌐ ⌐
to Judith and her mother makes me feel good; they think
we have made the right decision and Judith seems to have
the skill and the confidence to carry the idea through.

At the end of the afternoon, Judith joins the children for
their end of session 'quiet time'.

'She joined in!!!' the staff report delightedly afterwards.
'She seemed to know exactly what to do. The children
loved her! But will she apply? Will she want to work with
us?'

Yes, Judith will apply, despite the low pay. She has just
been made redundant from her job in London; she wants to
move North again to be with her parents because her
mother is ill. Since the job will be afternoons only, she

hopes to be able to get part-time work in the mornings or evenings. She will live in a city not too far away, and she has her own car so will not have to rely on buses. And she would love to work with Ben.

Now, I can't believe it. The many setbacks, the times we thought we had reached the winning post, only to have someone uproot it and replant it a mile away, have taught me caution. As the day of the interviews approaches; I force myself to stay calm, certain that something will go wrong.

June 28th dawns, bright and sunny. In the afternoon, at nursery, a small crowd gathers: the interviewing panel from the LEA, six—yes, six—deaf women, including one who has not visited the Nursery and one who used to have children there, and a group of interested onlookers, mums with children at Nursery who cannot conceal their fascination with this group of people who can converse without using their voices. The deaf people seem relaxed now, easy in each other's company, some very different now from the way they had appeared on their previous visits, jolly, full of life.

As I sit with them, watching, I feel how unjust I could have been. Here, the only hearing person in a crowd of deaf people engaged in conversation, I feel uneasy. Some parts of the conversation I can follow; at other times I am lost and I find myself gaping with concentration, struggling to pick up a hint that might clue me in on what is happening. Occasionally I might catch someone's eye, and, aware of my difficulty, that person will give me a clue, or explain something; meanwhile, the conversation goes on and when I return to it I am lost again. How like the deaf person's experience this is, isolated among hearing people. How like the experience of these deaf women when they first visited Nursery. For we were all well-meaning, we signed with them and we offered them semi-translations of bits of other people's conversations—but they were still at a disadvantage, and no wonder they were tense and nervous. At least, soon, thanks to one of these women, Ben will not have to suffer such isolation. At least at Nursery there will always be someone he can talk to on equal terms.

Before the interviews, an officer from the LEA has a quiet word with me. Obviously, he says, I cannot be allowed to participate in the interviews, but he would value my opinion. Which of the applicants do I feel would be most suitable? I give my choice, and the reasons for that choice, and the interviews begin. An interpreter is hastily found: a lot of the applicants have very little hearing and some have poor speech, so that even the carefully articulated English of the teacher of the deaf will be unreliable as a means of real communication.

Just as the interviews get under way there is a surprise: our 'signing assistant', the partially hearing woman who helps us with language, arrives. Hearing about our distress at there not being any applicants, she put in an application herself, just in case, for she could not bear the thought of Ben being without a deaf person to help him. Now, looking round, she is delighted, and she echoes the view of the other women there: how unusual it is to see a group of deaf people competing on equal terms for a job. Normally, the deaf are used to competing with hearing people and, in such situations, have low expectations of their chances. Here, each feels that she has something valuable to offer, that, in terms of this job anyway, deafness is seen as a desirable attribute rather than a disadvantage. She talks to us for a while, then, in between interviews, she speaks to the officer in charge. Then she leaves. He tells me later that she withdrew because she wanted one of the profoundly deaf people to get the job; she didn't want the fact that she had more hearing—and hence better speech—then they had, to influence the decision of the interviewing panel. How wise of her!

But it is not the best speaker who gets the job. After the interviews, Judith is called back in and is offered the post. And she accepts. And I am delighted.

The officer from the LEA comes to talk to me afterwards. He is amazed, he says, at what he has learned this afternoon about the deaf, and about deaf education. He is very grateful to have had the opportunity of being involved. He has mentioned to Judith, he says, the possibility of this project being continued into primary school, if she would be willing to stay on. He will follow our progress with interest, and he offers his very best wishes for next year. His attitude gives me great satisfaction—and confirms my faith in 'ordinary' educators, who, like the nursery staff, and the educational psychologist, are not afraid to give their backing to something new. If it were not for them, these 'unaffiliated' professionals, the events of today could not have happened.

As I go outside, and throw my arms around Julie, who has been waiting anxiously throughout, I am conscious, too, that if it had not been for her constant support, and that of all my friends, I might well have given up long ago.

At last, then, the work is really over. Now, for the first time in months, I can rest. When Ray comes home and hears the news he takes it quietly. Someone asks if we will celebrate. We haven't got the strength to celebrate. We are both absolutely worn out, me, from the pressure, Ray from coping with me under pressure. We both feel that now, maybe, we can get back to being an ordinary family again. I have done all this for Ben. At the moment, I hardly know the child, and poor Sarah, just reaching the end of her first year at school, has had so little attention recently that it is a wonder she still has any faith in us at all. But now we can start rebuilding. Now, we can begin our return to normality.

PART TWO

THE DIARY

During the very early years with Ben and Sarah, I kept a little diary—the five-year diary referred to in Chapter One. As life became more and more hectic, I abandoned it, and the only records I kept were very spasmodic ones, mainly concerning Ben's language development.

This summer, the summer of 1984, feeling happy, free, confidently optimistic about what the future holds, and hopeful that from now on I might have a bit more time to myself, I have taken up my diary again—not a five-year one, this time, but one large enough to keep a comprehensive record of events as they happen, day by day, week by week.

The following are extracts from that diary.

1 WITH JUDITH: THE FIRST TERM

4.9.84[1]

BACK TO SCHOOL! And Judith's first day. As I was filling in Ben's home/school book, as I have done every day since Ben started Nursery, it was lovely to think that it would be a deaf person reading the book, and that once she knew from the book what had been happening in the holiday she would have no problem at all talking to Ben about it.

I took him in as normal, settled him down—then Judith came in, with that lovely smile—and once again Ben was fascinated. I didn't really want to go home, I wanted to watch them—but in the end I had to leave them to it and rely on what everyone told me at the end of the day. Mrs Davidson was thrilled already at what's going on between Judith and Ben; she eavesdropped on them by the guinea pigs and was really impressed by the amount of signing and the length of time their conversation lasted. She observed the same kind of 'laid-back' signing that we've seen when Ben is with Ken. Judith felt they'd had a good day, too, although she was a bit worried by Ben's lack of concentration at 'quiet time'—feels that it might take a while for Ben to get used to looking to her for information.

5.9.84

I have never known such happiness and excitement in all my life! I've talked and signed so much today and achieved so much understanding . . . it might have been just an ordinary day for Ben—it's me who is feeling a transformation. It's hard to know what to write first—I'm signing in my mind and I keep expecting signs to come out of my pen instead of words. During the afternoon at Nursery, and a meal out in the evening, I got to know Judith so much better, and felt so very close to her—but other things were happening at the same time—real changes. During the afternoon I promised Judith that I would do my best always to sign if she or Ben were around—but actually signing with her during the meal I could *feel* myself learning and becoming more confident in what I was doing—it all felt easier, natural somehow. Plus, so many of the things she was saying were relevant to Ben and have, just in that one evening, increased my understanding of him and his needs. Judith can remember so clearly how she felt at that age, tells me what she thinks he is experiencing, and I believe her! And I can use this knowledge in the way I deal with Ben. I've always wanted to know what he's thinking, but in some ways he was a closed book to me—now it feels as if Judith has started to open up the book, and I feel so grateful to her . . .

6.9.84

Today has been full of new feelings—so much closer to Ben, and so confident in dealing with him. This morning, in his room, I felt able and willing to communicate so many things to him—as if a door had been opened into his mind and I could appreciate how he sees things . . . I pointed out the sun on the inside of the viaduct arches, told him about the meal with Judith last night, about Annette and Roger babysitting and Little Sarah sleeping in Big Sarah's room . . . I'm sure I must have been capable of signing such things before, and have done, of course, but far less often than I might have done. I've never felt inspired, never had the determination to keep it up. Judith's comments about being excluded from conversation, and her delight last night at being with a group of hearing people who could sign, and her determination not to miss out, without making me feel guilty, managed nevertheless to instil the urge to satisfy her needs in my dealings with Ben. Judith can give me a truer idea of how he feels than anyone else—and he has been missing out on a lot, unnecessarily. Today I have been trying to sign all the time she and Ben were about, and in situations where I was talking to someone who is learning to sign— which meant full-time at nursery and as often as not in the street, too. I still forget sometimes when I get carried away chatting, and it's impossible while holding one child—but I haven't made a bad start today and I can only improve.

When Ben was his usual bolshie self when the time came to get ready for Nursery, I told him that Judith would be at Nursery to sign to him; he was suddenly all co-operation— even stood still to have his face washed! When I came to collect him at 'quiet time' he and Judith were curled up on a settee in the Rainbow Room[2] looking at a book together, and when I asked him what he and Judith had been doing he said they'd been talking about rowing in boats. Julie said yesterday that he'd talked about Judith to her when she picked him up after Nursery. This is great!

7.9.84
Observed in the Rainbow Room—couldn't keep away any longer! Saw Ben sign really naturally to Tom, 'You pass round the chocolate biscuits'—but he did it in BSL style—You chocolate biscuits pass round!

Noticed how Judith is able to help Ben to experience things in the most effective way, e.g. she wanted to get him to feel the 'Happy Birthday' musical box. Just a week, and so many changes. I feel so happy—as if a great load has been lifted off my shoulders. Just having observed Ben and Judith for these few days, I've got so much confidence now about his future. I'm sure that he's going to be OK. It's a wonderful feeling, after all these months—years—of messing about, going in one direction and then the other, never really being sure. I feel that we've found the right way; I'm sure we've done the right thing.

Judith:[3] *When I first came here, all the teachers welcomed me to the school, and I felt a very warm welcome. When I first met Ben, he looked at my face; he was surprised, because he knew that I was deaf. And he knew that he could communicate with me . . . He knows that I'll be coming every day to talk with him and that he can talk to me in BSL . . .*

All the hearing children know that I'm deaf. And when I first came, they tried to speak slowly for me. But a few of them didn't realise that I was deaf, and they spoke too quickly so I had to ask a teacher what they were saying. And the teacher would then tell me what the child had said, and I'd see the child looking and realising that they had to speak slowly for me. They began to realise that they had to speak slowly for me in the same way that they speak slowly for Ben, and that we're the same, because we're both deaf . . .

Ben is the only deaf child in quite a large hearing school, and I'm the same—I'm the only one working with the teachers. And I want to feel equal to the teachers, and I want Ben to feel equal to the other children as well.

I feel I've got on very well with the children and the teachers. The teachers use sign language, and some of them are not really sure, and so I help them. And so I can also interpret for Ben. Some of the children are using signs for the first time. One girl was talking to Ben and she was using signs. I couldn't believe it! She said, 'You sit down,' and he sat down.

At first I thought it was a little bit difficult, but at the end of the week I've realised that everybody's done very well. The teachers are signing with me and to Ben. The children are using some signs with Ben. I feel it's very easy to get on with all of them.

I think Ben is paying more attention to me, because he knows we're both the same, we can communicate. I've been telling him we're both the same. We both use sign language. The other hearing people around have been watching us when we've been talking to each other. And they are trying now to use signs more.

I know what he means when he's signing to me and using his BSL. When he says something, I know what he means. The teachers don't understand him, and so I tell them what he means. So they're beginning to pick up a little bit of BSL.

Caroline H., Nursery Nurse: *I get on with Judith very well. We already seem to have built up a pretty good relationship. She's very friendly and she's really very easy to get along with. I think we have to be careful because we're not used to having a deaf person among the staff; we have to try to consider this, particularly where we talk in a group, to try and remember to look at Judith so she can read our lips. When we're talking generally in a group we don't want her to feel left out at all.*

Ben seems to be responding very well to Judith and he seems very co-operative with her. And he's responding a great deal to her signing. We see Ben signing much more frequently than when Judith isn't here. She's also a great help when we're signing to her or to Ben. If she sees us struggling with a sign she's very quick to give us that sign. So we're extremely pleased with the first few days.

Mrs Davidson: *I'm delighted with the way she has fitted into the school, fitted into our team. Ben is relating very well to her and she's got a very good relationship going with Ben. Not only with Ben, but with all the other children, too. Although she hasn't got nursery experience, she seems as though she's got an insight into the work. And everything is just working perfectly as far as we're concerned.*

We haven't found any difference with her, as if she were a hearing person really, apart from the fact we're signing, we're trying to sign a lot more. And the staff are all now very enthusiastic and wanting to do more signing. She—she's just an inspiration I suppose, to us, really.

Ben's signing has improved. It's quite unbelievable really, how things have changed, in just one week. Even after one day, the change was noticeable. He seems to be signing in quite a different way. I can't explain how. He's signing much more readily. When he signs to us he just does the odd sign whereas when he's signing to Judith he keeps on signing for a much longer period. And it seems almost an artistic way he's signing. It's a different way of signing from what he does to us . . . It's more or less as though it's a continuity to his signing which we haven't seen before.

The children are going up to her, which I didn't think they would. I thought they would have stood back a little bit but children are going up to her and talking to her . . .

10.9.84
Wonderful signing group with Judith and nine others, after which Judith said she would never forget tonight. It really was good. I tried to organise without being dominating, and let Judith take over when she felt like it. Everyone seemed to enjoy it; by the end of the night we had five pairs communicating with each other without voice, and Judith going round joining in.

Before the class Judith came here for tea; Sarah played with her for a while, then whispered, 'She's nice!' Ben and Sarah fought over who would sit next to her on the settee. The difference between a mealtime without her at home and a mealtime with her is obvious: we were all really conscientious about signing for Judith's benefit, but Ben benefited as well, and he gazed at her for so much of the time, obviously expecting to get meaningful communication from her.

11.9.84
I feel Ben's social skills are improving all round, like he decided, himself, not to stand up at the table at lunch, and he accepted several explanations that went contrary to what he wanted to do . . . Mrs Davidson told a lovely story about Ben dropping a wooden brick on her foot and Judith taking him into a corner and persuading him to say 'sorry'. The situation at home feels so much easier; he seems to expect much more from communication: instead of opting out or withdrawing he pursues conversations. Everyone's noticed an increase in copying of lip-patterns and attempts at saying words, too—and he's altogether easier to get through to.

14.9.84
Judith says she's really happy with her week and really proud of Ben. Both signing and lip-patterns are improving —I saw him *say* 'no', today. He is showing a renewed interest in sound, keeps asking for the headphones on the stereo and giggling when there's music. He and Ray are in the bath together now, shouting into each other's ears, and it's amazing how similar Ben's shouts are to Ray's. In the bath yesterday Ben and Ray were splashing each other. Ray said, 'I'll splash you six times,' and Ben said, 'I'll splash you ten times', and did, without signing in between. Can he count to ten in his head???

17.9.84
Judith says her dream is that the whole village ends up signing. This morning Ben apologised to Sarah, spontaneously. She was quite amazed.

21.9.84
Nursery is going great! Judith still very happy, proud of Ben; she says he's talked and talked (signed!) today, and I can see that at home. His attitude to communication seems to have changed; he initiates a lot more conversation— today at teatime he was asking us if we liked what we were eating. He's always been a happy little boy but he has this bouncy, joyful, carefree air about him now. I can talk him

out of things sometimes, instead of just saying no and removing him from temptation or temptation from him. I stopped him from sticking a piece of wood into the plug socket without actually taking the bit of wood away from him . . . High spot of the day was seeing little Sarah Stainthorpe interpreting for Judith—Caroline told her it was Rainbow Room time and she went and tugged Judith's arm and signed, 'Rainbow—come on!' Apparently she carried on during quiet time—wish I'd been there to see. It really is a good experience for these children. Earlier, I was talking to Caroline and Judith when another girl, who has always been shy of signing, actually came and joined in the conversation, and did really well with her signing. I think I'm remembering to sign more when Ben's around, too. It's not the signing that's hard now, it's just remembering.

8.10.84
Ben went to the hospital this morning to see the audiologist. I was unsure whether to take him because he woke up full of cold . . . Anyway, we went and, after a lot of persuasion and explanation, he co-operated in the play audiometry enough to get the start of an audiogram—another first. We all thought he responded to some sounds, and the audiologist said he would prescribe Ben some new Phonak post-aural aids like Judith's now, in the hope that he might be influenced by the fact that she wears them.

16.10.84
Our educational psychologist observed Ben at Nursery yesterday and was very impressed. She noticed a lot of the improvements that we have noted, which is reassuring because she is not as biased as we are. Today everyone concerned with teaching and supporting Ben met to have an informal chat about his progress. It was good to have Judith at a meeting like this for the first time; her presence made sure that Ben's point of view as a deaf person was represented, and her being there really kept things balanced; it was like giving him a voice. I managed to interpret the whole thing to Judith's satisfaction, and everyone was delighted with his progress.

17.10.84

Judith is in a fair old state; when I got to Nursery she told me she'd been awake all night worrying and thinking about the meeting. We had a long and detailed conversation that I am trying my best to remember and note down.

There was a lot of the usual kind of talk at the meeting about hearing aids and particular aspects of English—this time the bone of contention was 'the' and 'a'—but it could have been anything—the sort of English-orientated comment that Ray and I have learned to ignore, but which Judith must really have taken to heart as a criticism of her ability to teach Ben. She said—today, not at the meeting— that even she, at her age, could never get the hang of 'the' and 'a', that a lot of deaf people found it really difficult to understand what to use when. I told her not to worry; teaching Ben about articles was our job, not hers; she was there to extend Ben's BSL, not to teach him English. Her second worry was the same as Ray's and mine, i.e. hearing aids. She had said at the meeting that a lot of born deaf people just can't be bothered with hearing aids and that she always used to throw hers away or take them out when no one was looking when she was small. She feels she didn't derive any benefit from them until she was a teenager, then she decided she liked and was interested in the sounds she heard. Before that, they had no meaning for her (this despite an *oral* education). From her point of view, she says, she'd never heard sound, so didn't miss it—used the other senses instead. She said, you never see teachers trying to force a blind child to wear glasses, or someone with no legs to use the limbs he hasn't got . . . She feels really strongly that to force Ben to wear an aid is unnecessary and unfair, and the same with the auditory trainer . . . So I put the teachers of the deaf's argument to her, the one we're always getting, i.e. that we must at least give him the chance to use any hearing he has, to become aware of sound. Judith half-agreed, but then said (with such facial expression that I can't hope to do justice to her feelings in words on a page) that a lot of deaf people forced to wear aids feel strange when they take them out, get weird vibrations in their ears and feel dizzy—and if Ben were being affected in this way he wouldn't be able to tell us. She really brought home to me how little we hearing people *can* know of what it's like to be deaf, especially if, as the teachers of the deaf are, we're only dealing with non- or partly-communicating children and hardly ever meet a deaf adult, let alone talk to one.

What Judith says makes me even firmer in my belief that there is no justification whatsoever in making Ben wear an aid, *or* having impressions taken, *or* persisting with the auditory trainer, if he doesn't actively want to.

Then we got on to education in general, which gave me the chance to explain to Judith why Ray and I want to opt out of the deaf education system for as long as Ben is happy. She was fully in agreement with a lot of what I said, particularly about what is true learning and what isn't, and she has tales of her own to tell about her schooling, about how the hearing teachers used to come at the children with the same things, in the same way, day after day, which Judith said just made her and her friends switch off; then the deaf Maths teacher would come along, producing new and interesting things, about which he could communicate and which they could understand and learn easily. Learning by sitting watching teachers talking was another thing we agreed wasn't true learning, and Judith said that happened for her right from nursery age and continued for much of school. She used to long to get home so she could ask her parents to explain what the teachers had been on about. I couldn't help thinking, what about the majority of children, those with hearing parents? Who—or how—could they ask, with the level of communication they must have had at home?

18.10.84

Judith's brother, Peter, rang and told me about an international congress on the education of the deaf which is planned for next year at Manchester University. He said he'd taken the liberty of sending for the information for me and thought I ought to submit a paper about our ideas. To Manchester???? I bet they wouldn't even read it. Signing doesn't exist in Manchester.

19.10.84
Some milestones: Ben answered a why? question. Me: This lightbulb is broken—why? Ben: I hit it with a stick.[4]

He's also learning rules of story telling. On Monday, when he was telling me about going to the fell race with Ray, he described the runners coming over the brow of the hill, then did the sign for 'finish', which grown-up deaf people use to show past tense, and growing kids use to split up parts of a story. Then he signed that he and Ray and Sarah walked a bit and had a sit-down. Ray has just remarked about the control Ben has over his facial expression when he's telling you something that's happened. He was describing how he'd shouted at Ray, and you could see him reliving the event; then when he'd finished that little bit he shut off all expression again—so it was obvious he was back in the here and now. Also, for the first time, I've seen him use the sign for 'talk' when signing to himself. I think that's a direct result of being exposed to adult conversation and being able to eavesdrop.

28.10.84
Another BSL feature appearing: use of eye-gaze, with the sign and lip-patterns for 'look': he shows the direction you're supposed to look in with his own eyes, without pointing!

He has been calling 'Mum-mum' to get my attention for a long time now, but yesterday and today we made a game of it and I got him to shout 'a' for Dad as well. A bit of speech therapy in the right place and he'd be calling 'Dad!' He really enjoyed shutting the door on us and calling for either one of us. But then he shut the door on himself and wanted us to call him . . . !

5.11.84
Fireworks at nursery. Compare my sign—'fire' + 'work'—to Judith's—fingers shooting into the air and a positive explosion expressed in the face—and you can see why they understand each other so well and why I'm finding it harder (in comparison) to get through. Fortunately I can see all these things as signs of progress and proof that Ben

is getting language from Judith that I would have been unable to give him—so, although it's sometimes frustrating in the short term, the long-term benefits far outweigh that and I'm not upset by it at all. Every time it happens it means that his langauge has gone one step further.

6.11.84

Ben's visit to Judith's has got to be the highlight of the week. He and her dad get on so well: they watched 'Thomas the Tank Engine' together, Roland signing what was happening for Ben; Ben played with the dog, flashed the flashing light doorbell, saw Roland's workshop and claimed two presents Roland had made for him and Sarah—friction propellers beautifully made out of wood, and fascinating to Ben. And everybody was signing around him all the time. We came back with Judith in the back of her car, signing about what we could see. Every time I come into contact with groups of deaf people where I'm in the minority it gives me the incentive to sign more.

7.11.84

Asked Judith if she could come to Ben's birthday party, and if she would come to the hospital on the 19th with Ben when he goes for his earmould fitting and to collect the Phonak (only one because the audiologist only got one impression). Both OK. Rushed back home to do some housework, only to be called back half an hour later because Ben had fallen against a wall and cut his head open and was with Judith in the doctor's surgery, having it stitched. *Ran* down again, panicking like mad, only to find a very quiet and calm Ben sitting on the floor with an equally calm Judith, playing jigsaws. Judith had been quite upset but it soon emerged that she had sorted out his needs perfectly, had done just the right amount of explaining and distracting to make the stitching (only one) bearable for him.

9.11.84

It was Ben's medical in the afternoon—not the best time, what with the bump on his head and a recurring ear infection—but quite interesting. The doctor said, 'I don't suppose you know if he can tell his colours?' and, 'Do you know whether he can count?' Together we surprised and impressed her on both tasks.

11.11.84
Ben is starting to ask questions about things he can't see, like where water and fire go to. We had a lovely conversation about the dark—the sun hiding.

13.11.84
Ben's fourth birthday. It was good to have Judith at the party, to make sure he knew what was going on. She is so used at Nursery to making sure he doesn't miss out on anything, she just carried on here, then stayed for tea with the grown-ups. She played for ages with Ben with his garage on the table. Mum took his rejection of her for Judith a bit hard. We adults got in lots of signing practice, and Ben thoroughly enjoyed himself. It was wonderful to see all the kids signing 'Happy Birthday'.

16.11.84
Just been colouring with Ben. We co-operated very nicely and did six pictures between us. His fine motor control is so good that it surprises me that he shows no interest in drawing or painting real things just yet. Funny that in 3-D —dough, wood and potato shaping—he will readily make real things: faces, a boat, a car, a horse, etc., but he won't draw or paint them.

18.11.84
We all went out for a 'proper' meal on Saturday night at a Chinese restaurant—Ben's first such experience. It made such an impression on him that he relived the whole thing today, re-telling in imitative play eating, drinking, the ice cream, the waiter, getting drink from one place, food from another . . . sometimes he went all the way upstairs pretending to do something and came back. When Sarah lost interest he fetched the dolls and set the scene with them so he could be waiter.
    Ray and I set ourselves the task of signing throughout

the evening meal. Direct results: Ben copying snippets of adult conversation, including signs he's never used before: will, letters; Sarah signing voicelessly, 'I want a drink.'

19.11.84

Judith came with Ben, his teacher and me to the hospital to collect Ben's earmoulds and new hearing aid. Before we left, Ben was refusing to go and see the doctor. Judith told him she was going to let the man look at her aid, so Ben came along. Judith sat in the back of the van with Ben and they were signing together at intervals all the way. He wanted both of us to come in with him to have the aid fitted, and we both tried it on, but not Ben—repeated 'no's, despite efforts by all of us to persuade him. We agreed to take it and try it in peace and quiet at an opportune moment at home. It's a very powerful low-frequency adjusted aid. With Ben's representative supporting me I felt much more able to express my point of view.

Interesting to note that by the time we left, the audiologist was making serious efforts to sign. Judith's influence? And he commented on Ben's increased communication. I left the hospital with a very different feeling from the one I usually have. Normally it's anxiety about something or other; today it was confidence.

Took the hearing aid to Nursery; told Ben to show Mrs Davidson his 'present'. He did, but wouldn't touch it, and wanted it back in its box straight away. Ray came home; Ben ran to show him the hearing aid and let Ray put it in for him after saying how beautiful it was (Ray, Ben just agreed). As soon as it was switched on (whistling), Ben took it off. We said OK and put it away. Judith said that at Rainbow Room time Ben said he wanted to go home for his hearing aid. Ben proudly showed Sarah the Phonak; she was very helpful and said it was beautiful, could she wear it? Ben said no and put it away again. Last attempt of the day: Ben brought the hearing aid to Ray; Ray said it needed trimming, the tube was too long. After it had been sorted out, Ben allowed it in his ear twice and tried it on Sarah, then took it out and gestured 'No'. So it's on top of the stereo again.

21.11.84
First thing this morning Ben again remembered the hearing aid, took it out of its box, said no and put it back. Again when Annette came he proudly showed it to her, then replaced it in its box. Took it to Nursery this afternoon, so that if he asked for it it would be there. He didn't ask.

22.11.84
More instances of Ben showing people his hearing aid and then refusing to put it on. I refuse to push him; it's early days yet. At teatime Ben was performing the 'Wide Eyed Owl' for us—very difficult to write down how he signs it—but he knows it all and even attempts a vocal 'To Whit To Whoo' at the end. Sarah was in stitches because what he actually said was 'Mer-Moo'.

23.11.84
There is more and more of Ben's signing now that I don't understand—I start off conversations then almost wish I hadn't because he loses me. I feel a real sense of achievement if I actually understand one of his strings of signs first time round when I'm not completely sure of the context. Fortunately he sometimes splits his chunks of narrative by using Judith's 'thinking' posture—finger on chin, head to one side—which gives me the chance to work out what he's just said before the next bit. I catch myself adopting the sympathetic smile and the so-called 'negative nod' of the well-meaning non-signer. The Phonak went to Nursery today but wasn't referred to.

24.11.84
Ben woke up and immediately started spelling practice. He started with names, then went on to do signs, asking me to fingerspell the words. We did all the family and then 'toilet', 'tent', 'camping'—and some I can't remember. He seems to have made the discovery that all signs can also be fingerspelled, and he was testing out his theory.

26.11.84
Signing class. Someone asked Judith if the deaf have their equivalent of whispering. She showed us how, with her eyes and face and barely noticeable movements of her body and hands, she could express something to someone without anyone else being aware of it. Her face was amazing, the expressions so subtle, yet the meaning unmistakable.

I have been thinking that when Sarah was at this stage in her language development I rarely answered a communication of hers with a one-word response. With Ben I often do, sometimes because I haven't got the time because of the constraints of, for example, having to get Sarah to school on time, to persist till I fully understand him or to stop what I'm doing to pursue a conversation. So I've tried today to extend my answers and the communication span, as I used to do with Sarah. The difference is, of course, that with a hearing child you can do this at the same time as other things, but with a deaf one you have to stop what you're doing in order to communicate about it—when you're as inexperienced as we are, anyway—though it's amazing what the deaf can do at the same time as they sign.

30.11.84
Visited Judith's family. Ben spent a lot of time with Ray and Roland in the shed making a boat. Ray took some photos. He's pleased that Roland is signing to him more now—the first time they met, Roland just spoke, possibly unsure of how well Ray could use and understand sign. Ray's signing is much closer to BSL and he finds it much easier to tune in and understand Ben than I do just now. I'm still restricted by my English, and I can see now that it's far easier to work out what Ben's on about if you try to concentrate on *his* language, what's coming from him instead of what's going on in your own head in English!

We spoke to Judith's parents about hearing aids. Both were very explicit about distraction and disruption of concentration, when the sounds coming through don't mean anything, and how they interfere with perception of vibration and sense of balance. They made the distinction again between people born deaf and postlingually deafened people who, they said, are more likely to take to a hearing aid naturally.

2.12.84
Tidying the kitchen with me Ben used a 'because' phrase—said he wouldn't put the stool in front of the cupboard because the door wouldn't open. Yet another example of him not using a specific sign (he doesn't use 'because')—but making the *meaning* clear because of his expression and choice of order of signs. I wonder how many people would agree that he had actually meant 'because'?

4.12.84
Ben brought the hearing aid to Ray at teatime—ate an apple while Ray put the aid in for him. He kept it in for half a minute or so and then put it away. Progress, nevertheless. In bed Ben was looking at the Ladybird Big and Little book—a picture of four candles reducing in size. He pointed to each in turn, smallest first, signing, 'Me, Sarah, you Mummy, and Daddy.' He refers a lot to the past now. He has learned the sign for 'a long time ago' and keeps testing it out, mentioning events and trying the different past tense indicators, with a questioning look on his face.

6.12.84
Day dominated by the receipt of the draft statement of Ben's educational needs, delivered by the educational psychologist this afternoon, before she went to observe Ben at Nursery. It's a collection of reports, mostly written in March of this year, detailing people's opinions about Ben's development, progress and likely requirements, and a draft compiled after consideration of all the reports, in Ben's case from the Nursery, the educational psychologist, the school doctor, his former and present peripatetic teachers, and us. The statement itself is OK, it includes that Ben needs and shall be provided with a native signer at his present place of education, and at first I was fairly happy with all the reports, picking out phrases like 'very lively, happy three-year-old', 'Shows no sign of frustration',

'Relaxed at home and in nursery', 'alert little boy', 'very friendly'. But then certain aspects of a report about his language development began to bother me. The language that Ben is developing now, with the help of Judith, is BSL, whereas the language of all his observers except Judith is English. An attention span (for watching) of three to four signs is quoted, for example, and a length of expressive utterance of three to four signs. But there's no indication in the same report of what he does with his face and body as he performs these three or four signs, or who he is signing to when he produces them—for example, when two deaf people are signing together they look to each other's faces for half the information, not hands, and it's well known that the deaf adapt their language depending on whom they are talking to. Ben simplifies his language for people he knows can't sign very well, elaborates it when he's with Judith. It's far too complicated an issue, his language acquisition, production and development, to be properly assessed, except by someone who is very familiar with the grammatical aspects of BSL and is either deaf or working closely with deaf people who are fluent. I've learned in the sign language workshops that the difficulty of assessment is one of the main reasons why so many professionals won't accept BSL as a teaching language, and I can see that here. It's obviously so much easier for hearing teachers to assess a deaf child's language if what they are looking for is English. Anyway, this three to four sign-producing child was telling us a lovely story at teatime about last Summer at our friends', having to pull the little rowing boat towards the big boat—really hard work and difficult to pull—and tie it on, with facial expression saying so much more than I've just said in words, and placement saying exactly where the big boat was in relation to the rowing boat. Coming up the lane from taking Sarah down, Ben (general output four signs plus repetition) was asking to look at the photos: 'Camping, eating and sleeping, gets really dark, and cuddling Mummy (Aaah, Mummy!) and—OOH! going to the toilet and (thinks) running and swimming—cold, swimming—and in the van to the pub—drink and running, getting slower, walking up the hill . . .' then, I must be honest, the repetition starts . . . Even this translation doesn't do justice to all the information he gets into what he signs—Judith would probably have seen much more.

Note the use of 'and' which has been creeping in over the last couple of weeks.

At Nursery Judith said she thought the educational psychologist had been pleased when she observed yesterday. So I went in and asked Mrs Davidson how it went.

I knew she was committed to the project but I hadn't realised quite how much it meant to her till today. She expressed such relief that the educational psychologist had approved of what she'd seen yesterday; she's really personally involved with it all. It was so good to hear that in the educational psychologist's opinion Ben's development had made strides, even since her last observation session on 15th October. She saw several nice little incidents that demonstrated Judith's usefulness as a facilitator of communication between Ben and other children.

10.12.84

Progress meeting today about Ben. These meetings really are awkward—because what we want from this year is so different from what the Advisory Service wants. They're always on about discipline, directed learning—and *English*, all the time. Here we have a golden opportunity for Ben to gain language incidentally, in a free environment—a proper nursery experience—and they keep wanting to pin him down, to 'make' him learn, in a language that's not his . . . However, everybody had their say, thanks to the educational psychologist's tactful direction; The new nursery teacher put up a really spirited defence of Nursery practice, and several people were able to reiterate that conditions are ideal for Ben to learn BSL this year, and that's what we should be aiming for.

11.12.84

Collected photos of Ben with Judith's father. There is one that says it all—Ben looking adoringly up at Roland while they work—beautiful.

Judith came with us for Ben's visit to the hospital for a

check-up on Ben's ears. We saw the consultant, who was concerned that Ben wasn't wearing a hearing aid. We had a little discussion about why he wasn't (me) and why he should (the consultant), at the end of which we agreed to differ . . . At home, Ray saw Ben spontaneously use the perfect 'when' sign, when we had both said at the last progress meeting that he didn't use it.

Ray found that Ben does know the shape of the number three—also contrary to what we said at the meeting. He was also using both hands to express the equal factors of even numbers, two plus two and three plus three, mirroring the numbers.

14.12.84

Ben asked to watch the video of *Insight*.[5] His understanding has increased since last time. Today he actually understood a whole story, the one where Wordworm is trying to commit suicide. He was signing 'poorly, sad, crying', etc. I left him watching, then he ran in to fetch me from the kitchen and told me that Wordworm was better: 'OK now, not crying, Supersign has picked him up, he's cuddling him.' I hadn't explained anything to him (naughty me); he had followed the story straight from the television.

Later, he made up a layout with the wooden railway. He was telling himself how many of each of the different engines and carriages there were, then he told me what colour they all were, then the different colours on each piece. It was a good long piece of communication—but still pretty basic. Maybe some aspects of Monday's meeting have made me too critical. I was thinking of someone's comment that he doesn't use his language to imagine with, and forgetting that we have seen him do just that, several times. That's the trouble with labelling, or attempting to assess, what is such a fluid situation. It's too open to error, as the two events I noted earlier show: we didn't think he used the sign for 'when?' or knew what the number three looked like; that's the information which went down in everyone's notes, and already, the information is out of date—if, indeed, it was accurate in the first place.

15.12.84
It's been bugging me ever since I wrote up last night's diary, this 'when and how?' business, these questions Ben isn't supposed to know how to ask or understand if asked. He *can* let you know if he wants to find out when something is going to happen or when it happened. He just tries out some of his tense markers (yesterday, a long time ago, tomorrow) and watches your face till he gets the right response. As for 'how?', in the right context you can read the question from his face. So much of the questioning in BSL happens in face and posture, but once again we're falling into the trap of using English as a model and looking for single sign translations of words. As for 'why?'—who's to say he doesn't have ways of expressing that which we blinkered hearing people are missing? If I wasn't so personally involved I'd find it fascinating, but as it is I find it frustrating and worrying that hearing people with so little experience and understanding of the language Ben is learning are trying to judge his development in it.

16.12.84
New sign plus lip pattern and vocalisation: 'ask'.

17.12.84
Today Ben wanted me to draw a 'Father Christmas tree'. Many rejected attempts later, I realised that he wanted the image I was getting down on paper to look exactly the same as our tree, with the little Father Christmas hiding in the branches—so I did my best, and once he saw that I was really copying what was there rather than giving him a stereotyped, simple drawing, he was satisfied. Both children are off school because of a spotty ailment which looks as though it might be contagious.

During the visit to the doctor's to get the rash diagnosed, the doctor mentioned that he had had a letter from the consultant—'Something about you not doing something that he advised you to do. Shouldn't Ben be wearing a hearing aid?' So I explained about the argument and gave my reasons for not doing as I was told, and he seemed to accept it OK. I suppose that now we'll be labelled 'awkward parents' by the medics as well. Judith came for the last signing class of the year—mince pies, wine, etc.—and cheered me up immediately.

18.12.84
Ray's birthday. During the day the kids made him presents. We asked Ben what he wanted to make and he signed that he wanted to draw round his hand and colour it to give to Daddy. I was impressed at the instantaneous understanding and immediate response.

Later, they made biscuits. Sharing the job didn't work this time so they worked separately, with very little help. Children usually find spacing things on baking trays difficult, but Ben produced a perfect three by four pattern.

Judith came to see how Ben was; she told him a long story about how upset she'd been to find he wasn't at school on Monday, how she'd looked everywhere for him, then Mrs Davidson told her he was unwell. Ben watched her intently, nodding and copying a bit, but the real proof of the pudding came as she was about to leave, when he remembered and signed the whole story back to her.

20.12.84
We were at the dinner table, conversing, when Ben pointed out something to me and said (vocalised), 'Mum, look.' It was a while before I realised that it was the sound I had responded to rather than the signs—his voice is just like Sarah's.

He is making a lot of use of his voice at the moment. He'll look at you and talk without signing, and expect an answer, just like hearing babies do when they are trying out communication tactics. In the same way, he'll rattle off whole strings of fingerspelling, mostly random, but usually containing one or two of the words he knows how to spell. Again he waits for an answer, which I usually give entirely in fingerspelled English, to his great amusement.

Christmas Eve, 1984
Communication between Sarah and Ben now is sophisticated enough for her to be able to explain about Father

Christmas to him, get him to hang up his stocking, and for him to be able to come downstairs and relate the whole thing to us. Mum came; she's very impressed at the length of the tales he tells her now, even if she doesn't always understand them. She had no trouble understanding the game he was playing towards evening: he was Father Christmas, he had this heavy sack; he gave Nanny a new wheel for her car, then said he was off to give presents to lots of children. He learned a new sign today: 'EXCITED!!!'

Christmas Day, 1984
Ben was too excited to use the sign for 'excited' today. He was trembling with it as he opened the presents in his stocking. I missed watching Sarah opening hers—she did it at 5 a.m. with Ray—bless them, they didn't wake the rest of us till seven! Of the presents in his sack, Ben liked the photograph albums (especially when he had helped fill them with *his* photos), his fit-together roadways and, most of all—he clung to the wretched thing all day—a flashing machine gun from Judith (I must have a word with her). We all watched *Mary Poppins* after lunch. Sarah was touched by the story, but for Ben I think it was the visual effects: he was totally amazed to see real people flying, popping up out of chimneys, riding amongst a field of cartoon horses. He watched, spellbound, for the full two hours.

26.12.84
Ben had a new jigsaw for Christmas, with numbers of things in very complex, brightly-coloured pictures. Ray and I watched him do the whole thing himself, not by looking at the completed picture on the lid, but by matching shape and colour. He didn't look up till he'd finished it, but then the expression of pride and achievement on his face was a delight to see. Later he coloured a pig in his new colouring book—as neatly as Sarah would have done it, but with more outrageous colours—half green, half black. If he's colouring, he is able to keep within the lines, but he uses lots of colours—six different colours for the six strands of a tassel, for example. He has such a good eye for shape, too: making a Christmas tree in playdough he used the

triangular cutter to get the right shapes for the edges. I think one of the reasons I'm so amazed at all this is his continued reluctance to draw in 2D.

Another improvement in communication involving Sarah: they weren't equal in terms of being able to call in adult help in disputes—to 'tell tales'. They are now. When there's a *fracas* going on he's just as likely to come and volunteer information as she is, which makes him harder to take advantage of and less easy to use as a scapegoat. They are getting on really well just now—pretend games and mock fighting with giggles, rather than real fighting with tears. She even prefers to play snakes and ladders with him rather than with us.

28.12.84

Watched Ben playing the 'Sizesorts' game on the Spectrum. Sometimes the difference in sizes is minimal, yet Ben is able to place the shapes in descending order of height or width, which involves moving a cursor to select the next shape, and pressing the 'enter' key to tell the computer to go ahead, as well as making a choice between the five shapes on display. We know he's got the concepts 'bigger than', 'smaller than', etc.; we can now add 'taller, shorter, wider, narrower' and the signs to go with them. The great thing with the computer is that he's in control of the situation. The achievement is genuine and observable, an instant product and reward of his own thinking.

Caroline:[6] *Ben seems to be much more calm in himself now since Judith's been working with him. He seems to be showing less frustration in things. Whether or not it's because he can communicate more than he could do . . . it certainly seems so. And there seems to be a kinship between Ben and Judith. Whether Ben realises that Judith is the same as he is in that she can't hear—they seem to get on very well. I think perhaps because Judith's experienced what Ben's going through, because she's gone through it herself, there seems to be a rapport between them . . .*

Mrs Davidson: *With the staff I think we're all signing very much easier. I don't know that we're signing all that much better but it comes more freely to us. We're not as selfconscious as we were to start with, any of us.*

The children are quite used to Judith now. At first one or two of them did just say, 'Her voice isn't like yours,' but now the children don't seem to notice that she's any different at all. And a lot of the children like to follow her around, like her to be with them, and like her to show them how to sign. Ben is certainly a much easier child, his behaviour is much improved through Judith's guidance. His signing appears to us to be much more fluent. And when we sign to Ben he responds quite easily to us, which he didn't do very much before.

Ray: *I think when we were first interested in the idea of a deaf person coming to work with Ben we realised that that was going to have implications beyond just affecting Ben. And that we really hoped it would affect lots more people in the village, and in particular it could affect us. And that really has started to develop. Lorraine's signing, when I see her with Judith, is so much faster, so much more fluent than it used to be. They hold perfectly natural conversations. And when Judith is in a group of people where conversation is bouncing round fairly quickly, Lorraine seems to find no problem in actually interpreting for her . . .*

As parents, when we think of other people influencing our child, I don't think either of us has this feeling that Ben is just our child. We don't feel that Sarah is just our child. Sarah is her own person, and Ben is himself. They don't belong to us. They're our children in that we've got to have a responsibility for them but they don't belong to us and they're going to come into contact with all sorts of different people who will influence them in different ways. And it's so obvious that a deaf child is going to be helped by coming into contact with a deaf adult. It doesn't take Ben away from me. I come home at night and he still rushes up to me and jumps up at me and we relate to each other in the way that any father relates to his son, son relating to father. It complements us. In fact it helps us. We can discuss things that I don't think we had any chance of discussing just a few months ago . . .

Mavis (Judith's mother):[7] *If I see a deaf child, maybe in town, I will go up to them, approach them, and talk to them, because I know it will make them very happy. They'll see someone they can talk to—'Somebody who can talk to me, I can understand what you're saying.' It's great.*

I remember myself, when I was on a bus with my mother—and my mother was talking to me, and mouthing. And I was just looking at her and nodding, and somebody tapped me on the shoulder. And there was a man sitting across the aisle. And he signed to me, 'Are you deaf?' I said, 'Yes, I'm deaf.' He said, 'School where?' so I spelt it out, and so he started talking to me, we were talking to each other. I was so pleased, because he could understand me and I could understand him. Somebody was chatting to me in my language. We were using the same language. I was so happy, when I got home I told my father, 'There was a big man on the bus and he was talking to me, I had a chat with him.' I felt great. It was super. So I know a young child will be happy just the same if a deaf adult approaches them and talks to them.

31.12.84
It turned out to be a good year, 1984. After the kisses and the whisky at New Year Ray and I went up and gave both children a kiss as they slept. I can see nothing but good signs for next year; as I kissed Ben I wished him a whole year that continued as this one has ended: with optimism and happiness.

Notes

1 At the beginning of this term, Tyne-Tees Television began filming for their documentary. Quotations from interviews have been incorporated where appropriate in the diary extracts, but no reference to the process of film-making has been included in the extracts.

2 A separate section of the Nursery, used for more 'school-like' activities, and for one group to retire to at the end of the day for a story.

3 From the Tyne-Tees Television interviews. Translation by Peter Llewellyn-Jones.

4 There are accepted ways of annotating signed utterances, of which this is not one. For the sake of the general reader, who might find the correct form difficult to read, I have provided translations instead, and I hope that professional researchers into sign language will forgive me.

5 ITV's educational programme for deaf children, with signs and subtitles.

6 From the Tyne-Tees Television interviews.

7 Translation by Peter Llewellyn-Jones.

2 THE SECOND TERM

2.1.85
Bad news. Judith's friend and social worker rang to let us know that Judith's mum has died. Poor Judith. Now every New Year she'll think of her mother. I feel I want to go and see her, but at the same time I don't know if she would want that . . . and poor Roland—apparently at Christmas they decided to have their dog put down because he was finding it harder and harder to get about, and was badly affected by the cold weather, so he's gone, too, and Roland will be completely alone. Odd to think that I've only known Mavis for a few months; I feel much more of a sense of loss than that, maybe because she was so friendly with us, right from the start—and so full of life. I keep trying to imagine what it will be like next time Ben sees Roland—how will Ben feel to find Mavis gone and no dog either?

3.1.85
Nursery without Judith. Mrs Davidson and Caroline said that Ben had been all right, thank goodness—he seemed to enjoy just being back after the holiday.

4.1.85
Mrs Davidson rang to ask if we had any news of Judith. She told me a lot about how Ben had coped at Nursery— everybody had been making a special effort to make sure he didn't miss out on anything, and all noticed a big difference in him as they played with him—better concentration, a lot more communication, and good use of the play materials. He chose really interesting things to do and persisted with them. He also related well to the staff—Mrs Davidson said that while Judith was at Nursery the other staff obviously

didn't need to spend much time with him, and it had been interesting for them to see what he was capable of doing now. They and we were relieved that his dependence on Judith wasn't so great that the ordinary staff couldn't cope with an absence such as this. He really is an adaptable little boy. I went to see Judith in the evening but there was no one at home.

8.1.85

Was filling in Sarah's school holiday dates on the new calendar. As I wrote 'back to school' on the 3rd September, it suddenly occurred to me that, for Ben, we don't yet know which school. It was a shock, realising that it was this year, and his future schooling is by no means decided. I suppose I'm aware of the situation, but I keep thoughts of it right at the back of my mind—I really don't feel ready for the next 'campaign'.

I suppose, if I have to think about it, I'd like him to go to Windy Hill with Sarah, and I'd like Judith to go with him, but I can't see the idea getting much support, even from Judith; despite their criticisms, most deaf people still agree fundamentally with the idea of schooling in a deaf environment . . . Anyway, I suppose the issue will come up before long and then we'll have to consider it.

I told Ben Judith would be at nursery. She hadn't arrived when we got there. Ben looked all round the car park for her car, then did his despairing act, arms and eyes and eyebrows raised. She arrived just as he was taking his outdoor things off, and his face changed immediately, brightened into this big smile. Judith was still very close to tears; she had a lot of first meetings to cope with, people offering sympathy, but when Ben wanted her she gave her full attention to him.

10.1.85

Ben's statement, the final copy, came this morning. It's OK in that it specifies that Ben will have the assistance of a native signer during the time that he is at Nursery, but I just wish we could go through it substituting 'primary school' for 'nursery school', instead of having to go

through the whole persuasion business again in preparation
for the next phase.

12.1.85
Intensive signing weekend: two days of constant exposure
to BSL; practice at decoding, story-telling. THINKING in
the way a deaf person does . . .

16.1.85
Ray was home all day, has gone down with some sort of
virus. Ben was very considerate, left him in peace until he
felt well enough to get up, then took him a book.
Remembering what we'd learned about storytelling, Ray
went through the pictures with Ben, then told him the
story. Ben was really interested, watched Ray all the way
through, and actually laughed, like when he's being tickled,
at the funny bits. That's the first time we've seen that, the
first time we've known Ben laugh at a told story. That feels
like real progress.

I have been watching Sarah and Ben playing tonight; it
was brought home to me quite painfully how much Ben
wants to communicate with Sarah, and how desperate he is
for her approval. They were co-operating well, though,
which is nice to see. Interesting, too, to note at Nursery
how often other children want to join in Ben's play, and
how well able he is to lead in the play situation. So, co-
operation is there, and communication of sorts, but he still
isn't getting as much language input as other children get
whilst playing. Sometimes it's because he is concentrating
on, and looking at, what he's doing, and without constantly
interrupting his play, it would be difficult to change that.
But sometimes it's because, although the other children's
communication is improving, they can't hope to converse
with him on equal terms. The solution to this is obvious—
more contact with deaf children—but lack of contact, at
school at least, is unfortunately one of the consequences of
'going it alone' as we are. It becomes more and more
apparent at times like this that mainstream education can't
be seen as a long-term plan for him if he remains the only
deaf child in the school.

21.1.85
Ben's peripatetic teacher came. We had just been drawing some more pictures on the January wall chart. Ben drew a house and the van, both recognisable, and remarkable when you consider the fact that he refused to draw anything much before Christmas. It's as if he's suddenly seen the possibilities. He signed a lot to me while his teacher was here. His use of direction and placement is coming on: he was looking for something in a book and couldn't find it; I offered to help and he described to me something that had to be a helter-skelter. It was a dictionary-type book and I found him one, and I was right. Both Ben and I were really pleased. His teacher asked how Ray was and how the family was: I said that coming up to decision time was always a strain, that whenever assessment meetings, etc., were on the cards I got anxious. At last! I found the courage to come clean about what upsets me. It was really good to be able to tell her how I felt.

24.1.85
Ben *wonderful* this morning. I'd been telling him how fed up I was with the mess in the playroom, complaining that it wasn't fair that it was always me who had to tidy it all up. He looked really sorry and began to help—I mean really help. He took one side of the room and I took the other and we both worked solidly for over an hour, until everything was in its proper place.

The significance of that is that firstly I am starting to talk to Ben about my feelings, and secondly, he is able not only to understand, but also to sympathise and actually decide to do something to help.

28.1.85
Very good session with the peripatetic teacher. Ben started off by piecing together the same little jigsaws he was interested in last week. Very impressive recall and both production and reading of fingerspelling. Then the teacher brought out some new picture cards, large colour photographs of various forms of transport: aeroplane, train, cars, buses, helicopter, three different kinds of

boat—very inspiring, and Ben was extremely interested, has enough language now to talk about lights, brakes, brake lights, landing gear, breakdowns, and to differentiate between the various boats. Basically he can talk in some detail now about a picture, rather than just giving it a name and being happy with that.

30.1.85
We really are signing more at home now. It shows in that Ben has begun to deliver these flowing monologues of pure nonsense (is it?) in imitation of conversation he sees going on between Ray and me.

I observed discreetly at Nursery again—lots of conversation between Ben and adults, but little with other children.

31.1.85
The fact that Ben is missing out on conversation with other kids is really preying on my mind, so much so that I told Sarah off very bitterly this morning for ignoring Ben's attempts to talk to her, trying to get her to realise that if she doesn't respond to him he'll be missing out on something very important. I did stress to her that she is special because she's the only other child he can have anything like a proper conversation with, but, looking back, I was maybe a bit hard on her, and I regret that now because she is usually very good with Ben . . . but funnily enough, something else happened today which might improve the situation for all of us.

I had a 'phone call in the morning from a woman who lives locally but in a different LEA. She'd heard about Ben, and wanted to meet us and talk. So Ray and I went over tonight and met the family—her husband and little three-year-old son—just diagnosed severely deaf, with two little post-aural aids, 20-word spoken vocabulary . . . he lipreads his mum really well, and watches and copies like a professional mimic. We all shook hands when we met; Andrew shook hands. I signed, Andrew signed. I played Peek-a Boo, so did Andrew. He and his mother, Lynn, use loads of gestures and handshapes, which are uncannily like conventional signs, without having had access to signing at all—amazing to watch their communication.

Ray and I were very careful what we said at first, until we'd grasped from listening to them how they felt, but as we talked it became obvious—particularly from Lynn, who used to be a nursery nurse—that they felt that to do their best for Andrew they had to learn to sign. They just didn't know how to go about it, and had found it difficult to get information. Lynn feels that despite Andrew's good progress with speech and speech reading he is getting frustrated because of lack of language. We're going to meet again soon with the boys and see how they get on together. Andrew is so bright and alert, I'm sure he'll pick up signs in no time, from us and from Ben. So here is what we've been hoping for—a little deaf boy locally for Ben to get to know—and another set of parents who think as we do.

3.2.85
To Elspeth's for tea. Good to have appropriate photos, so that we could be sure Ben understood where we were going, that Ken would be there and that we would go and see the trains. His language is perfectly adequate now for explaining things, except where names and places are involved, when it still helps to have visual aids. It was great visiting two people who can sign so well. Ben remembered going on the Santa Special last Christmas and was telling Ken about it. Ken was most impressed with Sarah's signing; she was pleased.

6.2.85
Morning of the dreaded booster injection for Ben. Judith came with us to the doctor's; Ben sat on my knee while Judith stood in front of him and talked to him, about what a fit and strong boy this injection would make him. She'd had the same when she was a little girl, she said, and look how big and strong she was now! She kept up a constant stream of patter, in the midst of which Ben had his jab without a tear.

7.2.85

Lynn brought Andrew to see Ben and to visit the Nursery and meet Judith. We all went down in Lynn's car. The children were really curious about each other but Ben took it all very calmly, which surprised me. I'd explained to him all about what was going to happen and who was coming, and I'd expected him to be excited, just as I was. In fact, as the afternoon progressed, there were quite a few surprises, especially for me—for example, I was signing all the time, and because of that I was expecting Andrew to understand . . . I went back two stages in time as I realised that even though Andrew watched, and attempted to copy some signs, it would be a long time before he actually understood —me, at any rate. It made me realise just how far we've come and how much hard work Lynn has ahead of her, even if she is quick to learn to sign. Also, I thought that by some kind of magic Ben would realise that Andrew was deaf and start signing to him, but it was only towards the end of the afternoon that he showed some indication that he knew that Andrew was deaf: he started chucking him under the chin to get his attention, like Judith sometimes does with him.

The nicest moment of the afternoon was just after we arrived, watching both deaf children sitting in the Rainbow Room playing with a spaceship together, paying close attention to what Judith was doing, and Judith radiating happiness. Quite an emotional few minutes, really, each of us probably thinking what an ideal situation this was and knowing that, simply because of the geography, it couldn't become a permanent one . . .

At teatime Ben told Ray that a little deaf boy with hearing aids had been to Nursery to play with Judith.

11.2.85

The language Ben is using to describe his 'mind pictures' is expanding: playing 'Hide and Seek' with Sarah he told us he'd been hiding *under* the TV. First time I've seen him use the sign when referring to something not actually within sight.

12.2.85

Went with Annette and all three children (there's only Paul at school now) to Pat's farm in the morning. Saw some lambs, including one very new, still wet one, and the children collected an egg each from the hen-house for their dinner. Pat noticed the improvement in everyone's communication: last time we visited we were still depending very much on visual aids to explain things, but now both Annette and I are able to give Ben elementary (I say elementary because they're nothing like as complex as Judith's) explanations of what's going on, and Ben is able to understand them.

13.2.85

Ben told his peripatetic teacher a story this morning. We were both thrilled, she because she's never seen him do that before, I because I was happy that she had actually seen it for herself.

14.2.85

I spoke to the speech therapist. She seems very pleased with Ben's response just now; he even managed to produce a 'K' sound in their last session. He brings what he learns with her back home and occasionally goes through his repertoire of sounds . . . just what the Manchester teacher used to ask of him, except that now he understands what is required of him and enjoys what he is doing. The speech therapist has persuaded a local charity to buy her a 'C-Speech' (a computerised voice-recognition set-up with visual display) to use with her pupils; she's sure Ben would benefit from being able to see a visual image of the sounds he produces.

21.2.85

Ben made a perfect 'V' sound in bed this morning, by experimenting adding voice to his 'F' in one of his little speech sessions. Good to have fingerspelling to show him the difference.

Saw a new and more mature way of negating today: sign plus shake of the head performed simultaneously.

It has just occurred to me, considering Ben's language development and comparing it with hearing children's (as I do all the time, what with memories of my Sarah and having little Sarah around developing like mad), we've never really taken account of the fact that it was seventeen months before we started to sign with Ben, and a lot more time before we were anything like fluent . . . so whatever we do now we can always expect there to be at least an eighteen-month difference between his language production and that of a hearing child of the same age . . . in some ways, a comforting thought, in others an indication of the tremendous amount of work still to be done . . .

24.2.85
More linguistic progress. Ben used his sign for 'and' to mean 'then'. He signed 'Build it up first, *and* put on the roof.'
It was a beautiful day; we all walked up to the reservoir and saw a heron. All very excited except Ben; after all, we're always seeing birds up there. I couldn't make him understand why this was different, special—which just goes to show how much further our language has got to go . . . also how difficult it is at this stage to distinguish between what is a gap in his language and what is a gap in his knowledge. It's so much easier for Sarah to amass information: she'd never heard us mention a heron before so knew immediately that it was unusual, whereas 'bird' for Ben means virtually all birds as yet: no one has talked about the different kinds of birds in Sign: although he's sure to have noticed differences, talking about them makes things so much clearer.

26.2.85
Ben and I played with the farm during the morning. I suppose I have been neglecting these morning play sessions a bit since Judith started at Nursery—it was so tempting just to hand over responsibility, but of course Ben needs all the input he can get; having the help of a deaf person is wonderful, but Ben needs education from all sources, as many as possible; I shouldn't have stopped

working just because Judith started. Anyway, this is a good time to get into the habit again.

I'm sure we're seeing another stage in Ben's signing ability. More and more he is using his hands independently of each other, one showing one thing, the other another, not just in forming signs, but in expressing complicated relationships—like one hand showing the shape of a staircase, the other—and his face—exactly how someone was walking up it. Also saw 'when' again, in 'When I grow up'. His teatime babble is looking more and more complicated—sometimes I'm quite at a loss how to respond. When Sarah used to do it in baby babble I used to say things like, 'Yes, we had one but the handle fell off'—but it feels wrong somehow to be signing nonsense to Ben—although he seems happy with any response, so long as you do reply to him.

We watched a 'Supersign' (*Insight*) video in which the sign for 'disappear' is used. I was talking about what was happening and used the sign myself a couple of times. By teatime it was a part of his vocabulary: when he had eaten his meal he said it was 'Finished. Disappeared.' More progress: two signs, same meaning.

28.2.85
I've noticed another question form, loosely translatable as 'What are you doing?' or 'What's that for?' He uses the conventional sign for 'What?' with a very quizzical expression and rapid glances from the object in question to the person he's asking. At first I misunderstood the sign and just gave him a name, like 'It's a letter,' or whatever, but that wasn't good enough, it was more information he was after.

2.3.85
LASER workshop in Bristol: a very lively and interesting morning spent going through Dr Mary Gutfreund's 'Bristol Language Development Scale—English Free Version'—an attempt to arrive at a means of assessing linguistic progress in BSL as opposed to signed English. She is a very approachable woman, open to any response. Some

interesting points were raised about what constituted language and what didn't. Ray was very interested in the philosophical distinctions between language and communication, and Dr Gutfreund was receptive and flexible. The morning had a very productive feel to it—a good workshop.

After lunch Ray and I spent about a quarter of an hour absolutely spellbound watching two deaf women signing (although that word on its own seems inadequate to describe what they were doing) to a baby of about one, also deaf. The communication skills of these women were amazing; there was just so much going on between them and the little girl. One woman was holding the baby first, then the other one came and took over. Every mother of a deaf baby should be shown a video of a scene such as that . . . Even though each woman in turn was holding the baby, so, in theory, 'had her hands full', the communication was there all the time; that baby was actively involved in conversation, was repeating the signs for 'go to sleep', 'bottle', 'Where is it?' She was waving to people, even attempting to copy the different styles they used, and her attention was complete. Teachers —and parents—of little deaf children talk of the problem of 'getting the baby to look'. No such problem here. Eye contact was easily gained and held for as long as there was something to communicate, and it looked easy, so effortless and relaxed. So Ray and I had the best introduction possible to the next item on the agenda: a panel of deaf parents talking about bringing up their deaf children. We watched that baby's mother tell of her experience with the baby's peripatetic teacher and of how amazed she was to learn that the function of a peripatetic teacher of the deaf was mainly to teach, guide and inform the parents. She saw that as totally inappropriate in her case and, having watched the previous scene, we had to agree! It was OK for the peripatetics to dole out that kind of advice to hearing parents, she said, because of course they do need support and information on how best to communicate with their deaf children—but I don't!

There were lots of stories with, it seemed, a recurring theme: the inappropriateness of the advice given by the professionals as regards education, and the damage incurred by individual deaf people as a result. Parents of very young deaf children were determined to get what they wanted for their children; some had been encouraged to hear what we have gained for Ben, and we got a lot of encouragement.

Gloria Pullen spoke of her follow-up study to Conrad's research into deaf school-leavers.[1] Her signing, once I was used to it, was easy to follow, very expressive; she covered lots of ground and told a great many stories in a very short time; wonderful to watch, but again highly emotive, with once again this thread running through of *damage*—the damaged lives of so many families because of a system of education which prepared them all for speech and abandoned them when they, between them, failed to produce it. Some of her stories were amusing, but by the end of her talk I felt almost ashamed to be hearing. And at the same time I could feel and understand the guilt and despair of those hearing parents who had been badly let down by those employed to advise them, feeling at the end of it all that they had failed their children, not that their children had failed, and desperately looking for some way to make amends. Some even asked Gloria if she would teach them to sign. Upsetting, too, after hearing all that, was Gloria's discovery that, for employers, it wasn't the ability to speak well that mattered. The deaf people in the good jobs were the best *readers*, not the best talkers . . . Powerful stuff, and I wished I could have had sitting beside me all those parents I know who believe that their child is going to be the one in twenty who makes it orally . . . see if they would still think it was worth the risk.

3.3.85
There was a letter waiting for me when I got home: my paper has been accepted at Manchester. I'm to present it in 10–15 minutes at a 'panel session', whatever that is. Panel of one other committed Total Communicator, perhaps? I saw it as an omen, a very positive end to a weekend that has increased my determination to *do* something to try to change some of the terrible things that are happening in deaf education.

9.3.85
Ray took Ben into town shopping. When they came home Ben told me all about it; his storytelling is really coming on. I could actually see the roundabout, how fast it was going, where Daddy was standing, where Ben was and what he was eating at the time. Very accurate eye-gaze, rôle-taking and swapping . . .

11.3.85
First proof that Ben understands the conventional sign for 'How?' Talking about Saturday again, I asked him how he'd got to the top of the bus on the roundabout and he said he'd climbed a ladder.

14.3.85
Went shopping with Mum and Ben and had lunch in a café. We sat at the window upstairs and Ben marvelled at all the different lorries going past on the road. He's so interested in everything, so very responsive when you point things out to him or explain about things. He's such good company, really seems to enjoy what he's doing while he's doing it, isn't preoccupied with whatever's going to happen next, concentrates really hard on what's going on *now*. Lovely to be with.

15.3.85
Spring Fayre at Windy Hill tomorrow; Sarah wanted to enter the dressed egg competition. With very little help from me she made a Humpty Dumpty on a wall. So did Ben. He faithfully and steadfastly watched and copied everything Sarah did for the one and a half hours it took her to complete her model. So now we have two smiling Humpties in plasticene cloth caps sitting on plasticene brick walls in green meadows encircled with alternately placed white and yellow tissue paper flowers, almost identical except that Ben's Humpty bears a distinct resemblance to Ken! It was a joy watching them, helping when I was asked, fascinated by Ben's ability to observe and imitate.

16.3.85
Gave Ben his own money for the first time and persuaded him to buy his own bits and pieces from the stalls, culminating in one independent purchase. We really should work on money with him; he hasn't really had much experience of using it himself and is not sure of the signs connected with it. Still, he managed, and Ray and I could sit and chat over a cup of coffee without having to check up on either child—another indication of their developing maturity, and pleasant for all of us.

18.3.85
Caroline is doing an excellent language skills course at the moment. I was talking with Mrs Davidson today about how we could help Ben to benefit from what she is learning in the same way as the other children will. The course tries to enable participants to be more aware of language uses in young children and how to extend their language in the nursery situation. We've both seen, watching Ben, that his language is adequate for most purposes, and feel that it is time now that he was encouraged to use it more widely: Judith's communication with him is excellent, and he's learning his BSL from her, but they both need to be given opportunities now to expand a bit more. I was trying to explain to Ray, who was expressing some doubt as to how much you can influence a child's learning by engineering language input. There are certain techniques you can use in conversation with preschool children, which develop their use of language and encourage imagination and abstract thought, relating play materials to real experiences in their lives and going on from there into abstract and imagination. Closed questions (What colour is this? How many wheels are there?), for example, have limited value, but open questions (Where do you think the train is going? Who is travelling on it? What will happen if the people miss the train? Could there be anyone you know on that train? etc.) catch the child's imagination so that a teacher can clue in on and follow the child's interests and continue the conversation, aiming to let the child set and control the subject matter. These techniques are fundamental to

nursery education, and easy to learn, but not many people think about them unless they are pointed out. I've been thinking back to Susan Phoenix's letter.[2]

You asked for advice on your first deaf nursery assistant. Although you say it is a non-teaching rôle, we have found it just the opposite. I feed in the ideas and Agnes, my deaf partner, teaches the two little deaf girls very effectively . . . You see although I am a fairly fluent TC user now, I know that I cannot compete or trust myself to add all of the so necessary innuendoes a native signer uses. Agnes and I have spent one day a week, with the assistance of an interpreter, at a local college's playgroup course. This has proved invaluable not only for Agnes, but also for me to gauge Agnes' own knowledge. She is without doubt one of the most intelligent deaf adults in Northern Ireland, but . . . how we all suffered when Agnes came to realise how much in life she has missed because no one told her . . . However, all this learning has to be subtle and carefully supported. The average deaf adult feels desperately inferior to us chatting 'paragons'. I continually have to remind Agnes that many hearing women have never been interested in further education or any of the interesting psychological concepts of child development. After one year she is now beginning to believe me and will now stand up at parents' meetings and sign her feelings about the education of the deaf.

Agnes was fortunate in that Susan was able to make sure that she got some training, but Judith has had no training other than what she has observed—and since she can't hear, how is she to know what kind of questions other teachers are asking kids? Anyway, Mrs Davidson has decided that it would benefit all the staff to be told in some detail what Caroline is learning on the course, and she is going to make sure that Judith is included, and that she gets the opportunity to practise what she has learned, in a planned way, with the other teachers, so that she gets used to working with Ben, now that he has enough language, in the same kind of way as the other staff are working with the hearing children.

At home, we watched a video of child-teacher interaction in a school for the deaf. I saw no open questions. All that was required of the children were yes/no answers or single-word responses. And these children were six, not four. It was heartbreaking. What a contrast there is between the concerns of our nursery teachers and the concerns of these teachers of the deaf. Yet both are in the business of language development.

19.3.85
I had a letter from Miranda. She says that in her heart of hearts she would love to see Ben at a school for the deaf, with qualified teachers and a deaf adult. I'm coming round to that idea myself, some of the time, but watching that video yesterday—how could I live with the thought of Ben being 'educated' like that? And I doubt if we could persuade either of the schools to take on a deaf adult with Ben . . . And I wonder if she realises how far away the schools are? She says that as a friend she can see why we're trying to do this our way and educate him locally, but as a teacher of the deaf she can envisage lots of problems . . . We certainly have plenty to think about these days.

21.3.85
Lovely conversation at teatime again today, and quite a few instances of Sarah signing to Ben. He is using his voice a lot and is also very interested in other people's response to sound: he plays drums and blows whistles as hard as he possibly can to see our reaction, or he talks into our ears and stands back, waiting for a reply. Sometimes he asks if things are making a noise. Tonight he was watching *Top of the Pops* and he asked, 'Are they talking?' I said, 'No, they're singing.' He signed, 'Can you hear that?' This morning, after one of those conversations, I tried to explain a little about hearing, and gave him a list of deaf people and one of hearing people. He's certainly curious about the whole business.

22.3.85
After another noise session this morning I asked Ben if he wanted to try and listen to it with his hearing aid. Inside I felt very foolish—as if I'd just said something like, 'Would you like to try and grow another pair of legs, Ben?' But anyway, he was willing; he said OK and we got the hearing

aid and warmed it up and put it in and I gave him a hammer and told him to listen as he banged. He hammered a few times, smiled politely and put the aid back in its box . . .

24.3.85

Ben is having quite a few mini-tantrums at the moment. It reminds me of the time just before the Summer break when it seemed to me that his language had become inadequate for his needs as regards communication. There are other possible reasons, of course—he has had chicken-pox and quite a few minor illnesses, and he's recently had to come to terms with the loss of his bedtime bottle—and Ray and I are wrestling with the 'which school' business . . . Tonight he had one of his worst ever: he threw his construction set out of its bag so that bits of it scattered all over the room, and when I asked him to pick them up he refused, so I insisted and got pretty angry with him, at which he screwed up a picture that Sarah had just painted . . . I put him to bed, and he was heartbroken. Serious outbursts like this are so rare with both our children now, I do find myself wondering what's caused them . . .

28.3.85

I think Ben thinks he can hear. Ray and I keep saying, 'Aah, poor little thing,' but should we? I don't really know how to respond when he insists on having the tape recorder on beside his bed, and messes about with the volume on the TV until it's 'just right'—for hearing people—and all this without hearing aids. Do we say brightly, 'No, you're deaf, you can't hear it but you can feel it'? Do we assume, as most teachers of the deaf would, that his interest in sound, and his production of it, mean that he must be hearing something, so run for the hearing aid and try and get him to listen? When he talks on the telephone, he definitely understands that there's someone at the other end from whom information can be gained, because he not only wants to know who we're talking to, but also what has been said. But how does he think it's done? And why does he talk on the 'phone?

We had lunch out today, and I had my first embarrassing

experience directly connected with Ben's deafness. He had a big glass of lemonade in the café, and he drank it very fast, then began to belch. He really enjoys burping, so he makes happy little singing noises with it. The café was quiet enough for people's heads to turn, and Ben doesn't look the innocent babe any more. The belching went on and on, Ben wondering why I kept telling him to be quiet. Eventually I felt I had to explain to the assembled company, and then of course it was the other people's turn to be embarrassed. Fortunately I can tolerate quite a high degree of 'bad manners' in little children, because Sarah and other people's kids have convinced me that it's something no amount of nagging can cure—I've seen Sarah grow out of it as she became more aware of adults' manners and the sort of situations which require exceptionally good behaviour —and decided to appear 'grown-up' herself . . . So I wasn't devastated and could laugh it off quite easily. But I suppose it is time to begin to acquaint Ben with the noises people don't generally find acceptable in company. I remember Judith telling us with great relish about how she had to remind her parents that they must try to eat quietly in public . . . how they didn't realise how much noise cutlery made on plates if you weren't careful . . . and just how noisy the physical act of eating can be if you don't control it. It must be very easy to seem uninhibited if you're deaf!

3.4.85

In searching for 'gaps' in Ben's language, a lot of people have been commenting recently that Ben never uses the 'Why?' sign. Hearing children go through an observable 'WHY?????' phase, which we have not noticed in Ben. Well, he has arrived there today. His little sign for 'Why?/What for?/How?/What are you doing?' appeared so often tonight that I was able to get him to use the conventional 'Why?' sign—and I wasn't doing anything particularly interesting or mysterious. This proves—to me at any rate— that you can't just decide what you want to teach and then teach it. You have to wait for the right moment and then use it if you want a child to learn. Ben hasn't really had the urge to find things out from me in the past. Now, suddenly, he has the urge—either that or the urge to keep my attention for longer and longer periods of time—so he needs to use 'Why?'

4.4.85
Miranda came. She is so POSITIVE! We both feel very privileged to have her help. She said that Ben's signing is coming on beautifully, and offered various suggestions to help it to develop further. It was really enlightening to observe that the techniques she was suggesting were very similar to the ones the Nursery staff use as a matter of course—the ones we've been discussing. She said that Syd—though of course naturally inclined that way—has learned to use them brilliantly—can really get the most out of each little exchange.

8.4.85
Ray got Ben to wear his hearing aid again, but only for a couple of minutes, by getting it in then immediately distracting him. Ben seems to think that that's enough. I made a half-hearted attempt to bribe him by saying that I'd play with him if he kept the aid in (whatever came over me?) but he wouldn't accept that, just slunk off on his own—without the aid—and who can blame him? It all feels so familiar, and at least now I have the confidence to trust his judgement. It just doesn't seem fair on him to make an issue of it; even though he's still interested in sound and keeps asking if certain things make a noise, he doesn't make any connection between sound and the hearing aid.

An old friend came today, a nursery teacher from our old home. She is supposed to be taking on a profoundly deaf five-year-old next term. His deafness was diagnosed at $2\frac{1}{2}$ and so far the LEA has done nothing about it apart from allocating him one of their very few nursery places. She is really worried about how she'll cope; he has hardly any communication: no sign, no speech. And we think we've got problems.

9.4.85
I've been thinking about thinking we've got problems.

Really, we have got no problems now, in terms of daily life with Ben—it's lovely, really enjoyable. But we still have problems—it's thoughts of his schooling now that are making me miserable. I hate not being able to *do* anything; I can see the time slipping by and I'm pessimistic about the chances of us managing to talk the LEA into keeping Judith at all, let alone on better money, and even though we shall have Mrs Davidson's support and, hopefully, the educational psychologist's, the responsibility weighs heavy. It would be so much easier just to let the 'powers that be' get on with it. At the same time, I read yet another research paper today which casually mentioned that the reading ages of the group of deaf 13–16 year-olds in its sample were from 6–8½, and that makes me feel that there's got to be something we can do to prevent Ben from becoming one of those statistics in ten years' time, and that we have to carry on fighting to do our best for him as *we* see it, not as the people who have been happy with the status quo for X number of years and are *still* failing to see it—and that means continuing to avoid 'traditional' deaf education— and that means 'mainstreaming', and that means incurring disapproval from both the teachers of the deaf and the deaf themselves.

Notes
1   CONRAD, R. *The Deaf Schoolchild*, London: Harper & Row (1979).
2   Susan Phoenix ran the very successful Total Communication playgroup referred to in Part One, Chapter 8, with the help of a deaf adult, and sent me a very helpful letter when we were looking for a deaf person to work with Ben.

3   THE THIRD TERM

12.4.85
Ben's descriptions are getting more and more detailed and accurate: Ray brought some games home for the Spectrum and when they were setting up the computer Ben came down and asked me for the four-way socket adaptor, one of the connecting leads, and the new program with the wheels and cogs in it. A big step forward, far better than pointing or taking your hand and showing what he wants. And what a lot of things to remember at once.

19.4.85
The speech therapist called to see me before she goes to London to have a look at the RNID's display of technical aids for the deaf. She says the more she sees of Ben, the more convinced she personally is that we're doing the right thing by signing to him, because he is developing so well. I spoke to her about the schools dilemma; she wondered about trying half-days at a school for the deaf. She said that in her experience 'special' kids in mainstream schools can cause their teachers quite a bit of panic (Am I really capable of dealing with this child???) but that if Ben did go up to Windy Hill she would give the class teacher as much support and encouragement as she possibly could.

20.4.85
Ben seems to have gone back a stage, to before he was capable of understanding explanations. He wants something and if he can't have it you explain why; he watches the explanation, understands it, but carries on stamping his feet and grizzling. I've given up repeating the information once it's gone in, I just let him get on with it and hope it doesn't last too long. But trying to think of reasons . . . Lack of contact/easy communication with other deaf

children? My state of mind? Or maybe just that Little
Sarah—who is his best mate at the moment—is throwing
some fairly impressive wobblers just now?

22.4.85
Ben's teacher came in the morning. Ben was already
excited about going back to Nursery but he was co-
operating nicely, though not concentrating very well,
when suddenly he told me to hold up both hands in front of
me, and played a perfect rhythmic clapping game on them
like Sarah does: 1-2-1-2-123 and 1-2-1-2-123, etc.. The
teacher was impressed. She often gains insight into his
true ability coincidentally like this; in a typical teaching
session periods of intense interest are quite rare, not
because of incompetence on her part—she has lots of good
ideas and tries her best to follow his interests—but because
of the constraints imposed by Ben's *having* to perform at a
given time on a given day whether he feels like it or not—as
with most schools, of course. A few weeks ago in a similar
session he had lost interest and his teacher and I were
talking, when he casually fetched two very complicated
puzzles and completed them in front of us on the table,
quickly and without help,when he had appeared incapable
of completing a much simpler task only minutes before.

23.4.85
The earliest date for Ben's review is to be the 14th June.
It's very late for a decision to be made—not a lot of time to
prepare Ben for whichever school he's to go to. Ray's
reaction to the late date was that we should have to make
the decision ourselves before then and proceed accordingly.
I wish I had his confidence.
    A memorable conversation with Ben just before bed,
worth recording in full. I was drying him after a bath,
playing about with him.

    Ben: Can I blow a raspberry in your ear?
    Me: No, it would hurt my ear.
    B: Would it go down your neck and hurt your
           throat?

M: No, just my ear.
B: Would it hurt your eyes?
M: No.
B: Would it go through here and hurt your nose?
M: No, just my ears. I can hear, so loud noise hurts my ears.
B: Loud noise doesn't hurt my ears, does it?
M: No, you're deaf, you can't hear, so loud noise doesn't hurt your ears.
B: My ears don't hurt.
M: No. You're deaf. That means your ears are broken. You can't hear noise.
B: My ears are broken?
M: Yes, your ears are broken. They don't work. Same as Judith, her ears don't work, her ears are broken, she's deaf, like you. And Ken (etc., same phrases repeated for all the deaf people we know, Ben watching intently all the time).
B: Are your ears broken?
M: No, I can hear, I'm hearing. My ears are OK.
B: Are Daddy's ears broken?
M: No, Daddy's ears are OK. Daddy's *eyes* are broken, that's why he needs glasses. His eyes don't work very well; he can't see very well. He needs glasses to make his eyes better. Little Andrew has hearing aids to make his ears a bit better.
B: When Andrew grows up will his ears be better?
M: No, Andrew is deaf. When he grows up he'll still be deaf. But his hearing aids can make his ears a little bit better. When Andrew is a man he'll be deaf; when you're a man you'll be deaf, your ears will still be broken.
B: Are men's ears and women's ears broken?
M: Yes. Ken is a grown man and his ears are broken. Judith is a woman and hers are still broken.
B: Are Tommy's ears broken?
M: Yes, but he wears hearing aids to make them a bit better.
B: Did the doctor make them better?
M: Yes, sometimes he goes to see a doctor.

That was enough for him. I wonder if he'll come back to it tomorrow and if I've done the right thing in explaining that way, because in his experience broken things are upsetting . . . but he didn't seem at all upset, just interested, and at least now he's gone some way towards understanding what being deaf means . . .

26.4.85
Plucked up courage at last, to talk to Judith about next year. She says that if the job is full-time she will go with Ben to Windy Hill.

30.4.85
Wonderfully inspiring visit to Miranda's unit with Judith and Ben. Came back full of ideas. Judith spent ages chatting to Syd, comparing experiences and passing on ideas. A good bit of in-service training for her, and Syd said he learned a lot, too. I wish we were closer in distance so we could have more contact. Ben had a great time joining in at the unit—in fact the main problem with him was over-excitement rather than boredom. He joined in a lot of activities, including a play about Peter and the Wolf, which the boys performed after Syd had told the story. Ben played the cat. During the lunch break Ben sat with Judith and Syd (and behaved far better than he would have done with me) while I sat and talked to Miranda about schools and the fact that Ray and I are fairly convinced now, having seen all the options again, and talked to Judith about how she would feel about staying on, that the best way to continue Ben's education will be for him to go to Windy Hill. She was disappointed, but I think at least she understood our reasons. If we want BSL in the classroom for Ben, as a beginning to a bilingual education, Windy Hill is the only place locally which will provide it.

1.5.85
Introduced Judith to Windy Hill. I sensed quite a bit of shyness/embarrassment in the other staff but the class teacher took it all very well. She has been a member of our

signing class for a year now, and had made up her mind to do her own communicating; she asked me to leave once the introductions had been made so that she wouldn't be tempted to use me as an interpreter. I took the first twelve books in the reading scheme home and, having looked at them and thought carefully about all the other activities that go on at school (TV programmes with text in English, mathematical and scientific language, etc.), I decided that it would be just too much to put into practice my idea of trying the sort of signed reading scheme with Ben that Miranda is using in her unit. It would need a resident artist and a lot of planning and wouldn't really benefit the other early readers at all, whereas if we followed one of the computer reading schemes or converted the Bristol one[1] to use with the existing scheme, all the early readers would gain from it and it would be a better use of resources.

2.5.85

I spoke to the class teacher at Windy Hill this morning—spent three quarters of an hour in the classroom with Ben while the others were in assembly. He was very interested in an empty aquarium, and watched intently while I explained to him, first using a book, then drawings, that they were hoping to get some frogspawn for it and what would happen if they did. The teacher was very impressed at his concentration and attention: we've told her it exists but she's never seen it for herself. She was quite pleased at the way the afternoon went yesterday but annoyed with herself for not managing to say all she'd meant to say to Judith. The children loved her, of course, and were queueing up to fingerspell their names to her, with help from her and a very important-feeling Sarah. The teacher said the children weren't at all inhibited, which was a relief to me; I'd wondered whether they might be just that bit more conservative than nursery-age children. We hammered out a few problems: TV programmes, Assembly, PE, stories . . . All do have solutions, which will take a bit of organising, but it is possible. Ben found reading books with his name in the title[2] and was allowed to take them home. Judith had enjoyed her visit, said that the teacher could sign fairly well and was easy to lipread, and she was sure that things would work very well.

We have a bit of a problem with the light evenings at the moment—Ben refuses to believe it's bedtime. Tonight, in one of our regular 'discussions' about whether or not it was time to come in, I said he could have another ten minutes. Quick as a flash he signed back 'twenty'. I had no idea he was capable of that.

5.5.85

Ben was upset today because Ray and Sarah rode their bikes to the baths while we went in the van. Thank goodness we have the means of making promises for the future and explaining why not now. When Ben and I chatter now it feels so *normal*—the way I like to think a deaf child and deaf mother would be, sometimes we use our voices, sometimes we don't . . . it all seems so easy, and he is always initiating conversation now, wanting to know and talk about things.

8.5.85

A very fraught day, with a terrific hour-long argument with someone new to the advisory team about the viability of using BSL. Thank heavens we ended the day with a visit to town and a talk by Clark Denmark. From the denial of BSL as a language, to which I had been subjected in the day, to living proof of its existence, in the shape of Clark expressing in full and complex sign language his intention to train 200 native users of BSL to teach it to hearing people,[3] and BBC Television showing a pilot programme for their new BSL teaching series, to be transmitted in 1987, where BSL ranks as a language alongside and equal with any other. Wonderful, just the confirmation I needed, and just at the right time. As usual with their foreign language series, the BBC did extensive audience research before planning the programmes, and found that 14 per cent of the general public has contact with a profoundly deaf person, and that 13 per cent of the general public over the age of 16 would be interested in a TV series for learning BSL. The programmes will stress the need for students to get involved in local classes, and the BSLTA is being established to cater for the projected demand by providing qualified deaf tutors.

Judith was satisfied with the outcome of the meeting; it appears likely that because of her having deaf parents and having BSL as a first language, she will be able to follow one of the new training courses; they are being organised so that people can follow them even if they are working at the time, and LEAs are being actively encouraged, at separate meetings with the BDA and the BBC, to provide the funding (about £650 per place). Judith would be an obvious candidate for our LEA—but would they pay? We live in hope . . .

13.5.85

LOVELY conversation with Sarah; she has been following the schools saga with bated breath. She really does want Ben to go to school with her, and when I told her tonight it looked as if we had finally beaten down the last of the opposition and he would be able to go to school with her, her little face positively shone.

Some research was brought to my attention today—apparently it suggests that the reason profoundly deaf children reach a reading age of eight and then stop is that they are unable to learn to read beyond the level of their language competence. That seems to make a lot of sense—but I was led to wonder how the teachers of the deaf can fail to admit the connection between language deprivation and the fact that their profession insists on deaf children learning English first—a language in which very few prelingually profoundly deaf people ever achieve competence.

14.5.85

The speech therapist rang and asked if she could come and see me this afternoon. I was a little nervous because I was worried about upsetting her with my doubts about Ben's potential for speech; I didn't want to make her feel she was doing nothing to help him. In the event the meeting was quite productive because she herself had decided that the best thing she could do for him at this stage was to encourage and develop his language in general rather than his speech—which suits me very well. From September she was planning to do this using Judith as an interpreter, much as the nursery staff are doing now, if nothing goes wrong and Ben does start at Windy Hill.

17.5.85
In the afternoon Ben and I and Judith went up to Windy Hill to watch the concert and the maypole dancing. Judith and Ben sat at the front with a book of the play (*Rumpelstiltskin*), and Judith explained and answered Ben's numerous questions. Really it was a very good public relations exercise, because those at the school who might have doubted how Ben would fit in couldn't fail to have been impressed by his concentration and Judith's ability to keep him interested, even during the instrumentals and the many songs. Not that I would expect him to sit through events like that normally (Assemblies, etc.)—but it was good for everyone to see that he could do it if necessary, and to see Judith in action.

Mrs Davidson had a letter from the head of adult education in Judith's home town today, asking for a reference for Judith since they were considering employing her to teach a night class in signing (she teaches it already, but on a voluntary basis). Mrs Davidson wrote the reference during the afternoon and showed it to Judith and me when we came back. GLOWING, it was. Judith was quite choked. I was proud of both of them today. I don't mean to be patronising—the two of them together were just so different from the man in the street's picture of poor handicapped deaf people.

22.5.85
Little Sarah is with us at the moment while Annette does a few days' supply teaching; before Ben's teacher came this morning the two little ones had weeded the garden, collected stones and filled up a hole with them, played with the milkman's dog, painted the Christmas trees they started yesterday, played Mummies and Daddies with the doll and pram and had a terrific battle about who was

going to wash the doll's hair, which was the only time I had to intervene.

Ben's teacher had to join in washing the 'baby' and putting it to bed, but when that was done the two children got up to the table, alert and ready for a repeat of Monday's auditory training session. Little Sarah shouted 'Ben' on the auditory trainer and got a response; even I am convinced now that he does have some awareness of sound in his ears, but I still wouldn't call it hearing—at that volume it's just as likely to be tactile, and the discovery won't make any difference to the way we treat him—I would have thought that such a gross perception of sound would be superfluous to Ben's needs: he knows when people are talking because he can see their mouths moving, and he'd *feel* a lorry coming before he heard it. But anyway, at the moment he's enjoying the speech and listening games; he's experiencing nothing but success, and no one is conning him, so I can't object. He attempted to say each of the colours, and he got the lip patterns exactly right, if not the sounds.

An interesting conversation with the speech therapist at Nursery: she is doing the Reynell language test with Ben, using Judith as interpreter—just out of interest, because neither of us feels that the test is entirely suitable, for lots of reasons. However, it is helping her to discover some gaps in Ben's language that she found surprising, until she came to the conclusion, for herself, that Ben's experience of language is completely different from that of other children of his age. She's realised that it's much harder for Ben to gain the sort of everyday information that the rest of us take for granted, such as what a scarecrow is, for example. If nobody tells Ben things, or he doesn't experience them for himself, there is no way he can know about them. So she has set herself the task of filling in these gaps—not so much in language, but in the knowledge behind it, as she comes across them, by providing suitable materials and using Judith's help, which is great. So maybe tests—no matter how unsuitable on the surface—do have a purpose, and she reckons that anyway his language level according to Reynell is about $3\frac{1}{2}$, which can't be bad for someone who had such a slow start, however ill-adapted the test is.

25.5.85

Return of the 'Shall I be deaf when I grow up?' conversation. Actually, he started off by asking me if I could hear something, then signed, 'I'm hearing.' I signed, 'No, you're deaf.' He signed, 'I'm deaf. I'll be hearing when I grow up.' It runs very deep, this conviction that all grown-ups can hear. I've heard the same story lots of times about deaf children who have no contact with grown-up deaf people—and heard how upset they were when they found out the truth, when they'd assumed for years that they would be able to hear one day. Thank goodness we do know Judith and Ken, and I can give Ben examples of grown-up deaf people to tell him he'll be the same. And that he can see Judith teaching, and running a car and living in a lovely house, so that he can see deaf people achieving the sort of status he might hope for for himself, rather than thinking, as deaf kids must do when they never meet any deaf adults, that only hearing people can be successful.

Went to town shopping. Again LOADS of questions, about buildings this time. 'What's that place? What's in there? What's that for?'

Came home, checked the information for the International Congress in Manchester and found that my paper had to be in by June 1st, and since we plan to go away next week I had to get it done. So I spent the evening writing it, pleasantly surprised by how easily it took shape. During the writing it became an argument for BSL for the under-fives. I like it that way, but whether Manchester will is another matter . . . (The version of the paper which I gave at Manchester is reproduced in the Appendix.)

30.5.85

Ben has got the idea that unless you're looking him straight in the face you're not really 'listening'. Which is true. He insists that you look and carry on looking until he has finished whatever he wants to say. It's very tempting (for us hearing people—I know with the deaf it's different) to look away once we're fairly sure what is meant, but Ben won't have that now. He has actually told me to put down what I am doing and watch him. Proper attention is an absolute requirement of signed communication—you just cannot do the equivalent of 'Yes, dear, lovely' with Ben now. He's reached the same stage as Sarah when she caught on that when I said 'Mmm, mmm,' I wasn't really listening.

Visited York. We walked along the walls, had a horse and carriage ride (and a ride on the horse's back once the driver saw Ben was deaf), stared at an emergency fire tender (and got to sit inside, try on a helmet and wield an axe once that driver found Ben was deaf) *and* got a free Kit-Kat, this time not because Ben was deaf but because the man in the shop where we went to buy it was drunk and was giving them away . . . So it turned out to be Ben's lucky night. I don't believe in all this stuff you read in Freddy Bloom's work[4] about deaf children having to be *more* polite and *better* disciplined than hearing children, and not letting people treat your child any differently just because he or she is deaf. I think being particularly nice to Ben makes people feel good; it allows them to make contact with him and it helps them over their embarrassment rather than increasing it as a refusal would. I'm sure it doesn't do Ben any harm. After all, he *is* different; he does miss out on some experiences because he can't hear . . . if people want to compensate him, let them. As parents we do it all the time, by trying to arrange for him to do as many things as possible and gain lots of experience for himself, and I think it's great when other people want to come in on the act. The deaf themselves, even though sometimes they resent the 'handicapped' label, still want to keep the concessions made to them, and rightly so, I think. I think this business of 'sameness' is all hung up with the idea of trying to turn deaf kids into pseudo-hearing kids, not letting them 'impose' their deafness upon a predominantly hearing society. It's nonsense. Hearing people are ready and willing to adapt . . . Look at Clark's figures about the number of hearing people who will want to take advantage of the opportunity to learn to sign during and after the BBC's series . . . Five million ordinary people interested! How much easier life would be for the deaf if they all went ahead and did it!

3.6.85

Some memorable moments during Ben's teacher's session: again a definite response to sound through the auditory trainer, but not to his own voice, which shows how loud and clear sound has to be before it registers. After some discussion about whether he knew the sign for purple, the teacher showed the die to Ben and asked him what colour this spot was. Ben *said* 'Bur-bur'. Pleased with our astonished response, he went on to make good attempts at all the colour names as we said them.

4.6.85

This morning Ben surprised us all again. He asked what I'd got and my hands were full so I said very clearly, 'Cheque books.' He made an attempt to copy, then Sarah said it again, very clearly, and Ben said, 'Eck boo,' in a flat, deaf voice, but recognisable. I might turn oralist yet!

I wonder if he—or we—would have got so much pleasure out of these attempts at speech if we'd already spent years slogging away at it as a first priority . . .

6.6.85

Little Sarah's birthday. Ben spent the whole day with her; he didn't want to miss anything; didn't let her out of his sight until she went to bed—but once home he got really excited at the prospect of going to school with his sister tomorrow. He said he would do some writing. I'm feeling very sure of Ben; he is lovely at the moment and I'm very confident and optimistic—maybe because now he is actually going to start at the school, and once he's done that it will be very difficult to change plans . . . I only hope they have a good afternoon with him tomorrow.

7.6.85

Ben's first afternoon at school. I had thought he was adequately prepared, but I realised on the way that all I had actually said was, 'You're going to Sarah's school.' I hadn't explained how long he would be staying or that I wouldn't be there—so I had quite a bit of last-minute explaining to do to make sure that he really understood. I told him that

Judith would be meeting him at school and that they would both stay, and he was happy with that, until we arrived and Judith's car wasn't there, at which point he got anxious and gripped my hand—but Sarah came to the rescue. I was reminded of his first days at Nursery, when he had Sarah to rely on and had such a happy start . . . and Toddlers . . . in fact she's seen him through all his 'firsts'. She led him into the playground and he was soon joining in a game of 'Hokey Cokey'. His first move after that was to start a play-fight with Sarah, which wasn't at all what she had expected ('If Ben comes to my school I'll always have a friend')—but he was told that was bad, and distracted with another game, and all was well again. Once in the classroom he clung onto Sarah's hand, but kissed me goodbye just as easily as he does in Nursery. I had offered to stay until Judith arrived, but his teacher was sure she'd cope, with Sarah's help, so I left.

I hadn't expected to feel so nervous and worried about Ben; even after I'd seen Judith's car hurtling along the main road towards the school I couldn't rest, wondering how they were all managing and thinking that the class teacher could still change her mind . . . Anyway, 3.30 came at last and everything had gone smoothly; the teacher was quite happy and Judith was very pleased at how interested Ben was in the classroom itself, asking about the things on the walls, what the words meant, what the different pieces of equipment were for. The teacher was easy to lipread at storytime and Ben had sat still and watched as he does at Nursery. So all looks well.

10.6.85

Judith had a streaming cold at the weekend; today she was off Nursery, and the educational psychologist was due to observe, so Mrs Davidson was in a terrible state, very fed-up and unlike herself, and I spent another afternoon pacing the floor, imagining the worst. But Ben came up trumps again. Depite Judith's absence the educational psychologist was very complimentary. She had observed very discreetly as usual and Ben had—thank goodness—not had one of his off-days. She thinks it's been a marvellous year, that the

Ben she saw today is your average, well-adjusted, *normal* 4½ year-old. What better compliment is there when the child you are describing is supposed to be severely handicapped? Her enthusiasm was catching, and by the time she dropped me off at home I was almost flying. Annette had seen that I was enjoying talking, so had taken Ben home and met Sarah; when I got home, shortly followed by Ray, we decided that we should celebrate, which we did.

12.6.85
Ray has seen an interesting bit of information: an HMSO report of noise levels which recommends that more than two hours of exposure to a noise level of 90dB is likely to damage hearing. Yet professionals in deaf education and audiology advocate constant input of 120 decibels and more for children such as Ben . . . now where's the logic in that?

13.6.85
Read Ben a story from a Ladybird book in bed. He kept turning the pages forward to see what happened next from the pictures, then going back to where we were so I could sign it, always remembering where we left off. Earlier he saw me reading a book without pictures to Sarah; he asked if I was talking, and what the printed words were. I explained that it was written English, and showed him how it could be signed in English. I don't know how much of my explanation he understood, but he certainly asks the right kind of questions!

He has started, sometimes jokingly, to request detailed agendas of events, sometimes two days' worth, asking, 'Then what?' after each item. He obviously has to think quite hard about it, but he will run through a day's activities, e.g. 'First asleep, then wake up, then go downstairs, then get dressed, then breakfast, then take Sarah down the lane to meet Barbara, then Sarah goes to school, then come home, make the beds, then go to Annette's house, then play, then follow Little Sarah about, then play, then have dinner, then Nursery, see Judith's dog . . .' etc. You have to watch him all the way through these monologues or he starts the whole thing again. Also he's getting clearer and clearer about the future, thanks to Judith's skill in explaining it to him in a way he can understand and use himself. He's looking forward to the Gala day and going camping, and locates each fairly accurately in the strings of days and nights that are his future tense.

14.6.85
THE REVIEW! Annette entertained me all morning; I had the sort of nervous tension I haven't felt since my driving test—the same sort of preoccupation with passing or failing . . .

Everyone presented a report, and Ray and I were invited to comment where we felt it appropriate. We had agreed to be extremely careful and only to dissent if absolutely necessary, so during the usual half-hour discussion about hearing tests, hearing aids (or lack of them) and speech work we kept very quiet, in fact I found it very hard to keep a straight face because of all the totally uncharacteristic nodding and smiling Ray kept doing, and my nerves disappeared. The educational psychologist's report was lovely to hear, complimentary to all concerned, especially Judith and the Nursery staff. She felt that, apart from the obvious problem with speech and hearing Ben's development was keeping pace with that of an ordinary child. The speech therapist was able (thanks to those tests I was so wary of) to provide evidence of linguistic competence at least up to the $3\frac{1}{2}$-year level, which she thought was very impressive given the delay in the onset of expressive language. His peripatetic teacher had very positive things to say about his speech, hearing and lipreading progress. Mrs Davidson praised his social and intellectual development and the help Judith had given to the staff at Nursery. We went on to stress the beneficial effect Judith has had on ourselves and in the community, as well as the more obvious effect on Ben's signing. Then I read out the conversation I had with Ben a few weeks ago about his deafness, to show his capability in language as well as his developing attitude to being deaf and the desirability of contact with adult deaf people to prove that deafness is permanent but no great disaster.

We then discussed his needs as of now, which everyone agreed were, basically, an accurate hearing test, continuing access to deaf rôle models, extending his use of BSL, filling in the gaps and developing his descriptive skills, continuing access to the NORMAL curriculum appropriate to his age and intelligence—and the beginnings of English as a second language. Once agreed, we had theoretically to decide how best to meet those needs. It was obvious to most people there that the decision had already been made; some still sought to follow the rules exactly and circumnavigate a bit, but eventually Mrs Davidson gave her opinion: 'Somewhere which offers the normal infant curriculum, a class with very small numbers, preferably where the teacher can sign, preferably where there are some children Ben already knows . . .'—the twinkle in her eye was getting brighter, her smile getting broader, till the LEA representative interrupted to say: 'Somewhere like Windy Hill School, shall we say?' at which point everyone gave up the pretence and laughed.

The teachers of the deaf were duty-bound to express reservations, which they duly did, but very tactfully, about the desirability of Ben getting his teaching second-hand . . . at which we made the point that the class teacher has had more signing practice in the past year than any teacher of the deaf employed by the LEA . . .

Ironic really. There we all were, pontificating about what might be best for Ben next year, while he was up at Windy Hill, enjoying a normal Friday afternoon at school, despite having been dropped off there by someone other than me, not having Judith's help, and Ray and I being late to pick him up . . . hardly ideal circumstances for his second afternoon at school—but his teacher said that he had been fine. At storytime Sarah had helped with the signing.

The teacher and Ray and I had a long chat while the children were playing. The conversation, about next year, was relaxed, productive, easy, *equal*. I have great hopes for September.

So, the climax to months of frenzied thinking, arguing

and talking has come and gone, and I am immensely
relieved, but very conscious that, far from being an end,
this decision marks the beginning of another phase,
possibly the hardest yet in terms of real work, but
hopefully easier in terms of the mental strain involved.

18.6.85
Spent the whole day in the Windy Hill classroom. Was very
impressed with the teacher's methods and with what the
children are doing but was conscious, as she is, that a lot of
the ordinary routines, like discussions, TV programmes,
stories, are going to be difficult to make accessible to Ben. I
took detailed notes of the day's events, thinking of ways
round the difficulties as I went along and discussing them
with the teacher. There are ways round most things, but
they will involve a lot of work for Judith and me as well as
the teacher. It was comforting to note that she does
prepare well in advance, have resource and topic information books, lesson plans and timetables, which will make
preparation a lot easier for Judith. I feel very enthusiastic
and confident about being able to work with this teacher; I
just hope that Judith will get on with her OK, and won't
mind doing the extra preparation. We have worked out
that there will be times in the day when she isn't needed to
work with Ben (PE, for example) and she can use these
times to prepare, but it looks as if next year will be quite a
challenge, for everyone.

Judith:[5] *I hope some deaf adults like me will work with deaf children in
other hearing schools. Maybe in deaf schools as well, because the hearing
teachers are using sign language with many more deaf children now.
And some of the deaf children maybe miss something that the hearing
teacher is saying, or maybe the teacher misses something they're saying,
whereas a deaf adult will much more easily know what they're saying
and be able to respond much more quickly.*

2.7.85
I went up to Windy Hill to give the dinner ladies a signing
lesson, at their request. This time I didn't make the mistake
of taking along a vocabulary list! I took two big sheets of

paper, talked with the women a lot about the skills they already have and got them to write down those skills in big letters in the middle of the poster. They wrote, in their own words, 'FACIAL—MIME—HAND SIGNALS—POINT-ING'. One of them had obviously been thinking a lot about what life must be like for our family; she asked first if I minded her asking questions, then she asked such a lot of really thoughtful ones and made some very accurate observations. Yet another ordinary person, interested, open-minded and concerned to help in any way she could.

When I got back to Nursery Mrs Davidson told me she'd been on the point of ringing me this morning—she had had a nightmare about losing Ben in a crowd of cyclists and she wondered whether anything had happened to him . . . 'Losing' him is very much on her mind; it must be awful for her, to have got so close and done so much for Ben, and then to lose him. All those skills, too, which the Nursery staff now have and which won't be used.

Mrs Davidon:[6] *Judith has helped not only Ben but the staff and the parents and everybody . . . especially the children, to have someone who has a certain type of handicap, particularly deafness, which children— and we—don't usually come across as much as other handicaps . . . I certainly think it's been very good for them, to come across somebody, know that they are an ordinary person, that their deafness doesn't really come into it very much . . . It's been a very exciting and a very rewarding year . . . We'd very much like to think we would have another deaf child at some time . . . so that all we've learned would not just fade away.*

Ridiculous, really; there are so many so-called units for the deaf in this country which don't have one member of staff between them who can sign as well as the Nursery staff can now . . . or who would know how to integrate a deaf adult into the team . . . or who would want to . . . What a system. And what a waste.

Lynn and Andrew came. The two boys played with Little Sarah, and are starting to sign to each other—in very short bursts, but actual signing now, not universal gesture— which says a lot for the amount of work Lynn and her husband must be putting in. Unlike us, they have no help from anybody; no one else signs with Andrew, not even his peripatetic teacher, and he is in an ordinary nursery now.

Lynn is fighting off depression; it has suddenly hit her how much work there is ahead of her, both in helping Andrew to communicate, in sign and speech, and in sorting out the best way to educate him. Her feelings made me remember my own of two or three years ago . . . It has suddenly become too much to cope with; then there's the added burden of the different advice she's getting from everyone about what she should be doing for Andrew and how. 'I just want to let him be a normal little boy,' she said, 'without all this pressure.' I remembered it all so clearly as Lynn was talking . . . Two, three years ago I thought I was going mad . . .

Notes

1 CHAPMAN, B. L. M., and WILBY, J. F. *Catchup*, School of Education Research Unit, University of Bristol.
2 *Reading 360, The Ginn Reading Programme.* Ginn & Company Ltd. (1980).
3 The British Sign Language Training Agency, Department of Sociology and Social Policy, University of Durham.
4 BLOOM, F. *Our Deaf Children*, Gresham.
5 From the Tyne-Tees Television interviews. Translation by Peter Llewellyn-Jones.
6 From the Tyne-Tees Television interviews.

CONCLUSION

I thought I was going mad. But I did not go mad. I came through it—we all came through it, thanks to our families, thanks to our friends, thanks to the nursery staff and to those other professionals who believed in what we were doing and supported us through it; thanks, eventually, to our faith in what we felt was right—and above all, *thanks to Judith*. She, more than anyone else, has shown us how we can be happy with Ben, the way he is; how he can, he really *can* be a normal little boy.

Someone asked us recently if we would change things if we could:

'Ah, but you'd have him hearing, wouldn't you, if you had the choice?'

The reply took a bit of thinking about, but it came out straight and true: NO, we wouldn't. OK, life is different with Ben; we have to allow more time for things because communication takes time; as a family we have a fair amount of interference by professionals to put up with; and yes, we do have to think very carefully about schooling. But we can cope now; we've learned how to handle these things without letting them get on top of us—and we are very happy with Ben. No, we do not wish to change him.

Throughout his nursery years, we have resisted the pressure from those who would have changed him, and we have won for him an education that allowed him to be himself. We would not wish him hearing any more than we would wish him red-haired or green-eyed. We love him as he is.

In September Ben starts school at Windy Hill with Judith.

'What are you going to do with yourself now?' friends

ask. For a long time I viewed the day Ben started school as the day I would start a long period of recuperation—but now I don't feel any need to 'sit with my feet up eating chocolates'.

I am full of energy now, full of enthusiasm, full of optimism, and I know exactly why that is.

When Ben starts school, I am going to write a book, about Ben and about us, about the first five years of our life with him . . . and I am going to dedicate that book to Judith.

POSTSCRIPT

You've seen the beginning of a deaf child's education in this book. Now, just for a minute, let's look at the end result: what happens when the deaf school-leaver goes out looking for work.

Remember what oralism sets out to do: it sets out to prepare deaf children for life in a predominantly hearing society by teaching them to speak and lipread.

Now, imagine the scene: a job interview. A deaf teenager who has worked hard while at school to learn and speak and lipread and has been successful, takes her place (for most of the 'oral successes' are girls) alongside the hearing candidates who have applied for the same job.

'Well done,' says the interviewer. 'You're deaf but you can speak and understand what I'm saying. So can the other applicants. What else can you do?'

Will that girl have anything else to offer? Or will she have spent so long on speech work at school that her general education has suffered?

Picture the same scene, different actors. A deaf teenager who has worked hard while at school to learn to speak and lipread—but has not quite made it—takes his place (for most of the 'oral failures' are boys) alongside the hearing candidates who have applied for the same job.

The interview cannot take place. Neither person can understand what the other is saying.

'Right,' says the interviewer. 'What else can't you do?'

No one is as cruel as that, really. In all probability the situation would never have arisen because the chances are that the deaf boy in this story would not have possessed the necessary skills to fill in the application form—that is, if he could read the advertisement in the first place.

And his is the position of the majority of deaf school leavers.

*   *   *

Now, back to Ben.

'What happened next?' some readers may ask. Did Ben and Judith stay at Windy Hill? Are they still there?

Well, that's another story. At the time of writing, Ben is in his second year at Windy Hill. Judith is now working full-time in the Further Education Department in a College for the Deaf. Annette has taken over as Ben's signing assistant/interpreter. This year (1987) Ben will be leaving the 'mainstream' and transferring to a special school or unit.

We hope that when he does join the deaf 'system', it will not be the one which is still failing children like the ones in the stories I have just told. We hope that when Ben joins the system it will be the one currently evolving in a city in our area, where the LEA now recognises the deaf as a cultural and linguistic minority.

There, what I see as the ideal education, not only for Ben but for any deaf child, is at this moment being mapped out.

BSL is now officially recognised there as the first language of profoundly deaf children; teachers of the deaf are learning BSL from deaf adults whose pay and status reflects the respect accorded to them by their employers, and deaf adults will be first trained, and then employed, to work alongside teachers in classrooms where a bilingual approach to education will be followed with children of all ages. That means that all deaf children in the school will be able to acquire language early, and that their education will be able to proceed at the same rate and with the same degree of complexity as that of their hearing contemporaries, as it does in Sweden, where a similar approach is followed.[1]

Educators of the deaf in this city will no longer attempt to teach children using a pidgin combination of two languages; they will treat BSL and English as separate languages, with distinct and separate uses—*but of equal worth*. Similarly, they will treat all deaf children equally, whether or not they have the potential to develop speech. 'Non-oral' deaf children will receive as good an education as 'oral' deaf children. Interpreters will be available at all levels, so that good English will no longer be a prerequisite of successful progress through the system. Deafness itself will be no barrier to a proper education. For the first time in this country, the deaf will have equal rights in education.

This is not a dream. It is actual Education Department policy in the city. I hope that, soon, Ben will be part of it. I hope that our LEA will be prepared to allow him to build on the start he has made and continue to benefit from an approach which *encourages* him to use his own language in the classroom—an approach which, at the time of writing, as far as I am aware, is not available to young deaf children anywhere else in the country—except at Windy Hill First School.

Notes
1 See WIKSTRÖM, L. A., in *British Deaf News*, September 1986.

APPENDIX

EARLY COMMUNICATION—A PARENT'S CHOICE
Paper presented at the International Congress on the Education of the Deaf, Manchester, 1985.

My son, Ben, is four-and-a-half years old. He was born profoundly deaf. In giving this paper I speak also for his father, who has taken as great a part in his upbringing as I have. Both my husband and myself are trained teachers.

Our approach to Ben's education has been based on the following facts, and on accepting them wholeheartedly: Ben is deaf. He is not and never will be a hearing person. There exists an active and flourishing deaf culture, which has its own language.

These truths are fundamental to our treatment of Ben, and in consequence the following assumptions can be made:

1 Because of the extent of his hearing loss, acquisition of language via the oral/auditory channels will be a slow process, if indeed it happens at all. Even using the most powerful form of amplification available, even with the help of dedicated parents and teachers, no one can guarantee that a child as deaf as Ben will ever develop intelligible speech.

2 As Ben grows up, deaf culture will play a significant part in his life. For relaxation and ease of communication he will probably choose as his friends other deaf people. If he marries, his wife will most likely be deaf.

3 Ben will find it difficult to read and write English (profoundly, prelingually deaf children commonly leave school with reading ages of $8\frac{1}{2}$ years and below). If he does not learn to read beyond this level, one of the primary means of gaining information in our culture

will be lost to him. Coupled with lack of easy access to the spoken word this would severely restrict his intellectual development, despite his being of normal intelligence and with the same potential for development as any other normal child.

Ben's deafness was confirmed when he was ten months old. Shortly afterwards it became apparent to us that unless we established a means of communication *very* quickly, Ben's development during the early years would be severely retarded. The experiences of the preschool years are extremely significant in determining the future quality of life of any child. Yet if we pursued an oral-only method of education during those years we could not reasonably expect language to be established before the age of five, so we would be depriving our child of experiences which relied upon unambiguous, effective communication, for precisely those years which we believe to be the most important of a child's life.

In the course of our reading we had discovered Total Communication, a new development in the education of the deaf, in which every possible means of communication, including manual communication, was made available to the child in order to get through to him or her in as effective a way as possible.

At that time we had the services of a peripatetic teacher, employed by the Local Education Authority to support us and to teach Ben. In common with many peripatetic teachers, then and now, she knew about Total Communication, but had not passed this information on to us. Once we had made the first move, however, she began to sign with Ben and arranged for us to attend courses in signing as and when they became available. So we were able to *begin* to talk to our child in a language that he could understand when he was about 17 months old, and communication slowly began to establish itself.

But as time went by it became apparent to us that this in itself was not enough. There were drawbacks.

In our attempts to combine signs learned at vocabulary classes with spoken English, Ben was getting little more than clues. For a long time, we could add only one or two signs to a spoken sentence, and Ben's development was of course correspondingly slow. Even now, with our fluency and vocabulary extensively increased, and communication with Ben vastly improved, when we attempt to combine signing with speech we are producing, in effect, a pidgin, which bears no resemblance to English.

So, whilst Total Communication was successful in alleviating many of the difficulties and frustrations we and Ben would be suffering if we were not signing, approached in this way it was not giving Ben a language.

At this time, we were also becoming aware that despite widespread use of signing in the classrooms of schools for the deaf, linguistic competence and reading ability, in English, in the prelingually, profoundly deaf, are still dismally low. In most schools deaf children are receiving a highly imperfect form of English and, given this fact, it is hardly surprising that the English encountered in their reading books still presents enormous difficulties for them.

We saw that it would be impossible for Ben to learn English quickly, if at all, and when he was about three-and-a-half we decided that for him to gain full linguistic competence early our target language would have to be sign language.

I have said that the quality of English Ben was receiving via the attempted simultaneous use of English and signs was poor, but it must be understood that the quality of sign language thus conveyed was just as poor.

In sign language, the language which deaf people use when communicating with each other, the positioning of the signs within the signed utterances is not random but essential to the grammatical structure of the language, and facial expression is of paramount importance: over 50 per cent of the information is conveyed by the face alone (and here I do not refer to the lip patterns normally associated with speech). To present signs from that language in English word-order and accompanied by speech is to rid it of many of its essential linguistic components, including many of those conveyed by the face.

Sign language was evolved by deaf people and reflects

their thought processes. Having been born deaf, Ben's natural perception of the world is that of a deaf person. He thinks in pictures, using highly developed visual skills. There should be no barrier to Ben's learning sign language —except our own and his teacher's lack of fluency in that language. He needed an expertise which we did not have.

But that expertise was available. We had seen the experts in action during visits to the local deaf clubs, where we all benefited enormously from the experience of meeting and signing with deaf people. To learn sign language properly, we and Ben would need prolonged contact with a native user of that language.

Ben was, by this time, attending our local Nursery School, where the staff had made a determined effort to learn signs and use them with him, but they, like us, were feeling that the level of communication was much lower than they were able to use with hearing children. They felt that Ben was 'missing out', and they were looking for a solution. Between us, and with help from Ben's peripatetic teacher, the educational psychologist, doctors and local councillors, we persuaded our LEA that the only way to give Ben access to language which he could assimilate easily during the crucial early years was to employ a deaf person, fluent in British Sign Language, (BSL), to work with him at the Nursery, with the staff, and with us at home, using his or her own language.

Judith, herself profoundly deaf and with deaf parents, has used BSL all her life. It is her native language. The LEA offered her a one-year contract and in September last year, when Ben was almost four, she started work at the Nursery School.

She has become a figure much loved and respected in the community, and she is living proof to all of us that deafness is by no means the tragedy which some professionals make it out to be. There is no need to 'cure' Judith: she is intelligent, happy, lively, confident, articulate; she leads a full and active life. If Ben is anything like her when he grows up we shall be happy.

We believe from our observations that BSL is an ideal first language for very deaf children. Its structure is far better suited to their mental processes than that of English: the born deaf do not think in strings of words.

To illustrate, let me take just one of the grammatical features of BSL: topic prominence. It proves to be ideally suited to the needs of a deaf child just making sense of his first signs. Hearing babies can pick out the important word in a spoken sentence just from tone of voice: in typical 'Motherese'—'Where's the *car*? Has Daddy gone to fetch the *car*?' Deaf babies do not have this facility, but in BSL the important word always comes first, thus: CAR WHERE? So the child can quickly gain the important information; he or she does not have to wait patiently through WHERE IS THE CAR? before beginning to grasp what is being talked about. One does not find deaf parents of deaf babies making the sort of complaints about attention span often heard from hearing parents and teachers trying to use signed English. In their language the skills of attention-gaining and attention-giving are fundamental and are learned very early. One of the first things we noticed when Judith began to work with Ben was his improved attention span.

Ben has made very good progress over this year. In his own language he can talk about the past, the present and the future. He can ask questions, he can tell a story, he can tell you what he is thinking and he can ask how you are. He can imagine, he can plan, he can reminisce, he can describe. He can even appreciate poetry!

But what about English? And reading? And lipreading? We hear this plea often, but we are in no great hurry about these. Our definition of Total Communication is seen over time. We do not have to do everything simultaneously. It is our firm belief that Ben has a far greater chance of learning English once he has mastered his own language. Once he starts to read, the lines of words will make far more sense to him if they can be explained in a language which he understands, and lipreading will be easier for him once he starts to read English. As I have explained, it is impossible to combine Sign Language and English, and we have opted for Sign Language first because it is so much easier for a deaf child to learn early. This plan seems logical to us and we are very happy with the results so far.

We do, however, have two regrets. One concerns the present experiment. Because of our insistence on BSL we have had to 'go it alone', and so has Ben. Although he has had the constant company of a deaf adult while at school, he has been deprived of the company of other deaf children. We, Judith and the Nursery staff would have preferred there to be a group of deaf children at the Nursery, but the other profoundly deaf children in our LEA continue to receive their education mainly orally at the local Partially-Hearing-Unit.

The other regret is about wasted time. Ben was almost four years old before he began to have regular contact with a native user of his language. By that age a hearing child has normally mastered most of the intricacies of the English language. If we had been introduced to Judith or to someone like her at the time of diagnosis, along with the social worker, the peripatetic teacher and the various medics with whom newly diagnosed parents are routinely put into contact, we and Ben would have had almost four years' experience of Sign Language rather than almost one, and Ben's linguistic development would most likely be on a par with that of hearing children of his age. At the same time, we and the family would, from knowing Judith, have had constant reassurance that Ben did have the potential to grow up into a normal, happy, well-adjusted adult.

So many parents emerge tearstained from their deaf child's diagnosis, feeling that a tragedy has occurred. So many profoundly deaf children reach the age of five with little or no language. This need not and should not happen. The tragedy is not that some people are born deaf, but that they are denied a means of communication appropriate to their needs. The tragedy is not that parents have deaf children, but that they are denied the opportunity to make an informed decision about the education of those children. Educational methods should never be imposed on parents and children at the discretion of teachers. Parents should be given a fair, comprehensive, unbiased picture of the options available and should then be allowed to choose.

Thanks to the 1981 Education Act, we were given that opportunity, eventually, by a sympathetic LEA, and we have been fortunate in seeing the sort of progress in our child which fully justifies our choice. We only wish that the opportunity were available to more parents and that more deaf children could benefit, as our son has, from being educated in the language of the deaf.

Lorraine Fletcher
22nd July 1985

RECOMMENDED READING LIST

HOLT, John. *How Children Fail*, Harmondsworth: Penguin Books (1969).

FREEMAN, R.D., CARBIN, C.F., and BOESE, R.J. *Can't Your Child Hear?*, London: Croom Helm.

LANE, Harlan. *When the Mind Hears*, London: Souvenir Press (1987)

MINDEL, E.D., and VERNON, M. *They Grow in Silence*, Silver Spring, Maryland: National Association of the Deaf (1971).

PAHZ, J.A. and C.S. *Total Communication*, Illinois: Charles C. Thomas.

SPRADLEY, T.S. and J.P. *Deaf Like Me*, New York: Random House (1978).

WOLL, B., KYLE, J., and DEUCHAR, M. (eds). *Perspectives on British Sign Language and Deafness*, London: Croom Helm.